Additional Praise for *Love in a Time of Climate Change*

"Climate change is the greatest challenge
tion. Meeting that challenge will require w
hearts. There are many primers that targe
target the latter. And that is why *Love in a*
such essential reading."

**Michael E. Mann, director of the Penn State Earth System Science
Center and author of** *The Madhouse Effect: How Climate Change Denial
Is Threatening Our Planet, Destroying Our Politics, and Driving Us Crazy*

"This book is an act of witness, and a powerful one. It reminds us that
if church is going to mean anything in a time of rapid climate change,
it's going to have to take on this toughest of all questions."
Bill McKibben, founder of 350.org and author of *The Comforting
Whirlwind: God, Job, and the Scale of Creation*

"Solutions to the world's problems must include the churches if they
are to be effective, and the churches must understand these challenges
theologically if they are to be mobilized. Sharon Delgado masterfully
articulates an unapologetically Wesleyan framework for climate justice
and, in doing so, gives the churches the resources necessary to bring
about lasting change. This book is a gift to Christians everywhere, one
that ultimately extends to all of God's creation. I highly recommend it."
**Jim Winkler, president and general secretary of the National
Council of Churches**

"With wonderfully readable wisdom, Sharon Delgado invites us, Christians and all, to follow her on this honestly hopeful and adventurously
holy way to our shared future: to live in love in a perilously changing
climate."
**Catherine Keller, George T. Cobb Professor of Constructive Theol-
ogy at Drew Theological School and author of** *On the Mystery: Discerning God in Process* **and** *Cloud of the Impossible*

"Sharon Delgado makes it clear that we, especially we who stand in the Wesleyan tradition, cannot choose between being scriptural in the fullest sense and activity to save as much as possible from destruction through climate change. There is no tension between biblical preaching and preaching on the overwhelming, life-determining issues surrounding climate change. Let's stop hemming and hawing and work with God to save God's creation."
John B. Cobb, PhD, Emeritus Professor, Claremont School of Theology and Claremont Graduate School; Founding Co-Director, Center for Process Studies.

"Honor the creation. Strive for justice for all our planet's creatures both now and in future generations. Sharon Delgado reminds us vividly and forcefully how today's Christians have a responsibility for tomorrow's Earth."
Ted Peters, coeditor of *Theology and Science* and Distinguished Research Professor of Systematic Theology, Pacific Lutheran Theological Seminary

"There is no more important challenge facing creation than the changing climate. *Love in a Time of Climate Change* gives a thorough understanding of the moral and spiritual implications of the climate crisis and emphasizes the injustice of not addressing the crisis. With love at the center of the conversation, it will motivate readers into taking urgent and serious action that will curtail the most catastrophic effects."
Rev. Canon Sally G. Bingham, president of The Regeneration Project, Interfaith Power & Light

"Love of God, love of each other, and love of God's creation are so masterfully intertwined by Sharon Delgado. Easy answers, a checklist of five things we can do to save the planet, are not found here. Delgado calls for a transformation of the world! How audacious to speak of love in an age of climate injustice. But isn't that our job as Christians, to love the world into a new reality? It will be a very difficult job to solve the climate crisis, but Delgado has unlimited hope that, in love, we can do it!"
Pat Watkins, Ministry for the Care of God's Creation

"Climate change is already impacting church ministries, from the fight against malaria to disaster relief and recovery. *Love in a Time of Climate*

Change is the book we need now to help us articulate a Christian understanding of the climate crisis and respond with boldness, urgency, and hope."
Jenny Phillips, Fossil Free UMC Founder, minister for Environmental Stewardship and Advocacy, Pacific Northwest Conference of The United Methodist Church

"We all know we're up against a cliff when it comes to climate change, and that we need a transformation in our culture, politics and personal behavior to protect life on earth. John Wesley understood what it meant to be in need of such a holistic and profound transformation, and Sharon Delgado brings a much-needed Wesleyan urgency and wisdom to bear on this issue. It's an important and eloquent contribution."
The Rev. Fletcher Harper, Executive Director, GreenFaith

"Sharon Delgado's *Love in a Time of Climate Change* is a timely and important book that deserves to be read widely by people of faith. Her call for Christians, wherever we may be, to look more closely at the issues of justice and creation care and to live out our faith in a time of climate change challenges us all."
Nicky Bull, chair of Operation Noah (UK)

Love in a Time of Climate Change

Love in a Time of Climate Change

Honoring Creation, Establishing Justice

Sharon Delgado

Fortress Press
Minneapolis

LOVE IN A TIME OF CLIMATE CHANGE
Honoring Creation, Establishing Justice

Cover image: Santa Cruz from Mission Hill, Circa 2125 A.D. by Russell Brutsché. Used by permission.
Cover design: Eileen Engebretson

Print ISBN: 978-1-5064-1885-8
eBook ISBN: 978-1-5064-1886-5

The paper used in this publication meets the minimum requirements of American National Standard for Information Sciences — Permanence of Paper for Printed Library Materials, ANSI Z329.48-1984.

Manufactured in the U.S.A.

This book is dedicated to the courageous souls who are living and working on the front lines of climate change. May this book support your efforts by inspiring others to join the rising tide of people working to honor creation and bring climate justice to our world.

Victims of climate change are the new face of the poor, the widow and the stranger that are especially loved and cared for by God. When creation is threatened in this way, churches are called to speak out and act as an expression of their commitment to life, justice and peace.

World Council of Churches

Contents

Acknowledgments

This book is the culmination of a thirty-year process supported by many people. My thanks go out to all who encouraged and supported me during the writing of this book and to the countless people who, over the years, helped make it possible.

I awakened to the dangers of global warming in the late 1980s, as did many who read Bill McKibben's groundbreaking book, *The End of Nature*. Bill's knowledge, insights, and leadership continue to inform and motivate me and millions of others, as the movement for climate justice grows.

In 1988, I entered Pacific School of Religion in Berkeley. While working on a Master of Divinity degree, I also worked on a Master of Arts degree focused on environmental ethics. Thanks to Carol Robb, Greg Bergquist, and Michael Mendiola, advisors for my thesis, which had the unwieldy title *Creation and Justice: The Wesleyan Quadrilateral as a Theological Method for Addressing the Ecological Crisis and Related Human Justice Concerns*. That thesis was a precursor to *Love in a Time of Climate Change*, which applies the same theological themes and systematic method to the topic of climate change, while incorporating what I have learned during the intervening years.

The impacts of planetary warming have progressed far more quickly than projected by computer models of that time. Changes to the earth's atmosphere, oceans, ecosystems, communities, and species are already more severe than what I feared my great-grandchildren would live to see. We all owe a debt of gratitude to James Hansen, Michael Mann, and other climate scientists who courageously sounded the alarm before others were willing to do so. They are still being vilified by those who refuse to admit that unless we change direction, we are heading for the climate cliff.

Albert Gore Jr.'s *Earth in the Balance* (1993) and *An Inconvenient Truth* (2006) helped educate me and made the science of climate change accessible to the public. Naomi Klein's *This Changes Everything: Capitalism and the Climate*, released in 2015, brought together the climate crisis and the crisis of democracy, showed how capitalism impacts the climate, and demonstrated hope for systemic change through the movement for climate justice. Other books that have influenced me appear in the Suggested Reading List.

I am grateful to the congregations I have served, clergy colleagues, and the United Methodist Church, which affirmed my gifts for ministry, including a specialized ministry of peace, justice, and creation care through Earth Justice Ministries. During the 1990s, Jaydee Hansen and Paz Artaza-Regan gave me many opportunities to work on environmental justice and climate change through the United Methodist General Board of Church and Society and the National Council of Churches. I am grateful for their mentoring, friendship, and the leadership they continue to provide the church.

United Methodist Women also deserves my thanks. The organization is often at the forefront of justice issues, especially those that disproportionately impact women, children, and youth, such as climate change. Over the years, they have published my articles in *Response Magazine*, including two Bible studies that included ideas for this book's third and seventh chapters.

I am grateful to family and friends who keep me grounded in personal relationships and the real world. Spending regular time with my grandchildren brings me joy and motivates me to continue working (and writing) for a world in which they will thrive. My husband Guarionex was my sounding board, companion, and primary support during the writing of this book.

Cappy Israel makes her guest apartment available to me for writing retreats in Santa Cruz. During a prayerful time there in the middle of one night, the framework and chapter titles for this book suddenly became clear. Santa Cruz artist Russell Brutsché painted the original picture that appears on the cover. My granddaughter, Anna Campbell, used her skills as a graphic artist to draft the initial cover design. Pamela Osgood edited an early draft of this book, as did Jenny Phillips, founder of Fossil Free UMC.

Thanks to Michael Gibson at Fortress Press, who has been helpful, encouraging, and accessible from the beginning. His suggestions for expanding some sections make the book stronger. Thanks also to

Michael Moore, Layne Johnson, and others at Fortress who helped bring this book to completion.

I am grateful for activist friends who stay the course even through trying times. You know who you are. I am glad to share time with you—singing songs, creating banners, developing programs, organizing demonstrations, engaging in nonviolent actions, and yes, even attending meetings. Being part of an extended community of people who are willing to work tirelessly for peace, justice, and the healing of creation continues to give me hope.

I am inspired by Indigenous people around the world who are rising up to protect the land, air, and water. My thanks go out to all who put their time, energy, and money into building a people's movement that is strong enough to transform the system that perpetuates climate change and a host of other ills. The God of love, whom John Wesley called "the soul of the universe," is certainly working through this global movement, bringing hope to the world.

1

Introduction: Love in a Time of Climate Change

Love bears all things, believes all things, hopes all things, endures all things. Love never ends.

—1 Corinthians 13:7–8a

Weather patterns in our region have changed. My husband and I moved from the Bay Area to rural Nevada County in Northern California as part of a *back to the land* migration of young people in the early 1970s. We rented a cabin in the beautiful pine, fir, and cedar forest outside Nevada City. It sometimes seemed that the trees themselves were raising their branches in praise of God. We planted a garden, acquired goats and chickens, and experienced the joys and struggles of raising our young children in the woods. We lived close to the rhythms of the natural world and enjoyed the cycle of seasons, including snow every winter. I remember looking out the kitchen window as I washed dishes, watching my husband walk through deep snow, creating a path for the kids and dogs who traipsed along single file behind him.

Now, just a few decades later, most winters bring some rain, but very little snow. When I started writing this book, California was in its fifth consecutive year of record-breaking drought. Reservoirs across the state were dangerously low and mandatory water restrictions were in place. The snowpack was seriously depleted. With rising temperatures, lack of water, and many dead and dying trees, the fire season started earlier, wildfires raged hotter, and more acres burned.[1] Sometimes smoke filled the sky for weeks at a time.

Then the fall and winter of 2016 brought rain, with snow at the higher elevations, which relieved and reassured us. Rain and snow storms continued, filling drained reservoirs and rebuilding the depleted snowpack. Still the storms continued, bringing record-breaking levels of both rain and snow. Now, as damage from floods has replaced drought as the immediate crisis, the California Department of Water Resources warns that climate change will continue to have a profound impact on California.[2] Scientists predict that our region will have more frequent droughts, more intense forest fires, and more severe storms and floods as the climate warms.[3]

Climate-related changes are taking place around the world. Many regions are being hit far harder than my community. Low-lying nations face storm surges, seawater encroachment, and hurricanes made more frequent and intense by warming oceans and rising seas. Island nations face the disappearance of their homelands. Several African nations struggle with record heat and drought, leading to water shortages, hunger, and disease.[4] Poor and vulnerable nations, which are hit hardest by climate change, often lack the infrastructure and resources to protect their people or rebuild. In developed nations, poor areas and communities of color are disproportionately impacted by weather disruptions. Yet the people in these regions have contributed little to the atmospheric burden of carbon emissions that cause climate change.

My purpose in writing this book is to issue a call to faithfulness and point in the direction of hope amid the climate crisis, which threatens the human family and God's creation. This book is geared toward Christians and people of other faiths who are willing to face the harsh realities of climate change, assess its implications, and develop a mature

---

1. Ed Joyce, "More Wildfires, Starting Sooner, Burning More Acres," *Capital Public Radio,* June 28, 2016, http://www.capradio.org/articles/2016/06/28/more-wildfires,-starting-sooner,-burning-more-acres/.

2. California Department of Water Resources: Climate Change, http://www.water.ca.gov/climate-change/.

3. Darrell Fears, "Climate scientists predict more blazing heat, drought, fires, and scores of dead trees in the West," *Washington Post,* June 23, 2016.

4. "Regional Vulnerabilities," 19.3.3, Climate Change 2007: Working Group II: Impacts, Adaptation and Vulnerability, Intergovernmental Panel on Climate Change (IPCC), http://www.ipcc.ch/publications_and_data/ar4/wg2/en/ch19s19-3-3.html.

response based on love of God and neighbor. With a challenge of this magnitude, only love will get us through.

The book highlights two primary themes: creation and justice. It is through *creation* that God blesses and sustains us. We are children of God and children of the earth, interconnected with all other parts of creation and called to honor and care for the earth. We lose sight of this reality to our peril and tragically, this is just what has happened. Ecosystems are being degraded at an alarming pace. The earth's changing climate is outpacing all other forms of environmental degradation and now threatens the stability of civilization and the balance of life on Earth.

A concern for *justice* reminds us of our responsibility for our neighbors. As followers of Jesus, we are called to be merciful and to establish justice for those who are marginalized. The concept of *climate justice* acknowledges that many poor and vulnerable human beings are already experiencing disproportionate harm due to the changing climate, other species are dying, and today's children and future generations will face increasingly harsh conditions as the planet continues to warm.

How can we face these realities, discern their implications, emerge with our faith intact, and respond with words and actions that demonstrate God's loving intentions for the world? This book proposes a process of discernment that will make this possible.

What does it mean to live in love as the consequences of climate change surpass predictions and the living systems of the earth succumb to the impacts of planetary warming? What does it mean to love God as life is diminished and the glory of creation fades? What does it mean to reach out in compassion to our suffering neighbors when disaster follows disaster with no end in sight? This book responds to these questions while affirming that no matter what difficulties we face, God's love envelops us and shows us the way. The book's premise is that love of God and neighbor in this time of climate change requires us to honor creation and to establish justice for our human family, for future generations, and for all creation.

Not everyone who reads this book will come to the same conclusions about what should be done to address the climate crisis. Readers come to this book with their own unique viewpoints, challenges, and responsibilities. This book is meant to equip people to come into their own as mature Christians, able to weigh the evidence and think for themselves, in community with others and with the help of the resources of faith.

Churches Respond to Climate Change

According to the US National Aeronautics and Space Administration (NASA), climate change is "a longterm change in the Earth's climate, or of a region on Earth," while global warming is "the increase in Earth's average surface temperature due to rising levels of greenhouse gases."[5] In this book I use these and similar terms interchangeably, since the earth's changing climate is characterized by rising average global temperatures.

Books and articles on global warming have been written for Christian audiences for twenty-five years. Most call on readers to respond by practicing good stewardship, reducing their carbon footprints, making their churches more sustainable, exerting their power as consumers by purchasing energy-efficient products, and exercising their responsibility as citizens by lobbying for stricter environmental regulations. In this book, I suggest such things myself. But as the rate of greenhouse gas emissions accelerates and average global temperatures continue to rise, these limited personal responses seem woefully inadequate for effectively addressing the grave and escalating climate disruptions seen around the world.

Why are our churches not sounding the alarm about the harm being done to God's creation? Why are our congregations not taking strong and concerted actions on behalf of God's beloved world? Some people may avoid the issue because of the magnitude of the problem. Many are struggling to feed their families, fulfill their immediate responsibilities, and make ends meet. Some of these day-to-day responsibilities may involve driving or other activities that require fossil fuels, and cutting back on their use may seem difficult or impossible. Even people who try to minimize their use of fossil fuels may feel hypocritical for speaking out about climate change if they still use coal, oil, or gas to power their lives.

A widespread and coordinated Christian response is also hampered by the denial of climate change among churches aligned with the Religious Right. Many of these churches insist on a literal interpretation of

---

5. "What's in a Name? Global Warming vs. Climate Change," National Aeronautics and Space Administration (NASA), http://www.nasa.gov/topics/earth/features/climate_by_any_other_name.html.

the creation stories in Genesis, leading to an anti-science bias that is characterized by the rejection of both evolutionary science and climate science. This active denial of climate change among many conservative churches prevents open discussion, inhibits action, and contributes to the air of controversy around the issue.

There is a strong political influence at work here, with most right-leaning churches adhering to Republican political and economic interests, which are invested in rejecting regulation and other climate action. In the US presidential election of 2016, 81 percent of white Evangelicals voted for Donald Trump, who denies the reality of climate change and demonstrates, in his policies, the antithesis of the love of God and neighbor that characterized the life and teachings of Jesus. The theological method proposed in this book provides a remedy for the authoritarian biblical fundamentalism of the Religious Right.

Many churches, however, have long acknowledged the value of science and the reality of global warming, including the Catholic Church, Eastern Orthodox churches, and many mainline Protestant denominations. Church leaders write pastoral letters on the topic. Denominational boards and agencies provide educational resources, pass resolutions, advocate for strong climate legislation, support binding international treaties, and call on church members to take action. Some congregations are rising to this challenge and are *greening* their churches by planting native plants or community gardens, offering Earth Sabbath celebrations, weatherizing their buildings, installing energy-efficient appliances, and putting up solar panels. Some church groups have participated in successful advocacy efforts by joining campaigns urging government leaders to establish fuel economy standards on cars and emissions limits on power plants. Some denominations are divesting from fossil fuels. Many individual Christians and church bodies work with ecumenical, interfaith, and secular organizations that focus on creation care. Yet despite these efforts, the church as a whole has not yet fashioned a coordinated response that is proportional to the magnitude of the threats that a warming world poses to God's creation, vulnerable members of our human family, and future generations.

Likewise, churches and faith communities of every kind engage in ministry with poor, sick, and hurting people in their communities and reach out in mission to suffering people around the world. Some of these projects seek to convert people to a particular religion, but many denominations now acknowledge the harm caused by early (and some contemporary) missionary efforts and have changed their ways, repenting for past harm and demonstrating a humble respect for diverse faith and cultural traditions. Reaching out in mercy without condition is an essential expression of faithfulness to Jesus's teachings on love of God and neighbor. Such acts provide a witness to the unconditional love of God.

Yet there is also a need for churches to engage in systemic analysis and to work for justice. Rates of poverty and inequity continue to rise in the United States and globally, as free-market austerity measures result in cutbacks to public infrastructure and social safety nets. Meanwhile, international organizations, governments, faith communities, and other charitable organizations continually organize massive relief efforts supported by the generosity of donors and the selflessness of volunteers. Organized efforts to offer charity and relieve suffering will become ever-more difficult and overwhelming as climate disruption progresses, leaving more people on every continent in need.

Some ecumenical and interfaith organizations, denominational boards and agencies, and other church groups call not only for *acts of mercy* but also for *acts of justice* on behalf of suffering people. Their statements do not always filter down to local churches or translate into congregational study on underlying issues or action for social change. Some inroads are being made as churches support campaigns for racial justice, immigrant rights, a living wage, prison reform, marriage equality, an end to human trafficking, and other justice issues. But churches mainly treat climate change as an environmental issue that only requires personal action and minimal lifestyle change.

Of course, it is important for those of us who live in the industrialized world to lower our carbon footprints, but there are reasons why many of us find this so difficult. Our social, economic, political, military, and even global institutions have been built upon cheap and abundant coal, oil, and gas. Effective climate action will require a transformation of the dominant ideologies, institutions, and systems that currently promote overconsumption and the profligate use of fossil fuels. Personal lifestyle change needs to be linked with communal organizing for structural change. Honoring creation and establishing justice go together.

The Movement for Climate Justice

Meanwhile, a strong and vital movement for *climate justice* has emerged, led primarily by marginalized people who live and work on the front lines of climate change. They do not speak quietly about sustainability, stewardship, or caring for creation. Rather, they demand justice for those who are experiencing the early effects of climate change, Indigenous people and others whose communities are being polluted by fossil-fuel extraction, young people and future generations, and other species with whom we share this planet.

Climate justice activists are not asking for charity, but are calling for justice. They refuse to dismiss the historic responsibility of wealthy nations, which developed on Indigenous lands, with the sweat, blood, and lives of enslaved African and Native peoples, by colonizing and waging resource wars against other nations, and by industrializing through the intensive burning of fossil fuels. Now people in poor nations and regions are suffering the early effects of climate change because industrialized nations have overwhelmed the global atmospheric commons with greenhouse gases. The injustice of the global system is not new—it is an ongoing pattern of colonization and subjugation that continues today. Indigenous communities are well aware of this historical context, and have been resisting the exploitation of their lands for centuries. They are also at the forefront of many contemporary struggles for climate justice.

Climate change is an unintended consequence of policy decisions put into place long ago, but its effects today are deadly. It not only impacts the present—it also forecloses on the future. Other trends also point toward a bleak future: poverty and inequity are increasing as the world's richest and most powerful people appropriate an ever-growing percentage of wealth by gaming the global system that they have designed.[6] As I wrote in *Shaking the Gates of Hell: Faith-Led Resistance to Corporate Globalization*:

> The system is designed for the results it is getting. . . . This becomes obvious when we look at the system of institutions that make up the global economy, and at who creates the rules, who benefits, and who pays the price. If we follow the money, we will see that the architects, rule makers, and enforcers of the global economy are reaping the benefits of what they have designed. . . . The rules of the global economy are not designed to provide a just distribution of the world's goods, but to protect and multiply wealth. They are not designed to preserve the earth, but to turn its gifts, such as forests and water, into money. They are not designed to

6. Megha Bahree, "The World's Richest Just Got a Lot Richer, While Everyone Else Didn't," *Forbes* (January 10, 2016).

improve the lives of the majority of human beings, but to bring financial benefits to the few.[7]

Climate justice activists call for changing the power structures that perpetuate planetary warming. They understand that an effective response to climate change includes working to reform democracy and transform the overarching system that reinforces multiple forms of injustice. Banners at rallies for climate justice frequently say, "System Change Not Climate Change."

Climate justice is comprehensive, and includes social, economic, racial, gender, and environmental justice. Organizing for solutions must begin at the local level, but changing the system requires the building of a global movement strong enough to pressure those at the apex of political and economic power. The growing climate justice movement is part of a larger *movement for global justice*, a broad alliance of groups working for fair trade, human rights, racial and economic justice, just international relations, peace, and participatory democracy. This has been called a "movement of movements," a "people's globalization," and "globalization from below." The ongoing refrain of this movement is: "Another world is possible."

This global movement has been bolstered and expanded by the release of Naomi Klein's bestseller, *This Changes Everything: Capitalism vs. the Climate*,[8] written for general audiences, and by Pope Francis's recent encyclical, *Laudato Si: On Care for Our Common Home*.[9] Both books link climate change with poverty and oppression, critique unrestrained capitalism, and propose a response that includes transforming dominant worldviews, ideologies, institutions, and systems. These ideas also appear in this book. As we explore the themes of creation and justice in the context of climate disruption, our exploration will be enriched by the theological method and teachings of John Wesley, who was born more than three hundred years ago.

The Relevance of John Wesley for Today

John Wesley, an Anglican priest, lived in eighteenth-century England during the Enlightenment, a time of great theological, scientific, and

---

7. Sharon Delgado, *Shaking the Gates of Hell: Faith-Led Resistance to Corporate Globalization* (Minneapolis: Fortress Press, 2007), 108–9.
8. Naomi Klein, *This Changes Everything: Capitalism vs. the Climate* (New York: Simon and Schuster, 2014).
9. Pope Francis, *Laudato Si: On Care for Our Common Home* (Rome: Libreria Editrice Vaticana, 2015).

social controversy and upheaval. He was a key leader in the spiritual revival that swept eighteenth-century England and led to the Great Awakening in colonial America. His insights still have relevance that will become clear as we consider them in light of the controversies and upheavals of our own time.

Wesley's unique teachings on *creation* highlight what is at stake with global climate change. They are based on his understanding of God's *omnipresence*, that is, the presence of God in and through creation. As we will see in later chapters, he taught that God is revealed through the natural world, God loves all creatures, humans are called to love and care for other creatures, and God's loving intention is for the redemption of all creation.

Wesley's teachings on *justice* center on the idea of *social holiness*, which emphasizes the connection between personal spirituality, community, and social concern. He preached, wrote, and acted on a variety of social issues, including slavery, wealth and poverty, materialism, workers' rights, the harms of industrialization, child labor, war and peace, and animal rights. His focus on social holiness establishes the centrality of justice for poor and vulnerable members of our human family, other species, and future generations.

Even more significant for us than John Wesley's teachings is his theological method. He appealed to scripture, tradition, reason, and experience as sources of authority in a process of discernment that has come to be called the *Wesleyan Quadrilateral*. This book will creatively adapt this process as it guides readers through an exploration of the themes of creation and justice. My hope is that this systematic approach will provide clarity and enable readers to effectively address climate change in a mature way that is consistent with their faith and values. Practical implications and general suggestions for action will be presented as the book progresses. More detailed suggestions can be found in several of the books, articles, and websites in the Suggested Reading List at the back of the book.

Book Overview and Organization

Part I of this book, "Discerning the Truth about Climate Change," introduces the book's primary subject matter and its theological method. Chapter 2, "Climate Change: A Sign of the Times," presents an overview of climate change and explains the likely impacts of a warming climate on church ministries and on creation. Chapter 3, "Scripture, Tradition,

Reason, and Experience: Tools for Discernment," describes how John Wesley used scripture, tradition, reason, and experience as tools for discernment in his search for truth and explains how they will be used to explore the themes of creation and justice in this book.

Part II, "Honoring Creation," presents the theological theme of creation through scripture, tradition, reason, and experience in the context of climate change. Chapter 4, "Scripture: Hearing Creation's Groans," shows how scripture illuminates our understanding of God's love for creation, the human role in creation, God's activity in and through creation, and creation's future. Chapter 5, "Tradition: The Wisdom of God in Creation," presents the theme of creation in general Christian tradition, summarizes John Wesley's views, and introduces several contemporary Wesleyan theologians' views on creation. Chapter 6, "Reason: The New Creation Story," explores conflicting worldviews, describes scientific understandings of the origin and nature of the universe, and explains how reason can help us think critically in order to find commonsense approaches to climate change. Chapter 7, "Experience: Creation as Sacrament," addresses the role of experience as it relates to creation, proposes a view of creation as sacrament, and explores the implications of experience in the context of climate change.

Part III, "Establishing Justice," develops the theme of justice in the context of climate change. Chapter 8, "Scripture: Transforming the Jericho Road," frames the theme of justice in the parable of The Good Samaritan by expanding the understanding of neighbor to include all creation, critiquing injustice, and calling for systemic transformation. Chapter 9, "Tradition: Social Holiness on a Warming Planet," develops John Wesley's concept of social holiness in light of climate change and introduces contemporary theologies of liberation that include systemic analysis of today's interrelated justice and environmental concerns. Chapter 10, "Reason: Climate Justice and Common Sense," examines climate change and related injustice through the lens of reason, reveals links that connect these problems, analyzes systemic causes, and makes commonsense suggestions for climate action. Chapter 11, "Experience: On the Front Lines of Climate Change," explores experi-ences of people living and working on the front lines of climate change, including leaders in the struggle for climate justice who can help us discern a faithful response to the climate crisis.

The Conclusion, "Love of God and Neighbor: A Faithful Response to Climate Change," integrates the themes of creation and justice as developed throughout this book and proposes a framework for climate action that is grounded in the love of God and neighbor and is expressed through honoring creation and establishing justice. By acknowledging that conclusions of readers may vary, this chapter encourages respect for the process of discernment and for individual perspectives.

Finally, a word of hope: Honoring creation and working to establish justice cultivates hope in us as individuals and equips us to offer hope to the world. First, as followers of Jesus, our primary hope is that we can live in faithfulness to the loving will of God in all circumstances, as he did. The fulfillment of this hope is possible only if we live under the influence of the Holy Spirit. As we do so, our ongoing growth in faith, hope, and love is expressed by our lifestyle choices and acts of mercy and justice in the world.

Second, we hope for the transformation of the world. I stress throughout this book that individual action is not enough to turn the rising tide of climate chaos. It will take many people working together to build a diverse and multi-focused movement that is strong enough to pressure policy makers, transform the system, and make possible the enactment of sane policies and practices that effectively address climate change.

It may be that the magnitude of the challenge of climate change will motivate the dramatic ideological and systemic shifts necessary for changing direction as a species. As we entrust our lives to God we are empowered to join with others in the growing movement for climate justice and to carry a unified message of healing, love, and solidarity as we live into God's future, offering hope amid the climate crisis that "another world is possible."

God is ever present, always with us. Love never ends.

PART I

Discerning the Truth about Climate Change

2

Climate Change: A Sign of the Times

When it is evening, you say, "It will be fair weather, for the sky is red." And in the morning, "It will be stormy today, for the sky is red and threatening." You know how to interpret the appearance of the sky, but you cannot interpret the signs of the times.

—Matthew 16:2–3

Humans have been interpreting the weather for millennia, but most of us are at a loss when trying to interpret the meaning of climate change. While many acknowledge its reality, most of us have not yet come to terms with its profound implications. Yet the earth's changing climate is one of the major signs of our time.

Weather and climate are two different but related concepts. Dr. J. Marshall Shepherd, President of the American Meteorological Society, put it in simple terms: "Weather is your mood and climate is your personality."[1] The earth's moods are becoming less predictable and more destructive, and the earth's personality is changing as average global temperatures rise and as record-breaking extreme weather events become more frequent on every continent. If greenhouse gas emissions continue to rise at current levels and warming trends continue, the

---

1. Becky Fried, "What You Missed in We the Geeks: 'Weather Is Your Mood and Climate Is Your Personality,'" The White House blog (October 1, 2014), https://www.whitehouse.gov/blog/2014/01/10/what-you-missed-we-geeks-weather-your-mood-and-climate-your-personality.

earth will have a completely different personality before the end of this century—a personality with increasingly dramatic mood swings.

To mitigate and adapt to a changing climate, avoid the worst damage, and begin regeneration, we need to understand its impacts on God's creation and on our human family, especially those who are most vulnerable. Those of us who follow Jesus and carry his message must also consider how rising temperatures and increasingly erratic weather will affect our ability to share the good news of God's saving love for the world, for these climate dynamics will impact all our ministries for the foreseeable future.

Exploring these realities in the context of ministry will give a concrete focus to our discussion about the present impacts and future projections of our changing climate. As the planet warms and weather disasters become more common, our congregations and all the people with whom we are in ministry and mission will be affected, especially those who live in the poorest and most vulnerable regions of the world.

Imagine More Malaria

In June 2014, three of my grandchildren went with me to the California-Nevada Annual Conference of the United Methodist Church. During a plenary session, Bishop Warner Brown invited Alex and Malina, ten-year-old cousins, to join him on the stage. He recognized them for raising money, rolling coins, and bringing it forward in a big jar for the Imagine No Malaria campaign.[2] This popular campaign provides mosquito nets for children in Africa, where many children die from malaria at an early age. The Bishop asked the children why they had worked on this project. Alex said, to great applause, "There's no difference. They're just like us." The Bishop gave each of the children a big hug. Malina said later, "He was proud of us."

Just ten years old, they already have empathy and can imagine how children who live halfway around the world must feel. Such ministries that teach our children to care about people in faraway places and enable us to reach out in mission in the name of Christ are incredibly valuable. What my grandchildren and church leaders do not yet know is that climate change will impact the Imagine No Malaria campaign and similar hands-on mission projects in almost unimaginable ways. According to the World Health Organization (WHO), malaria seems likely to be the vector-borne disease most sensitive to long-term

2. Imagine No Malaria, http://www.imaginenomalaria.org/.

changes in the climate. Global temperature increases of 2 to 3 degrees Celsius above pre-industrial times would increase the seasonal duration of the disease and increase the number of people at risk of malaria by several hundred million.[3] If greenhouse gas emissions continue on their current trajectory, we will have to imagine more malaria, not less.

This chapter explores how climate change is degrading God's creation, harming those who are most vulnerable, and negatively impacting ministries and missions at home and around the world. By understanding the scope and magnitude of this challenge we can open our minds and hearts to the Spirit's direction and dedicate ourselves to working together to bring healing and hope to the world.

The Scientific Consensus

As mentioned in the Introduction, many denominations have acknowledged the reality of climate change and have worked to raise awareness through statements, advocacy efforts, and recommendations for congregations and members. Some local churches have responded by *greening* the church in various ways. Many individual Christians struggle to limit their use of fossil fuels. Nevertheless, the extent of the threat of planetary warming and its stark implications for the future have not resulted in a widespread and coordinated response within our churches. We have not yet truly interpreted this crucial sign of our times.

Although the vast majority of scientists in climate-related fields agree that *anthropogenic* (human-caused) climate change is real, pastors and people in the pews are as prone to confusion and denial in the face of this challenging and sometimes controversial issue as anyone else. Later in this book we will explore some of the psychological, social, and institutional reasons why it may seem easier to avoid the issue, remain in denial, and maintain the status quo.

But avoidance and denial don't change our current predicament. They only postpone our inevitable confrontation with the impacts of a warming world and increasingly erratic weather, which people are experiencing now in countries around the world. If we are to awaken church members to these dangers and mobilize effective action on climate change, we have to educate our congregations about its reality, challenges, and implications. This requires us to use reason to discern

3. "Climate Change and Infectious Diseases," World Health Organization, http://www.who.int/globalchange/climate/summary/en/index5.html.

truth from falsehood and to ground our discussion in science so that we understand the basic facts and realize the implications of the earth's rising temperatures. Current knowledge is based on scientific evidence provided through observations, measurements, historical records, calculations, and projections. Scientific conclusions based on the weight of evidence provide us with a context for the work of developing a theological framework and discerning a faithful response to this great challenge of our time.

There is overwhelming scientific consensus that the earth is warming and that this measurable warming is caused largely by human-induced greenhouse gas emissions. The primary authority on climate is the Intergovernmental Panel on Climate Change (IPCC), which includes scientists from countries throughout the world. Their most recent report, published in 2014, states "Human influence on the climate system is clear, and recent anthropogenic emissions of greenhouse gases are the highest in history. Recent climate changes have had widespread impacts on human and natural systems."[4] The burning of fossil fuels is the main cause of recent planetary warming, but deforestation, industrialized agriculture, and other human activities also contribute. National scientific academies of every major country and 97 percent of papers published by scientists in climate-related fields conclude that we are observing anthropogenic climate change on a global scale.[5]

Since the beginning of the Industrial Revolution, greenhouse gases in the atmosphere have increased, with a corresponding rise in average global temperatures. For the first time in 800,000 years, levels of carbon dioxide (CO_2) have risen above 300 parts per million (ppm). In 2013, they passed the 400 ppm mark. If CO_2 emissions continue to rise at the current rate, we are on track to hit 600 ppm or beyond by the end of this century, causing global temperatures to rise accordingly.[6] Emissions of nitrous oxide (N_2O) and methane (CH_4), which are even more potent greenhouse gases than CO_2, also continue to rise.[7]

Meanwhile, the average surface temperature of the earth is getting hotter. According to NASA, with the exception of 1998, the ten hottest years on record have all occurred since 2000. The year 2015 set a record

4. Rajendra K. Pachauri et al., eds., *Climate Change 2014 Synthesis Report*, The Intergovernmental Panel on Climate Change (IPCC), 2, https://www.ipcc.ch/pdf/assessment-report/ar5/syr/SYR_AR5_FINAL_full.pdf.
5. "Scientific Consensus: Earth's Climate Is Warming," National Aeronautics and Space Administration (NASA), http://climate.nasa.gov/scientific-consensus/.
6. *Climate Change 2014 Synthesis Report*, 3.
7. Ibid., 5.

for the hottest year ever recorded[8] and was surpassed in 2016 as average global temperatures surged even higher.[9]

As temperatures rise, weather patterns are thrown off balance. We can't know whether a particular extreme weather event is actually caused by global warming, but we do know that it makes such events statistically more likely. In recent years, there have been thousands of record-breaking weather disruptions all over the world, which fits the pattern scientists expect with a warming planet. Heat waves have been setting new records, including in Korea, Australia, Argentina, and Europe.[10] This trend continued in 2016 with scorching heat waves in Russia, the Middle East, Southwest Asia, and the Southwest and Southeast United States.[11] Prolonged droughts have been breaking previous records in Africa, the Amazon Basin, Australia, the Arctic, India, Colombia, Somalia, and California. These droughts result in water shortages, diseased trees, crop failures, and in some instances, the deaths of animals and people.[12] With changing precipitation, drought, and heat waves, wildfire seasons start earlier. Huge wildfires are becoming more frequent, burning hotter, lasting longer, and burning more acres.[13] In 2016, out-of-control wildfires devastated forests in California, Alaska, Indonesia, Canada, Spain, Portugal, and France.[14]

Meanwhile, storms are getting bigger and more intense. As air warms, more water evaporates, drying out the land. Clouds carry the additional moisture, making storms more likely. This results in the excessive rainfall, super storms, typhoons, hurricanes, and floods that are creating disasters on every continent.[15]

As the climate warms, various species of plants and animals are

8. "NASA, NOAA Analyses Reveal Record-Shattering Global Warm Temperatures in 2015," National Aeronautics and Space Administration (NASA), August 14, 2016, http://www.nasa.gov/press-release/nasa-noaa-analyses-reveal-record-shattering-global-warm-temperatures-in-2015.

9. "2016 Climate Trends Continue to Break Records," NASA, July 19, 2016, http://www.nasa.gov/feature/goddard/2016/climate-trends-continue-to-break-records.

10. Brian Kahn, "Extreme Heat Defines Climate Change," *Scientific American* (November 5, 2015).

11. "Extreme Heat for an Extreme Year," NASA, August 11, 2016, http://earthobservatory.nasa.gov/IOTD/view.php?id=88547.

12. Bruce Wright, "Extreme Climate Change Pictures 2016: Amid Hottest Year on Record, Famine, Drought Grips Africa, Central America, India," *International Business Times* (July 22, 2016), http://www.ibtimes.com/extreme-climate-change-pictures-2016-amid-hottest-year-record-famine-drought-grips-2394114.

13. "Study: Fire Seasons Get Longer, More Frequent," NASA, July 28, 2015, http://climate.nasa.gove/news/2315/study-fire-seasons-getting-longer-more-frequent.

14. Anne-Sophie Brändlin, "How climate change is increasing forest fires around the world," Deutsche Welle (August 11, 2016), http://www.dw.com/en/how-climate-change-is-increasing-forest-fires-around-the-world/a-19465490.

15. "The Impact of Climate Change on Natural Disasters," NASA, http://earthobservatory.nasa.gov/Features/RisingCost/rising_cost5.php.

migrating, while those that can't migrate become extinct.[16] Vector-borne disease patterns are shifting, as temperatures, humidity, and precipitation rates shift.[17] The cryosphere (areas of permafrost, snow, and ice) has begun to melt rapidly, releasing greenhouse gases that had been sequestered in their historic frozen state and causing sea levels to rise.[18] The oceans are acidifying and heating up.[19] The earth's personality is changing as average global temperatures rise and as dramatic effects are seen in every country on earth.

Climate Forecasts

It is impossible to adequately visualize the future, especially as rising temperatures and extreme weather continually set records around the world. We can, however, read the signs of the times. Climate scientists tell us that if we continue along the current path there will be accelerating warming and more intense and frequent weather disruptions as persistent greenhouse gases continue to build up in the atmosphere.

Average global temperatures have risen by 1 degree Celsius (1.8 degrees Fahrenheit) since pre-industrial times.[20] These higher temperatures are causing far more damage than had been predicted and are contributing to more frequent and devastating weather-related disasters.[21] The IPCC, the World Bank, and other global institutions call for ambitious action to help countries avoid the worst projected climate impacts by limiting warming to no more than 2 degrees Celsius (3.6 degrees Fahrenheit).[22] But without significant cuts in emissions, climate scientists predict that average global temperatures could rise by 4 degrees Celsius or more above pre-industrial levels *in this century.*[23]

The World Bank's report, *Turn Down the Heat: Why a 4°C Warmer World Must Be Avoided,* warns of the dangers of such a rapid and dramatic temperature rise. Sea levels will continue to rise, inundating coastal cities, as the Greenland and West Antarctic ice sheets continue to melt.[24]

16. *Climate Change 2014 Synthesis Report,* 6.
17. "Turn down the heat: why a 4°C warmer world must be avoided," The World Bank, xvii, http://documents.worldbank.org/curated/en/2012/11/17097815/turn-down-heat-4°c-warmer-world-must-avoided.
18. "Sea Level," NASA, http://climate.nasa.gov/vital-signs/sea-level/.
19. *Climate Change 2014 Synthesis Report,* 4.
20. Susanna Twidale, "Global temperature rise to pass 1 degree C this year: Britain's Met Office," Reuters (November 9, 2015), http://www.reuters.com/article/2015/11/09/us-climatechange-summit-temperatures-idUSKCN0SY1F220151109.
21. Michael Le Page, "Climate Change: It's Even Worse Than We Thought," *New Scientist,* https://www.newscientist.com/round-up/worse climate/.
22. "Turn down the heat," xiii.
23. Ibid., xiii.

Rapid warming and acidification of the oceans will continue to have profound negative impacts on marine species, including coral reefs and entire ocean ecosystems.[25] Desert and coastal ecosystems, grasslands and forests (including tropical rain forests) will continue to change dramatically. Heat waves, droughts, wildfires, storms, floods, and other forms of extreme weather will continue to become more frequent and intense.[26]

Large-scale loss of biodiversity will occur, as the changing climate drives a transition of the earth's ecosystems into a state unknown in human history.[27] As population increases, destruction of agricultural lands due to heat waves, drought, salt water intrusion, or rising seas could substantially undermine food security at a global level.[28] In some regions, extreme weather events such as heat waves and massive floods will likely result in food and water shortages, malnutrition, epidemic diseases, injuries, and death.[29]

The World Bank report warns that the cumulative impacts of planetary warming could be catastrophic, as regional and global disruptions grow, combine, and interact. There is also the risk of "crossing critical social system thresholds," as climate change creates extreme stress on societies. Existing social, economic, or political institutions "could become less effective or even collapse."[30] The report emphasizes the risks:

> Thus, given that uncertainty remains about the full nature and scale of impacts, there is also no certainty that adaptation to a 4°C world is possible. A 4°C world is likely to be one in which communities, cities and countries would experience severe disruptions, damage, and dislocation, with many of these risks spread unequally. It is likely that the poor will suffer most and the global community could become more fractured and unequal than today. The projected 4°C warming simply must not be allowed to occur—the heat must be turned down. Only early, cooperative, international actions can make that happen.[31]

24. Ibid., xiv.
25. Ibid., xv.
26. Ibid., xv–xvii.
27. Ibid., xvi.
28. Ibid., xvi–xviii.
29. Ibid., xvii.
30. Ibid., xviii.
31. Ibid.

Climate change has been identified as an issue of national and global security. Institutions as diverse as the World Bank, International Monetary Fund, Central Intelligence Agency, and Pentagon warn of increased humanitarian need, migration pressures, and civil unrest. The Department of Defense's 2015 report, *National Security Implications of Climate-Related Risks and a Changing Climate*, states:

> The DoD recognizes the reality of climate change and the significant risk it poses to U.S. interests globally. The National Security Strategy, issued in February 2015, is clear that climate change is an urgent and growing threat to our national security, contributing to increased natural disasters, refugee flows, and conflicts over basic resources such as food and water. These impacts are already occurring, and the scope, scale, and intensity of these impacts are projected to increase over time.[32]

As emissions soar, temperatures climb, and weather-related disasters devastate region after region, earth's changing climate threatens to dramatically change the personality of the planet that has nurtured life, including human life, through the eons. As God's creation is degraded, human hopes for the future are foreclosed. We human beings, too, are part of creation, and we share in its suffering. We have a relationship of both kinship with and responsibility for the community of life on earth, and the outcome of this struggle largely depends on us. This is a pivotal time of choice between life and death. The ability of our earthly home to nurture life hangs in the balance. We can continue along the present course or we can repent, seek to discern God's will, and take action under the Spirit's guidance. We can organize now to mitigate greenhouse gas emissions, adapt to climate change, foster the earth's regenerative ability to sequester carbon, and transform the systems that cause climate change.

Calls for Climate Justice

In 1992, I traveled to Rio de Janeiro as part of the United Methodist delegation during the United Nations Conference on Environment and Development (UNCED), the first major gathering of world leaders to focus on global warming and other environmental and related development issues. It was clear even then that environmental concerns

---

32. *National Security Implications of Climate-Related Risks and a Changing Climate*, 2015 Report, Department of Defense, http://archive.defense.gov/pubs/150724-congressional-report-on-national-implications-of-climate-change.pdf.

could not be effectively addressed without simultaneously addressing poverty and inequity. The governments of the world agreed that *sustainable development* for poor countries was inseparable from global action on climate change.

Since that time there have been many summits, but greenhouse gas emissions continue to soar while poverty continues and inequity grows. Meanwhile, poor and developing regions experience disproportionate harm from the early effects of climate change. Negotiators from vulnerable and hard-hit nations are pleading with those from wealthier nations to take strong and binding action to limit emissions now.

As global temperatures rise, every place on earth will be affected, but many of the poorest regions will suffer the most severe effects. Rising temperatures and weather extremes will counteract efforts to reduce poverty, especially in developing nations. These are the very regions where faith-based groups and secular organizations reach out in mission to provide relief from suffering. As climate-related disasters trigger hunger, homelessness, regional conflict, and mass migrations, the continent of Africa will be particularly hard hit. Drought and water shortages there are already affecting agricultural production of basic crops like rice, maize, and wheat, causing food prices to rise, endangering food security, and threatening famine.[33] As glaciers melt and sea levels rise, low-lying regions and island nations experience disastrous flooding from monsoons, hurricanes, and other serious storms. Some islands and coastal areas will disappear; other places will become uninhabitable. Some poor countries and communities face multiple threats, compounding their risks.[34]

The Philippines, for instance, is extremely vulnerable to the ravages of climate change. Typhoon Haiyan, one of the largest storms ever recorded, hit the Philippines in November 2013, killing six thousand and displacing over four million people.[35] This disaster took place just days before leaders from more than 190 nations met in Warsaw, Poland, for yet another round of United Nations climate negotiations (the nineteenth Conference of the Parties, or COP 19). Yeb Sano, head of the Philippine delegation, fasted throughout the talks and pleaded

---

33. "Climate Change in Africa: What Is at Stake?" United Nations Environment Program (UNEP), http://www.unep.org/roa/amcen/docs/AMCEN_Events/climate-change/2ndExtra_15Dec/FACT_SHEET_CC_Africa.pdf.
34. "Turn down the heat," xv–xiii.
35. "U.S. AID Fact Sheet on Typhoon Haiyan," U.S. Agency for International Development (USAID), http://iipdigital.usembassy.gov/st/english/texttrans/2013/11/20131112286248.html.

with the convened delegates to institute binding targets for limiting emissions in order to spare vulnerable nations from further climate chaos. An interfaith group in Warsaw, together with people around the world, mourned and fasted in solidarity with the people of the Philippines.[36]

On the tenth day of Yeb Sano's fast, the "Group of 77," made up of developing nations, staged a walkout of the climate talks. What triggered the protest was the refusal by wealthier nations to 1) institute binding limits on emissions and 2) establish a financial mechanism to address *loss and damage* caused to poor nations by global warming.[37] This protest highlighted the fact that most accumulated greenhouse gas pollution has come from industrialized nations, especially the United States, while poor nations with minimal historic emissions lack the resources to respond to disasters caused by rising temperatures, rising seas, and extreme weather. These disproportionate impacts upon countries least responsible provide a key rationale for calls for climate justice.

Wherever disasters hit, women and their dependent children are among the most vulnerable. It is estimated that globally, women and children make up 70 percent of those living in poverty. In developing nations, women and girls often provide for their families' basic needs, such as water, fuel, and food. Their work increases as rising temperatures and weather-related disasters make these more costly or scarce.[38] When droughts cause crops to fail and food prices to rise, children suffer and sometimes die. The biblical exhortation to "care for widows and orphans in their distress" (James 1:27) surely applies today to the women and children who suffer disproportionately as the planet warms.

In industrialized nations, people in poor regions and communities of color bear the brunt of extreme weather. When food prices rise because of extended drought, those who struggle to feed their families are most seriously impacted. When Hurricane Katrina struck New Orleans, the hardest-hit neighborhood was the Ninth Ward, a poor, predominately African American neighborhood. Likewise, during Hur-

36. "'It's time to stop this madness'—Philippines plea at UN climate talks," Climate Home (November 11, 2013), http://www.climatechangenews.com/2013/11/11/its-time-to-stop-this-madness-philippines-plea-at-un-climate-talks/.
37. David Jolly, "Developing Nations Stage Protest at Climate Talks," *New York Times* (November 20, 2013), http://www.nytimes.com/2013/11/21/world/rich-and-poor-nations-spar-over-climate-damages.html.
38. "Women and Climate Change," Church World Service, http://hunger.cwsglobal.org/site/DocServer/CWS_Enough2.pdf?docID=1521.

ricane Sandy, the worst damage was inflicted on the Rockaway borough in Queens, largely made up of poor African American people.[39]

Environmental Justice and Climate Justice

People in poor countries and communities also bear the brunt of the pollution of land, air, and water caused by the extraction and processing of fossil fuels. As we have seen, when fossil fuels are burned they release greenhouse gases that cause atmospheric warming, but they also produce serious health and environmental impacts as they are extracted, transported, and refined. Mountaintop removal coal mining, hydraulic fracturing (fracking) for oil or natural gas, offshore oil drilling, and the destruction of forests to create vast tar sands mines pollute the land, air, and water and harm the people who live nearby.[40]

Areas that have been polluted over many years by toxic waste dumps, highly polluting industrial processes, or extractive industries have been called *sacrifice zones*. These include regions that have been polluted through coal, oil, or gas extraction, transport, or processing. Some sacrifice zones are in poor but oil-rich countries, such as Nigeria, where Royal Dutch Shell has extracted and refined oil for generations. While Shell and Nigeria's military leaders have gotten rich through oil sales, the land, air, and water have been ravaged by extraction, oil spills, gas flaring, and deforestation. This corporate plunder, supported by the government, has destroyed the subsistence economy of the Indigenous Ogoni people, who traditionally lived by farming and fishing. In 1995, Goldman Environmental Award recipient Ken Saro-Wiwa and eight other Ogoni environmental activists were hanged. In 2009, Royal Dutch Shell agreed to pay a settlement of $15.5 million related to complicity in their deaths.[41]

In developed nations, sacrifice zones are usually in or near low-income communities, usually communities of color. In the United States, *environmental racism* came to national attention in the 1990s under the leadership of African American churches. Environmental

---

39. Dominique Mann, "Hurricane Sandy Communities of Color Recount Their Struggle to Rebuild after Superstorm Sandy," *New York Times* (March 3, 2014), http://thegrio.com/2014/03/04/hurricane-sandy-communities-of-color-recount-their-struggle-to-rebuild-after-superstorm/#54564545.

40. "The Hidden Costs of Fossil Fuels," Union of Concerned Scientists, http://www.ucsusa.org/clean-energy/our-energy-choices/coal-and-other-fossil-fuels/hidden-cost-of-fossils#bf-toc-0.

41. "Fact Sheet: The Case Against Shell," The Center for Constitutional Rights (March 24, 2009), https://ccrjustice.org/home/get-involved/tools-resources/fact-sheets-and-faqs/factsheet-case-against-shell.

racism is "the intentional placement of hazardous waste sites, landfills, incinerators, and polluting industries in communities inhabited mainly by African-Americans, Hispanics, Native Americans, Asians, Pacific Islanders, migrant farm workers, and the working poor."[42] Activists in such communities have been working for *environmental justice* for decades, with some support from churches.

Today, many climate justice activists are engaged in struggles to defend communities threatened with pollution from the extraction, transport, or refining of fossil fuels. This aspect of climate justice incorporates environmental justice into the work of addressing the problem of climate change at the source. While continuing to call for strong international treaties, government regulations, and a rapid transition to renewable power, people engaged in these local struggles demand an end to the ongoing exploitation of fossil-fuel reserves and development of pipelines, refineries, and other related infrastructure. A common sign at climate justice rallies proclaims, "Coal, oil, gas—none shall pass." Another simply states, "Keep it in the ground."

Indigenous people are at the forefront of many of these struggles, calling for governments to respect their treaty rights and to protect the land, air, and water for future generations. For example, in 2016 the Standing Rock Sioux Tribe in North Dakota set up camp and took a stand against the construction of the Dakota Access Pipeline. The crude oil pipeline was scheduled to go under the Missouri River near the tribe's reservation, endangering their water supply. Members of hundreds of Indigenous tribes and thousands of allies sent financial support, shipped supplies, or joined the Standing Rock "water protectors" at their camp for peaceful and prayerful resistance.

Several denominations, including my own, have held services acknowledging and repenting for Christianity's past complicity in colonization, forced conversions, assimilation, and genocide. If we who are Christian intend to make amends and be reconciled with our Indigenous brothers and sisters, a big step forward would be to support them in their current efforts to protect their treaty rights, to stand with them as allies to prevent contamination of their lands and waters caused by the extraction of fossil fuels, and to learn from them about the value and interconnectedness of all parts of creation. By doing so, we honor creation and work for justice in our time.

---

42. *Almost Everything You Need to Know about Environmental Justice*, United Church of Christ, http://d3n8a8pro7vhmx.cloudfront.net/unitedchurchofchrist/legacy_url/421/almost-every-thing-you-need-to-know-about-environmental-justice-english-version.pdf?1418423801.

As we interpret the signs of our times, we must give special attention to the voices of those who live and work on the front lines of climate change but are generally ignored by the media. These include climate activists from the global South, poor people and people of color living in sacrifice zones polluted by fossil-fuel extraction, women farmers struggling to feed their families, young people speaking out for inter-generational justice, and Indigenous peoples calling for policies that protect the earth. Together this rising chorus of voices expresses the yearnings of people joining together in the growing movement for climate justice, which provides a critique of the global system of unrestrained free-market capitalism and demands systemic change. Their pleas, demands, and warnings urge us to demonstrate God's care and concern by raising our voices on their behalf and by taking actions that are consistent with the magnitude of the challenges we face.

The Last Beneficiary

Some churches have joined the global movement to divest from fossil fuels. I have been involved in helping to advocate for divestment in my denomination, the United Methodist Church, with a group called Fossil Free UMC, founded by the Reverend Jenny Phillips. In a 2015 article titled "The Last Beneficiary," Reverend Phillips called on the United Methodist General Board of Pensions and Health Benefits to screen out coal, oil, and gas from its investment portfolio. She explained that many of today's seminarians and young pastors will still be preaching in thirty or forty years. By the time they retire many climate forecasts will have come to pass. She wrote:

> If our hypothetical last pastor serves in the continental United States, he might spend years of his ministry working on recovery from extreme weather events—the kinds scientists tell us to expect more of—events like Sandy and Katrina. Or perhaps he'll work in a church whose endowment came from selling fracking rights, but whose tap water isn't safe to pour over the babies he baptizes.
>
> If he's appointed in Alaska, his church's building might have serious problems with its foundation, because warming temperatures are thawing the permafrost that has been the ground on which some Alaskan communities are built.
>
> The effects of climate change will make crop yields less stable, which could make food scarcer and more expensive. That's a challenge if our pastor is serving a missionary church in Thailand. Many communities

there depend on subsistence farming, and they expect more seasons of hunger.

When I think of that last beneficiary, the one whose pension you're charged to protect, I can't help but feel compelled to ask you to really, really explore the possibility that there can be a responsible path in which his retirement account isn't dependent on the flourishing of industries that will wreak such havoc and heartbreak and destruction and death upon the people he is called to serve.[43]

Of course, our concern extends beyond pastors and pensioners to our congregations and communities, to all the beneficiaries of the ministries and missions of our churches, and to all creation. As climate change accelerates, our congregations will have to do more than green the church. According to the National Council of Churches, USA:

The impacts of global climate change threaten all creation and will make it more difficult for people of faith to care for those in need. With expected increases in drought, storm intensity, disease, species extinction, and flooding, the impacts of global climate change will increase the lack of food, shelter, and water available, particularly to those living in or near poverty. . . .

Though many understand the devastating impacts that climate change will have on human communities around the world, few understand the impacts that climate change will have on core church ministries such as refugee resettlement, feeding the hungry, and disaster relief. The impacts of global climate change are already calling on the church to provide more financial resources and volunteer services to meet the growing needs of people in poverty in the U.S. and around the globe.[44]

Disaster relief efforts will claim an ever-increasing percentage of time, energy, and money, as heat waves, wildfires, storms, and floods become more frequent and severe. Church buildings destroyed in what used to be called natural disasters will have to be rebuilt or abandoned. Caring for the sick will require more commitment as malaria and other tropical diseases spread beyond their previous boundaries. Feeding growing numbers of hungry people will present a tremendous challenge as droughts increase, crops fail, famines spread, and food prices rise. In some areas life may become so difficult that alleviating suffering

---

43. Jenny Phillips, "The Last Beneficiary," Fossil Free UMC, http://www.fossilfreeumc.org/blog/2014/11/13/thelastbeneficiary.
44. "Climate Change and Church: How Global Climate Change Will Impact Core Church Ministries," National Council of Churches Eco-Justice Program, http://interfaithpowerandlight.org/wp-content/uploads/2009/11/ClimateWhitePaper_finalREV.pdf.

caused by rising temperatures and extreme weather may become the primary hands-on ministry of the church.

Ministries of hospitality and welcome for immigrants will be increasingly taxed by waves of migrants fleeing regions submerged by rising seas, made uninhabitable by extreme storms or drought, or engulfed in conflicts made worse by weather-related disasters. According to António Guterres, the UN High Commissioner for Refugees, climate change could soon become the biggest factor driving population displacements, both inside and across national borders.[45] Some regions will experience a mass exodus, while others will see an influx of climate refugees.[46]

If we ignore or evade the grave implications of the climate crisis, we contribute to the problem. As we seek to interpret this major sign of our times, we must heed the warnings of climate scientists and respond to the increasingly urgent calls for climate justice. With concerted and immediate global efforts we can avoid escalating catastrophe and begin the process of healing our world and establishing justice for those most vulnerable, justice for future generations, and justice for all creation. This is a task to which we are called as disciples of Jesus Christ in our time.

Intergenerational Justice

Intergenerational justice is fair and just treatment for the world's children, young people, and future generations. According to a 2013 Stanford University report, signed by 520 scientists, today's children will likely live in a world "irretrievably damaged" by climate disruption, extinctions, wholesale loss of diverse ecosystems, pollution, overpopulation, and overconsumption. The executive summary of the report states: "By the time today's children reach middle age, it is extremely likely that Earth's life-support systems, critical for human prosperity and existence, will be irretrievably damaged by the magnitude, global extent and combination of these human-caused stressors, unless we take concrete, immediate actions to ensure a sustainable, high-quality future."[47] Unless we take *immediate actions*, the children and young people of today will have to face not only the harsh conditions of an *irre-*

---

45. Melissa Fleming, "Climate change could become the biggest driver of displacement: UNHCR chief," United Nations High Commissioner on Refugees, http://www.unhcr.org/4b2910239.html
46. "Climate extremes, regional impacts, and the case for resilience," World Bank.
47. "Consensus Statement from Global Scientists," Millennium Alliance for Humanity and Biosphere (MAHB), http://mahb.stanford.edu/consensus-statement-from-global-scientists.

trievably damaged world, but also concern for their own children and grandchildren as the life-support systems of the planet continue to be degraded by runaway climate change.

Ministries with children and youth deserve a special look, since the impacts of a warming world will fall upon them most heavily. Some propose teaching children to care for the earth, to equip them for solving ecological problems left to them by previous generations. Of course, we must teach children to care for creation, but it is even more important to set an example for them to follow, for we cannot leave a threat of this magnitude to today's children to resolve. As adults who are responsible for the physical, emotional, and spiritual well-being of children and youth, we need to comfort them about the state of the planet, model alternatives to our profligate consumer culture, work for systemic change, and assure them that we will do everything in our power to protect them, defend God's creation, and pass on to them a livable world.

Working to protect other species and their habitats is directly related to intergenerational justice. We are in the midst of "The Sixth Extinction."[48] Studies suggest that up to half of the earth's animal species have been extinguished in the past forty years due to human activity,[49] with climate change threatening many more. Children have a special love for animals. God forbid that we should bequeath to them a degraded earth.

Indigenous people suggest considering how our choices impact our descendants to the seventh generation. Our biblical tradition, too, teaches that our decisions impact future generations. Deuteronomy 30:19 states: "Choose life, so that you and your descendants may live." As we consider our choices in the context of climate change, we can see that our action or inaction will influence the degree of harm that future generations may suffer, or open up possibilities for transformation and healing that they may enjoy. As people of faith, we can take heart from God's promise to "show steadfast love to the thousandth generation of those who love me and keep my commandments" (Deut 5:10). The witness of the Spirit confirms this hope in our experience and quickens our resolve.

48. Elizabeth Kolbert, *The Sixth Extinction* (New York: Henry Holt and Company, 2014).

49. Christine Dell'Amore, "Has Half of World's Wildlife Been Lost in Past 40 Years?" *National Geographic News* (October 2, 2014), http://news.nationalgeographic.com/news/2014/09/1409030-animals-wildlife-wwf-decline-science-world/.

Interpreting the Signs of Our Times

In this chapter I have presented an overview of the climate crisis, explained how various ministries will be affected by a warming world, and introduced the movement for climate justice. In the next chapter, I describe a discernment process that uses scripture, tradition, reason, and experience to inform faith and clarify thinking. In later chapters I employ these four sources of authority to develop the themes of creation and justice in the context of climate change.

As followers of Jesus, we are called not only to recognize and interpret the signs of our times, but to respond to them. As we face the painful realities of our changing climate, we hear creation's groans and are called to respond by working to preserve God's wondrous creation and the interconnected web of life. Behind the facts and statistics, we see the faces of God's beloved children, our brothers and sisters around the world, and are called to stand with them in solidarity, work with them to establish justice, and serve them in Christ's name. As we progress through the following chapters, gaining insight about these interrelated issues, it will become clear how this can be done.

3

———

Scripture, Tradition, Reason, and Experience: Tools for Discernment

We must no longer be children, tossed to and fro and blown about by every wind of doctrine, by people's trickery, by their craftiness in deceitful scheming. But speaking the truth in love, we must grow up in every way into him who is the head, into Christ . . .

— Ephesians 4:14–15

"Jesus loves me, this I know, for the Bible tells me so." These familiar words from a favorite children's hymn contain the core of the gospel: God's love for us through Jesus Christ as proclaimed in scripture. Sometimes we are able to accept this simple message, experience the assurance of God's transforming love, and step out confidently in faith.

At other times things may not seem so simple or clear. We may struggle with issues of faith. For instance, how are we to read the Bible and apply it to our lives? What weight should we give scripture as we seek its guidance in personal matters or in the issues of our time? How can we discern sound Christian understanding amid the babel of competing views? How can the varied strands of Christian tradition be reconciled? What beliefs can we affirm without abandoning our common sense? And how much can we trust our personal experience as we seek to understand what is true?

Instead of simply appropriating what other people tell us to believe, a mature faith requires us to develop and test our beliefs and come to our own understanding. We are each free and responsible to seek truth and make our own decisions. The discernment process described in this chapter will help us to grow in understanding and to come "to maturity, to the measure of the full stature of Christ" (Eph 4:13b).

When we view a topic from various perspectives, we gain insight from many sources. This helps clarify issues and inform decision-making. Scripture, tradition, reason, and experience provide four different lenses through which to explore issues, discern truth, and come to decisions. Albert Outler coined the term *quadrilateral* to describe how John Wesley used these four sources of authority as interactive and dynamic aids in his approach to theology.[1] In this book we will also use scripture, tradition, reason, and experience to explore the themes of *creation* and *justice* as we seek to understand and address the great environmental, social, and ethical challenges posed by climate change.

Scripture: Revealing God's Love

As we seek biblical guidance, we must come to terms with how the Word of God is revealed through the words of scripture. One dispute among Christians of different persuasions relates to the authority of scripture. In other words, how do we read the Bible and how much weight does it carry in our faith and life?

For John Wesley, the authority of scripture was paramount. He wrote, "I allow no other rule, whether of faith or practice, than the Holy Scriptures."[2] Nevertheless, he taught that the interpretation of scripture must be informed by Christian tradition, critical reasoning, and the existential experience of grace in order for its truths to be understood, evaluated, confirmed, and applied in daily life.

Wesley valued biblical understandings of Christian thinkers of the past, but he realized that scripture needs to be interpreted in each succeeding age and new cultural context. Although Wesley lived before the emergence of modern historical and literary criticism, he respected the biblical scholarship being done in his day. He taught that biblical

---

1. Donald A. D. Thorsen, *The Wesleyan Quadrilateral: Scripture, Tradition, Reason, & Experience as a Model of Evangelical Theology* (Grand Rapids: Zondervan, 1990), 22.
2. John Wesley, "To James Hervey," in *Letters of John Wesley*, ed. John Telford (London: Epworth, 1931), 1:285.

passages can usually be understood in their plain, simple, and obvious meaning, but he qualified this by saying that a text cannot be taken literally if it "implies an absurdity," seems "obscure," or is "contrary to some other texts," especially if it goes against "the whole scope and tenor of scripture." This is especially important if a text contradicts "all those particular texts which expressly declare 'God is love.'"[3] In such cases he advocated using reason to interpret individual passages in light of the whole of scripture, and interpreting obscure passages in light of clearer ones.[4] By putting qualifications on the literal understanding of scripture, Wesley opened the door to biblical criticism. George C. Cell has argued that although Wesley did not promote critical biblical interpretation in *theory*, he did adopt it in *practice*.[5]

Spiritual experience, according to Wesley, can help illuminate scripture, and biblical truths must be confirmed by experience. He said, "Experience is sufficient to confirm a doctrine which is grounded on Scripture."[6] Bible study is to be done in a spirit of prayer, since the same Holy Spirit who inspired the authors of scripture is also present with readers, helping them understand its true meaning and confirming its truth in their experience. He wrote, "All scripture is inspired of God—The Spirit of God not only once inspired those who wrote it, but continually inspires, supernaturally assists, those that read it with earnest prayer."[7]

In later chapters, we will explore several passages that provide a solid scriptural foundation for addressing today's climate crisis. As we seek divine aid in the context of a warming world, biblical passages on creation and justice can—with the aid of the Holy Spirit—illuminate the light of our understanding, quicken our conscience, enable us to discern the call of God, and inspire us to faithful action.

Tradition: Learning from the Past

The word *tradition* has several different meanings. It often refers to "an inherited, established, or customary pattern of thought, action, or behavior."[8] In this book, however, *tradition* refers specifically to

---

3. John Wesley, Sermon 110, "Free Grace," *The Works of John Wesley,* ed. Albert C. Outler (Nashville: Abingdon, 1986), 3:552.
4. Thorsen, *The Wesleyan Quadrilateral,* 144.
5. George C. Cell, *The Rediscovery of John Wesley* (New York: Henry Holt, 1935), 13.
6. John Wesley, Sermon 10, "The Witness of the Spirit II," in *John Wesley's Sermons: An Anthology,* ed. Albert C. Outler and Richard P. Heitzenrater (Nashville: Abingdon, 1991), 402.
7. John Wesley, *Notes on the Bible,* 2 Timothy 3:16 (Grand Rapids: Francis Asbury, 1987), 559.

Christian teachings and practices as they have evolved from the time of the early church until today.

How does tradition inform our search for truth? The varieties of Christian teachings that have developed throughout the past two thousand years make it difficult to know which strands of tradition to take seriously. Dominant forms of Christianity have supported empire in the name of Christ and have caused great harm. Other Christian movements have been true representations of Christ's love in the world. Aspects of the tradition that emphasize love are true to Jesus's life and ministry as presented in scripture.

As we look to tradition for insights, we will reflect on traditional Christian teachings about creation and justice, especially the teachings of John Wesley. He called himself a "man of one book,"[9] referring to the Bible, but he also read other books voraciously and encouraged other pastors to do so. He respected the insights and opinions of great Christian thinkers who had gone before. He took seriously the authority of tradition, particularly of early Christianity, "*the religion of the primitive church*, of the whole church in the purest ages."[10] He was convinced that the Methodist movement was the latest manifestation of this true, genuine Christianity, which he also referred to as "heart-religion," because it consisted of "no other than love: the love of God and of all humankind. . . ."[11] For Wesley, love was the key to an authentic expression of traditional Christianity—the foundation of both personal spirituality and social concern. In this book, traditional teachings and practices that demonstrate love of God and neighbor will carry authority for us as we seek to discern a faithful response to climate change.

Although Wesley was convinced that the truth of his theological convictions was upheld by scripture, tradition, and reason, and confirmed by experience, he approached other Christian traditions with open-minded tolerance. He wrote, "As to all opinions which do not strike at the root of Christianity, we think and let think."[12] He adopted an expansive view of ministry, saying, "I look upon all the world as my parish."[13] He preached several times a day in open fields, in the streets, in prisons and workhouses, in private homes where people gathered,

8. Frederick C. Mish, Editor in Chief, *Merriam-Webster's Collegiate Dictionary, Eleventh Edition* (Springfield, MA: Merriam-Webster, Inc., 2003), 1325.

9. John Wesley, "Preface: First Series," *Sermons on Several Occasions* (Grand Rapids: Christian Classics Ethereal Library), 12, http://www.luc.edu/faculty/pmoser/idolanon/WesleySermons.pdf.

10. Sermon 112, "On Laying the Foundation of the New Chapel," *Works*, 3:577.

11. Ibid., 585.

12. John Wesley, "The Character of a Methodist" (1739); in *The Works of the Rev. John Wesley in Ten Volumes* (New York: J&J Harper, 1827), IV:407.

and in his work with the poor and outcast. He said, "The Gospel of Christ knows of no religion, but social; no holiness, but social holiness."[14] This concept of social holiness reminds us that spirituality is not just a private affair, but includes the effects of our lives and actions on others. Following Christ does not mean simply tending to our own personal spiritual well-being; it also means loving others and acting for the well-being of the world.

We can't just superimpose Wesley's views about theology or social issues onto the contemporary situation. Still, his insights do carry the authority of tradition. His unique understanding of God's presence in creation and his concept of social holiness inform our views. His theological liberality and religious tolerance provide us with a model for working in our congregations, in ecumenical and interfaith circles, and in secular gatherings to communicate and cooperate about difficult and controversial issues. His open-minded approach to theology, science, and social issues encourages us to consider a variety of perspectives—both religious and secular—when seeking to understand and respond to climate change. His insistence upon love as basic to "true religion" grounds us in love of God and neighbor as central to authentic Christianity.

In later chapters, we examine Wesley's views on creation for their relevance today and explore what social holiness means on a warming planet. We also consider contemporary expressions of Christian tradition that may enrich our understanding. Our touchstone is love.

Reason: Seeking Truth

A third source of authority is reason. Wesley valued common sense. He insisted that the Christian faith is neither irrational nor anti-rational, and he used reason to defend its reasonableness. He said, "It is a fundamental principle with us that to renounce reason is to renounce religion, that religion and reason go hand in hand, and that all irrational religion is false religion."[15] Christian faith involves mystery, but it is not nonsense. It is important to maintain intellectual integrity in matters of faith and in all areas of life.

Wesley lived during the Enlightenment, and his positive view of

13. John Wesley Biography, entry from his Journal, June 11, 1739, http://www.biographyonline.net/spiritual/john-wesley.html.
14. John Wesley, "The Preface," Hymns and Sacred Poems (London: William Stratton, 1739), vii, http://quod.lib.umich.edu/e/ecco/004800840.0001.000/1:2?rgn=div1;view=fulltext.
15. Wesley, "To Dr. Rutherford," in Letters, 5:364.

reason was generally accepted in the intellectual milieu in which he lived. His theology reflects John Locke's empirical philosophy, the dominant philosophical worldview of the time. Locke's experimental approach to philosophy is evident in Wesley's experimental approach to theology. In a later chapter, we will explore questions now being raised about the value of empiricism itself, and about how such questions relate to our understanding of the universe.

According to Wesley, the faculty of reason is an invaluable tool for understanding scripture, discerning truth from falsehood, and making decisions for right action. He exhorted people to use their God-given powers of critical thinking when seeking truth, and to reason carefully and with integrity in order to come to right judgments and decisions. At the same time, he was aware of the limitations of reason in spiritual matters. He wrote, "Let reason do all that reason can. Use it as far as it will go. But, at the same time, acknowledge that reason is utterly incapable of giving faith, or hope, or love, and consequently, of producing either real virtue or substantial happiness. Expect these from a higher source, even from the Father of the spirits of all flesh."[16]

Science informed Wesley's understanding of creation. He lived in a time when the scientific revolution was bringing new theories and discoveries that challenged the biblical worldview. Wesley accepted the Copernican view of the universe, as did most Enlightenment thinkers. He was open to scientific theories and discoveries, and used reason to judge whether or not evidence supported particular views.

Reason enables us to incorporate contemporary scientific discoveries into our understanding of God's creation. It also enables us to educate ourselves about climate change, its causes, how it impacts creation, and its links to injustice and human suffering. Through reason we are able to think through the probable effects of various lifestyle and policy decisions on present and future generations and on the natural world, and make rational decisions for a just and healing response.

Experience: Knowing God

Wesley also used experience to develop and support his views. The grace of God acting through scripture, tradition, and reason bring us to a jumping-off point for taking a leap of faith. We can know about God and even believe in God based on the teachings of scripture and tradition. Reason can convince us of the reality of God based on the evi-

---

16. Sermon 70, "The Case of Reason Impartially Considered," *Works*, 2:600.

dence of God's action in creation or in people's lives. But believing in God is not the same as knowing God. Only when we experience God's presence for ourselves, does life-changing faith become real.

Although Wesley valued reason, he rejected the view that religion simply means the rational acceptance of doctrines. Rather, true religion consists of a living, heart-felt faith characterized by love. This "heart religion" comes about through inner experience; through direct knowledge given by God to the soul. He said, "And we then see, not by a chain of reasoning, but by a kind of intuition, by a direct view, that 'God was in Christ, reconciling the world to himself, not imputing to them their former trespasses,' not imputing them to *me*."[17] This experience of assurance of God's forgiveness and love is the foundation of faith. According to Wesley, the evidence of the truth of such intuitive knowledge can be seen by the fruits of the Spirit in the lives of those who have experienced it, especially as expressed through love.[18]

What does it mean to be open to the authority of experience in this time of climate change, as weather patterns change and disasters take place in countries around the world? The temptation is to ignore or deny the reality in order to avoid unbearable pain, or to shrink our circle of concern to more manageable proportions by focusing solely on our personal lives. Either of these choices makes effective climate action less likely and diminishes hopes for a livable future. The alternative is to open our eyes and hearts to the truth of whatever presents itself. By exploring the theme of creation through the lens of experience, we will see that our joyful experiences of the divine through the natural world as well as sorrow caused by its destruction may move us to compassionate action. By listening to people harmed by climate change, crying out for justice, we may be moved to join them in solidarity and make their cause our own.

Love makes this possible. In chapters that follow we will explore how the experience of God's love for us enables us to face the reality of climate change and how our love of God and neighbor can motivate us to compassionate action as we follow in the footsteps of Jesus, whose love for others took him all the way to the cross.

17. Sermon 62, "The End of Christ's Coming," *Works*, 2:481.
18. Sermon 112, "On Laying the Foundation of the New Chapel," *Works*, 3:585.

Discerning a Way Forward

In this chapter I have described how John Wesley used scripture, tradition, reason, and experience to formulate and support his views. In chapters that follow I will use these four sources of authority to explore the themes of creation and justice in the context of climate change. A deeper awareness of the value of creation supports actions to preserve and restore the integrity of the natural world. An understanding of justice that includes climate justice supports efforts to be in ministry with those who are most vulnerable to planetary warming, to establish intergenerational justice, and to work for justice for all creation.

Honoring Creation

4

Scripture: Hearing Creation's Groans

We know that the whole creation has been groaning in labor pains until now, and not only the creation, but we ourselves, who have the first fruits of the Spirit, groan inwardly. . . .

—Romans 8:22–23a

We move now into Part II, "Honoring Creation," which explores the theme of creation from the perspective of scripture, tradition, reason, and experience. In this chapter, we look to scripture as a source of authority to guide our understanding of creation in the context of our changing climate. How we understand biblical teachings about creation affects how we see and treat the natural world. If we see the earth and all creatures as beloved by God, we will honor creation and care for it.

We begin by acknowledging the ongoing debate among Christian groups about whether the creation stories in Genesis should be taken literally. According to the Bible's first creation story in Genesis 1:1–2:3, which was repeated around campfires for generations before being written down, God created the heavens and the earth in seven days. Conservative churches that insist on a literal reading of scripture expect believers to take this story literally and reject the theory of evolution as a matter of faith. Choosing between *creation and evolution* becomes a litmus test, leading some to believe that they must reject scientific evidence about the origins of life in order to be Christian. Submitting to this kind of closed belief system leaves people susceptible to following authoritarian church leaders or accepting doctrines that are untrue.

Taking the Bible literally doesn't prevent people from reading scripture from a purely subjective standpoint. Years ago, a conservative Christian was explaining to me that God created the world and everything in it for humans to use for our own ends. He pulled out his Bible and showed me the passage in the first creation story, in Genesis 1:26, that says, "Then God said, 'let us make humankind in our image, according to our likeness, and let them have dominion over the fish of the sea, and over the birds of the air, and over the cattle, and over all the wild animals of the earth, and over every creeping thing that creeps upon the earth.'" This passage has been misused historically to authorize a utilitarian approach to creation, as if God has granted human beings a license to use the earth for our own advantage without considering the well-being of the whole.

I decided to point out an alternative perspective by bringing up the second creation story in Genesis 2:4–24, which describes a completely different order of creation than the first story. It casts human beings in the role of tenant gardeners, entrusted with the task of tending the earthly garden: "The Lord God took the man and put him in the Garden of Eden to till and keep it" (Gen 2:15). I told my friend that I understood this passage to mean that we are responsible to care for creation, but at that point he ended the conversation. He shut his Bible and said, "I like my interpretation better."

On another occasion this same person quoted the words of Jesus out of context by saying, "For you always have the poor with you" (Matt 26:11), in order to rationalize poverty and inequity. He claimed to take the Bible literally, but he actually approached scripture through his own subjective cultural biases. In practical terms, he used the Bible as a source of authority to justify his perceived right to exploit the earth and ignore the needs of the poor.

By acknowledging not only scripture but also tradition, reason, and experience as sources of authority, we avoid the pitfalls of both literalism and subjectivity, especially if we study the Bible in community with others who seek truth. In this way scripture can help us find spiritual guidance for all aspects of faith and life, including our understanding of creation.

The Whole Tenor and Scope of Scripture

The stories in the first three chapters of Genesis were not written to present a scientific account of creation, but to offer spiritual truths, which include the following themes. God created the universe and delights in it, declaring it "very good." The Holy Spirit that "swept over the face of the waters" was active in creation from the beginning. Human beings are created along with all other beings (made on the same "day" as the other animals) and are included as part of the original goodness of creation. At the same time, humans have a unique role: to reflect ("image") God to each other and to the rest of creation. Although we are able to greatly impact—even dominate—the world for good or for harm, we are given the specific responsibility of caring for creation. The story of Adam and Eve about humanity's *fall* into sin (Gen 3:1–24) is an early theological explanation of why there is suffering and evil in a world created by a God of love. These stories at the beginning of the Bible provide the context for our human story within the created order. They offer a spiritual and theological starting point for reflecting on creation, ourselves, and our Creator.

There are many other creation-centered texts throughout the Bible that provide a foundation for reflecting on creation in the context of our changing climate. Several claim that God is revealed through creation. Psalm 19:1 proclaims, "The heavens are telling the glory of God; and the firmament proclaims his handiwork." This psalm speaks to me on nights when, looking up at the stars, I am struck by God's majesty and my heart is filled with praise.

Job suggests looking to the natural world to learn about God: "But ask the animals, and they will teach you; the birds of the air, and they will tell you; ask the plants of the earth, and they will teach you; and the fish of the sea will declare to you" (Job 12:7). This passage reminds me of the elation I feel when I hear the chorus of frogs who sing here in the evenings and the birds who take over at dawn, of the satisfaction I find in vegetable gardening, the joy of taking my grandchildren on nature walks, and the love I feel for the animals in my life. These experiences affirm God's presence in creation and confirm this scriptural truth.

Not all biblical texts describe the human role in creation as either domination or stewardship. Psalm 104 presents human beings not as masters of the created order but as members of the community of life, dependent on God's loving generosity for sustenance, as are all other beings. Although people in ancient times had no understanding of modern terms like *ecosystem*, this remarkable psalm portrays balanced ecosystems in which all species are provided for by a loving God. The psalm describes how God creates habitats and provides food and water to wild donkeys, birds, badgers, cattle, lions, sea creatures, and yes, humans. It goes on to praise God: "These all look to you to give them their food in due season; when you give it to them, they gather it up; when you open your hand, they are filled with good things" (Ps 104:27–28).

In light of this psalm, it seems apparent that damage caused by climate change to forests, agricultural lands, waterways, coastal areas, and other ecosystems violates the integrity of creation. How can we raise our voices to praise God for sustaining all creatures if we are in the process of destroying their homes? Other species, too, have a right to their habitats, since God loves them all and has created the means to provide for them. This truth is affirmed by Jesus, who spoke about God's care for the lilies of the field and the birds of the air, assuring his hearers that God cares for all parts of creation, even the most humble (Matt 6:26–30).

The story of Noah and the Ark offers further relevant insights (Gen 6:1–9:19). God instructs Noah to take two animals of every kind with him into the ark, thus ensuring the continuation of the diversity of animal life on earth. When the great flood ends and the waters subside, the covenant God makes is not just with Noah, but with all creatures: "This is the sign of the covenant that I make between me and you and every living thing that is with you, for all future generations. . . ." The image of the rainbow is a sign of promise and hope, not only for humans but for all creation (Gen 9:13–17).

Noah serves as a prototype for humans who seek to be faithful in protecting other species. In the 1990s I was part of an organized group of church leaders working to defend the Endangered Species Act, which was under attack and in danger of being dismantled by anti-regulatory conservative lawmakers. We described our support for the Endangered Species Act as a moral issue and called it "a modern-day Noah's Ark."

Under the Trump Administration, the Endangered Species Act may itself "be heading for the threatened list," as Republicans seek to limit the protections that it provides. In this time of climate crisis we are called to defend the wondrous variety of species so that they may continue to reflect the glory of God.

New Testament passages that shed light on our understanding of creation include stories about the life of Jesus. He often spent time outside in prayer (Mark 6:46)—a practice we can relate to as it immerses the person praying in the experience of relationship with God in creation. According to Mark, Jesus was "with the wild beasts" when he was tempted in the wilderness (Mark 1:13). Although no details are given, the presence of wild animals must have increased the drama of his sojourn, reminding Jesus (and us) of his human vulnerability. When the disciples feared that they would drown, Jesus stilled the storm (Mark 4:35–41). He walked on water (Mark 6:47–51). Other stories also stress Jesus's power over nature, including accounts of healings and other miracles, which demonstrate the power of the God of creation working through him.

Many of Jesus's parables relate to the natural world. He used metaphors that were familiar to his listeners, who lived in an agrarian culture. The parables of the Sower (Matt 13:1–23), the Mustard Seed (Matt 13:30–32), the Weeds among the Wheat (Matt 13:36–43), and the Lost Sheep (Luke 15:1–7) not only imparted spiritual lessons to his followers, but affirmed their role as caretakers of creation.

In the Parable of the Wicked Tenants (Matt 21:33–46), Jesus links human sin with the refusal to care for the earth's gifts on behalf of God. He uses the image of tenant gardeners to represent the human race. These "wicked tenants" not only refuse to give the owner a share of the harvest, they reject the owner's servants and finally kill his son. Jesus used this parable to both predict and interpret the meaning of his death. It places the central story of Jesus's crucifixion in the context of creation.

This survey of creation-centered texts demonstrates a consistent pattern, making clear that "the whole scope and tenor of scripture"[1] upholds the value of creation. These and other passages affirm that God loves and cares for creation; we humans are dependent on God and interconnected with the rest of creation; we are responsible to care for the earth; and there is hope for creation to be renewed.

We turn now to Romans 8:18–26, which is the focus of the rest of this chapter. The above biblical passages complement and shed light on this text. We will also use tradition, reason, and experience to illuminate our understanding of this mystical passage in which creation is personified as a woman ready to give birth.

---

1. John Wesley, Sermon 110, "Free Grace," *The Works of John Wesley*, ed. Albert C. Outler (Nashville: Abingdon, 1986), 3:554.

I have chosen Romans 8:18–26 as a primary biblical text because it points to hope for the redemption of creation, which is particularly relevant in this time when creation is threatened by climate change. This passage also affirms the interrelatedness of human beings with the rest of creation, highlights the presence of the indwelling Holy Spirit, and offers universal hope. This remarkable passage is found at the center of Romans, Paul's most systematic work:

> I consider that the sufferings of this present time are not worth comparing with the glory about to be revealed to us. For the creation waits with eager longing for the revealing of the children of God; for the creation was subjected to futility, not of its own will but by the will of the one who subjected it, in hope that the creation itself will be set free from its bondage to decay and will obtain the freedom of the glory of the children of God. We know that the whole creation has been groaning in labor pains until now; and not only the creation, but we ourselves, who have the first fruits of the Spirit, groan inwardly while we wait for adoption, the redemption of our bodies. For in this hope we were saved. Now hope that is seen is not hope. For who hopes for what is seen? But if we hope for what we do not see, we wait for it with patience. Likewise, the Spirit helps us in our weakness; for we do not know how to pray as we ought, but that very Spirit intercedes for us with sighs too deep for words.

This mysterious text portrays creation groaning "as in the pangs of childbirth," yearning to be set free. Here we see our fate as humans tied up with the fate of creation. We participate in its suffering. We participate in its hope. Creation's groans are our groans, and in them we discern the very voice of God.

Tradition: The General Deliverance

As we look to Wesleyan tradition, we focus on John Wesley's sermon "The General Deliverance," which was based on this text from Romans 8:18–26. Wesley began by making the case that God's universal love extends to all creation, then went on to ask the question he believed was central to this passage and to faith: "If the Creator and Father of every living thing is rich in mercy towards all . . . how comes it to pass that such a complication of evils oppresses, yea, overwhelms them? How is it that misery of all kinds overspreads the face of the earth?" He looked to this passage to answer this question, "which has puzzled the wisest philosophers in all ages."[2]

Next, Wesley described what he understood to be the role of the human in relation to the rest of creation. He based his understanding on the concepts of dominion (Gen 1:28) and stewardship (Gen 2:15). He understood human beings to be made in the image of God and originally "endued with all these excellent faculties, thus qualified for their high charge" of caring for the rest of creation.[3]

Wesley's view was that, tragically, human sin has led to utter disorder in God's loving design for creation. It is not only humans who suffer the painful consequences of human sin, but the non-human creation as well: "Since man rebelled against his Maker, in what a state is all animated nature! Well might the Apostle say of this: 'The whole creation groaneth and travaileth together in pain until now.' This directly refers to the brute creation."[4] Wesley bemoaned the state of other creatures under subjection to humanity:

And what a dreadful difference is there, between what they suffer from their fellow-brutes, and what they suffer from the tyrant man! The lion, the tiger, or the shark, gives them pain from mere necessity, in order to prolong their own life; and puts them out of their pain at once: But the human shark, without any such necessity, torments them of his free choice; and perhaps continues their lingering pain till, after months or years, death signs their release.[5]

Still, God does not intend for creation to go on suffering indefinitely. Wesley's sermon culminates in a rousing claim that God hears creation's groans and will respond by alleviating its suffering:

But will "the creature," will even the brute creation, always remain in this deplorable condition? God forbid that we should affirm this; yea, or even entertain such a thought! While "the whole creation groaneth together" (whether men attend or not) their groans are not dispersed in idle air, but enter into the ears of Him that made them. While his creatures "travail together in pain," he knoweth all their pain and is bringing them nearer and nearer to the birth, which shall be accomplished in its season. He seeth "the earnest expectation" wherewith the whole animated creation "waiteth for" that final "manifestation of the sons of God"; in which "they themselves also shall be delivered" (not by annihilation; annihilation is not deliverance) from the present "bondage of corruption," into a measure of "the glorious liberty of the children of God."[6]

2. Wesley, Sermon 60, "The General Deliverance," *Works*, 2:438.
3. Ibid., 440.
4. Ibid., 442.
5. Ibid., 445.
6. Ibid.

Wesley emphasized that this promised deliverance includes not only humans but all creatures. He said, "Nothing can be more express: Away with vulgar prejudices, and let the plain word of God take place. They 'shall be delivered from the bondage of corruption, into glorious liberty,' even a measure, according as they are capable, of 'the liberty of the children of God.'"[7]

Wesley's sermon informs our interpretation of this passage, but tradition continues to develop and interpretations continue to evolve. We turn now to reason as we seek to make sense of this passage in our context today.

Reason: Biblical Criticism

This text becomes clearer as we use reason to explore it critically. Its placement at the center of the Book of Romans is significant. Throughout Romans, Paul systematically explains how we are justified solely by faith in Jesus Christ, given new life in the Spirit, and offered hope for future fulfillment in God. The first half of Romans presents the inner conflict and futility of trying to live according to the Law, and contrasts it with life in the Spirit. This culminates in Paul's poignant cry lamenting our human inability to make ourselves into the people we want to be: "For I do not do the good I want, but the evil I do not want is what I do. . . . Wretched man that I am, who will rescue me from this body of death?" (Rom 7:19, 24). Paul responds by praising God, who offers the solution to this dilemma: "Thanks be to God through Jesus Christ our Lord!" (Rom 7:25). Paul continues this response by pointing to life in the Spirit as a way to freedom and right relationship to God: "For all who are led by the Spirit of God are children of God" (Rom 8:14).

These preliminary themes prepare us for the pivotal Romans 8:18–26 text, where Paul puts human salvation into a cosmic context by claiming that creation itself is in bondage because of human sin and that creation is yearning for the renewal that will come when human beings assume their rightful place in the created order. Paul acknowledges present suffering in light of his expectation of "the glory about to be revealed to us." He portrays creation itself as yearning for this revelation "with eager longing," which in Greek is *apokaradokia*, "attentive expectation or looking for, as with neck stretched out and head thrust forward."[8] Creation is craning its neck in anticipation, waiting for the

---

7. Ibid.

"revealing of the children of God," that is, for "all who are led by the Spirit of God."

Why is creation so invested in the revealing of people led by the Spirit? Because creation has been "subjected to futility" (Rom 8:20). In the original Greek, *futility* (*matelotes*) can also be interpreted as "vanity, nothingness, worthlessness."[9] Creation has been devalued and made worthless because of this subjugation, which is the same as "bondage" or in Greek, *doleno*, "a state opposed to liberty" or "a condition of servitude or slavery."[10] Scholars have suggested that this subjugation refers to human dominion over creation and humanity's fall into sin—human dominion gone wrong. No wonder creation is yearning to be set free!

The passage goes on in Romans 8:23 to link our groans with the groans of creation: "and not only the creation, but we ourselves, who have the first fruits of the Spirit, groan inwardly while we wait for adoption, the redemption of our bodies. For in this hope we were saved." The focus turns to the inner reality of those who seek to be led by the Spirit and who yearn along with creation for the promised renewal.

What is the hope presented here? Although some interpret "the redemption of our bodies" as hope for resurrection after death, here it is primarily used to clarify the meaning of adoption as God's children, which Paul has already defined as those who are led by the Spirit of God. In Greek, the term *redemption* (*apolutrosis*) means to "release from slavery on payment of ransom."[11] Paul often refers to sin as slavery and freedom from sin as redemption. (See, for instance, Rom 3:24–25.) The promise of redemption culminates in the profound promise at the end of chapter 8 that nothing will be able to separate us from the love of God in Christ Jesus, not even death itself (Rom 8:37–39), but here it directly relates to the themes that come immediately before and after: the struggle of enslavement to sin, the futility of trying to live according to the Law, life in the Spirit, and universal hope. The key for the renewal of creation is that humans assume their rightful role in relationship with God and with the created order.

In this time of climate change these ideas take on new significance. Wesleyan theologian Michael Lodahl said, "Obviously this Pauline passage (Rom 8:18–26) should play a central role in the development of

---

8. Spiros Zodhiates, ThD, Executive Editor, *Hebrew-Greek Key Word Study Bible* (Chattanooga: AMG Publishers, 1991), 1692.

9. Ibid., 1736.

10. Ibid., 709.

11. Ibid., 1692–93.

a Christian interpretation of this wondrous universe we inhabit. It instructs us to look, hope, and labor for redemption for all of creation, not only for humans and certainly not only for a select group of humans. . . . It hints at a deep, suffering divine presence groaning and interceding in and for the world's own straining toward deliverance."[12]

Experience: Sighs Too Deep for Words

We have used scripture, tradition, and reason to explore Romans 8:18–26. We now go on to consider how this mysterious passage is confirmed by experience, for it is in our own experience that the Holy Spirit brings the words of scripture to life so that they become for us the Word of God.

Scripture proclaims that creation reveals the glory of God. As we open our eyes, ears, and hearts to the sights, sounds, and wonders of creation, we experience the voice of God—in the song of a bird, the sound of a flowing river, the vision of a snow-capped peak, the hush of an old-growth forest, a cool breeze on a sunny day, the laughter of children.

We also hear creation's groans. At this time of peril, creation's groans are growing louder. From a distance we hear the groans of drowning polar bears, starving emperor penguin chicks, and the many species of plants and animals that can't adapt fast enough to changing conditions. We hear the groans of Pacific Islanders whose lands are being submerged, people in African nations experiencing ongoing drought and famine, climate refugees fleeing disaster, and people around the world whose local weather patterns are changing.

We humans are not separate—we are part of creation. We are children of God, but also children of the earth, part of the interconnected web of life. Even now, we experience alarm at the escalating damage visited upon our beautiful earth. Our anguish is intensified by knowing that the damage is caused by the human impact upon creation, by patterns of overconsumption, industrial development, and our fossil-fuel-driven civilization. Guilt mixes with grief as we consider our contribution to creation's travail. We may get discouraged as feelings of futility, hopelessness, and paralysis set in. As followers of Christ, we seek to be faithful, but as we find ourselves unable or unwilling to take significant action on climate change and other threats, we may expe-

12. Michael Lodahl, *God of Nature and of Grace: Reading the World in a Wesleyan Way* (Nashville: Abingdon, 2003), 213–14.

rience the inner struggle that Paul expressed when he said, "Wretched man that I am, who will rescue me from this body of death?"

We share the suffering of this present time. Not only does creation groan, but "we ourselves, who have the first fruits of the Spirit, groan inwardly . . ." as we experience the suffering and bondage to which we and our fellow creatures are subjected. Could it be that God, too, suffers with us and yearns for creation's healing? Apparently so. The Holy Spirit, God's active presence, is with us in our suffering and yearning, and we experience this presence in "sighs too deep for words." These sighs are a form of prayer.

Our Challenge Today

Our challenge is to apply this text to our contemporary situation, keeping in mind the reality of climate change and our search for a faithful response. As we learn more about its dangers, we realize the extremity of our situation. Oil spills, methane plumes from natural gas storage wells, and crude oil train explosions highlight the accidental disasters caused by fossil-fuel dependency. Ecosystems and communities are destroyed by extreme forms of fossil-fuel extraction that include mountains blown apart to access coal, water pollution and earthquakes resulting from "fracking" (hydraulic fracturing of rock to extract natural gas), and vast wastelands created by tar sands extraction. Many other environmental and social harms result from industrial society's addiction to fossil fuels, including mountains of garbage, islands of plastic, persistent herbicides and pesticides, geopolitical conflicts, and resource wars. Damage to the climate system is a less visible threat but in the long run is even more catastrophic.

The earth's changing climate is not just one issue among many, but the overarching situation in which all of humanity's other challenges are embedded. We have been arrogant and careless in our relationship with creation, and under the illusion that advanced technology and industrial society insulate us from nature. Ultimately, they do not. Like all created beings, we are utterly dependent upon God and interdependent with all other parts of creation. What happens to the natural world affects us, especially the most vulnerable among us, and will affect future generations.

It is not easy to be hopeful when considering the accelerating release of greenhouse gases, rising global temperatures, and ever-increasing, weather-related disasters. Creation's groans are starting to sound more like death groans than labor pains. Yet this text invites us to trust that God intends for new life to be born out of creation's current travail. There is still hope that human beings will live in right relationship with God, with each other, and with creation. To commit oneself to this hopeful vision is an audacious leap of faith, an act of hope that itself engenders new life.

Taking Scripture Seriously: Hope for the World

Honoring creation begins with appreciating the world around us. By expanding our prayers and other spiritual practices to include the natural world we experience our connection with the whole. Moments of transcendence may take place while sitting on a beach, swimming in a river, walking in the forest, gazing at stars, working in the garden, or watching a sunset. Such moments immerse us in the grace of God that is present throughout creation.

Prayerful reading of scripture challenges, comforts, inspires, and motivates hopeful action. The point of studying scripture is not to reinforce or prove what we already believe but to open ourselves to new insights, deeper understanding, and spiritual transformation. Reading the Bible with an open mind allows the Word of God to break through in surprising ways.

Leading or participating in Bible studies that focus on creation enables us to explore together how scripture guides us into right attitudes and actions. Are we living as responsible members of the community of life? Are we working for the common good and living in ways that bring hope for creation's future? These are questions to keep in mind as we seek guidance, challenge, and inspiration from scripture.

As people experience creation's suffering, many are laboring for new life by simplifying their lifestyles, creating resilient communities, advocating for climate-friendly policies, and engaging in public actions to protect creation. People from every continent are organizing, networking, and joining together to build a global movement for climate justice strong enough to bring about the changes that are required. The question for us is: Where is the church of Jesus Christ in this struggle?

There are signs of hope. But as God's people, even when things seem impossible we are called to live in hope: "Hope that is seen is not hope, for who hopes for what is seen? But if we hope for what we do not see, we wait for it with patience" (Rom 8:24–25). We are not called to wait *passively*, but *patiently*. We may not yet know what to do. We may have to wait for guidance, but we are able to lift our hearts in prayer, trusting that "the Spirit helps us in our weakness; for we do not know how to pray as we ought, but that very Spirit intercedes for us with sighs too deep for words" (Rom 8:26).

As we listen to creation's groans, we hear the voice of God calling us to hopeful action. As we groan inwardly, yearning for new life, the Holy Spirit intercedes for us and urges us forward. By living and acting in hope, we embody hope and become signs of hope for the world, trusting that God's activity in and through us contributes to the coming birth of a renewed creation.

5

Tradition: The Wisdom of God in Creation

Now the wisdom, as well as the power of God, is abundantly manifested in his creation, in the formation and arrangement of all his works.[1]

—John Wesley

I have a collection of children's books about creation that I read to my grandchildren and to the Sunday school children in my church. Some of the books present the seven-day sequence from Genesis 1, with colorful pictures showing the emergence of light and dark, heavenly bodies, plants, sea life and birds, and finally animals and human beings. Some books are based on the story of Adam and Eve. Jane Ray's *Adam and Eve and the Garden of Eden* introduces the creation story by saying: "At the very beginning of the world the earth was a dry and dusty place, where nothing could live and nothing could grow. So God made a mist which watered the ground all over. Then with his great hands, he formed the first man of the clay of the newly watered earth."[2]

Other picture books on creation are more loosely based on scripture. *And God Created Squash* by Martha Whitmore Hickman portrays God as an old man with long white hair and a beard, thinking up things to

---

1. John Wesley, Sermon 68, "The Wisdom of God's Counsels," *The Works of John Wesley*, ed. Albert C. Outler (Nashville: Abingdon, 1986), 2:551.
2. Jane Ray, *Adam and Eve and the Garden of Eden* (Grand Rapids: Eerdmans, 2005), 1.

create. He puts his ear to the ground and says, "I'd like to hear something growing."[3] As he creates he walks around smelling flowers, tasting food, and enjoying the abundance of life. At the end he says, "I'll be around. You may not see me. But I'll be here—and there—wherever you are, whenever you need me. Even in the middle of the night."[4] *Big Momma Makes the World* by Phyllis Root presents a feminine image of God: "When Big Momma made the world, she didn't mess around . . . she rolled up her sleeves and went to it."[5] Big Momma, with a playful baby on her hip, takes mud and knits it together to create the world and everything in it, culminating in a huge ball of mud out of which emerge people of every race, size, and shape. They are, apparently, naked, to the delight of the children.

Each of these books is a creative contemporary expression of Judeo-Christian traditional teachings on creation. Each has its own unique twist based on the theological interpretation of the author. Christian tradition is not static. It develops in an ongoing way.

A Christian understanding of creation doesn't rule out respect for science. I also read the children a science-based book about the origins of the universe called *Life Story* by Virginia Lee Burton, author of children's classics such as *Mike Mulligan and His Steam Shovel* and *The Little House*. *Life Story* begins with the birth of the Sun, "one of the millions and billions of stars that make up our galaxy."[6] It proceeds with a fascinating walk through geological time and the evolution of life on earth right up to the present. "And now it is your Life Story. . . . The stage is set, the time is now, and the place wherever you are."[7]

I have never felt there was a conflict between reading the traditional storybooks that talk about God creating the world and children's books based on science. These accounts of creation complement each other. The children aren't confused. They know the Bible stories, they know about Jesus, and they know God's love. They also know about stars, black holes, dinosaurs, and fossils. The scientific story of creation doesn't negate teachings about God as Creator, Redeemer, and Sustainer of the world.

---

3. Martha Whitmore Hickman, *And God Created Squash: How the World Began* (Morton Grove, IL: Albert Whitman and Co., 1993), 8.

4. Ibid., 29.

5. Phyllis Root, *Big Momma Makes the World* (Cambridge, MA: Candlewick, 2002), 1.

6. Virginia Lee Burton, *Life Story* (New York: Houghton Mifflin and Co., 1962).

7. Ibid., 69.

Creation in Christian Tradition

As is true with children's picture books, traditional Christian teachings about creation have varied over the centuries. Some traditional views have emphasized the glory of God revealed through creation, the kinship of human beings with other creatures, or the human responsibility of stewardship. These attitudes support an understanding of the value of creation and the human role in caring for the earth.

Other teachings, sadly, have done more harm than good. In fact, Christianity has been widely criticized for promoting a view of *dominion* that has contributed to ecological destruction. In "The Historical Roots of the Ecologic Crisis," a now-famous article written in 1967, author Lynn White Jr. charged that the Christian religion is primarily responsible for the ecological crisis, because its underlying ideology has supported unfettered exploitation of the earth. White's primary arguments centered around Judeo-Christian understandings of dominion, the origins of the scientific revolution in natural theology, the idea of perpetual progress rather than cyclical views of time, and the dualism of man versus nature. White pointed to differences between Eastern Orthodox churches, which have focused more on creation spirituality, and churches in the West. He claimed that Western Christianity is "the most anthropocentric religion the world has seen."[8]

There are merits to White's critique of Christianity, but he based his primary argument on a particular interpretation of the Genesis creation stories, which he explained by saying, "God planned all of this explicitly for man's benefit and rule: no item in the physical creation had any purpose save to serve man's purposes."[9] As we have seen, there are people who understand the stories of Genesis in this way, but White went further by claiming that this view undergirds Western culture. He wrote: "Our science and technology have grown out of Christian attitudes toward man's relation to nature, which are almost universally held. . . . Despite Copernicus, all the cosmos rotates around our little globe. Despite Darwin, we are not, in our hearts, part of the natural process. We are superior to nature, contemptuous of it, willing to use it for our slightest whims."[10]

The election of Donald Trump, whose support by white Evangelicals

---

8. Lynn White, "The Historical Roots of Our Ecologic Crisis," in *Science*, vol. 155, no. 3767 (March 10, 1967), http://science.sciencemag.org/content/155/3767/1203.

9. Ibid.

10. Ibid.

helped him win the election, seems to support White's thesis. Trump is appointing leaders and enacting policies that will be disastrous for creation and will bring further injustice to people. But this is just the latest and most extreme manifestation of a pattern of destruction that has been going on for centuries. Christian farmer and poet Wendell Berry asks a question that should be deeply considered by anyone who professes to follow Jesus: "How can modern Christianity have so solemnly folded its hands while so much of the work of God was being destroyed?"[11]

Rather than argue against White's thesis, it seems more fruitful to acknowledge that attitudes he describes have done their share of harm and have contributed to ecological destruction. We can also affirm his suggestion that Christians adopt an alternative theological model that motivates care for creation, as we seek to do in this book.

Another problem with traditional Christian teachings is that creation has often been ignored. Especially since the Reformation, creation-centered themes in Christian writings have been overshadowed by the emphasis on human salvation. The created world has largely been viewed as a stage or backdrop for a drama played out between God and human beings, and between human beings and each other. This narrow focus ignores the fact that we humans are part of creation, interrelated with other species and intimately connected to the natural processes of the earth.

In recent years, perhaps motivated by ecological concerns, theologians have searched scripture and historical writings to see how prominent Christian figures from the past have viewed creation. These studies shed light on traditional Christian views and inform contemporary theological perspectives on creation and our place in the universe.

Throughout the centuries, movements such as Celtic Christianity, Benedictines, Franciscans, and other contemplative orders cultivated spiritual connection with the natural world. Creation-centered writings of mystics such as Hildegard of Bingen and Meister Eckhart continue to inspire people today.

Francis of Assisi (1181–1226) expressed a view of humans as part of creation, related to all other parts. In his "Canticle of Brother Sun" he invites Brother Sun, Sister Moon, and other parts of creation to join him in praising God.[12] In our day Pope Francis, who chose his own name after Saint Francis, has similarly spoken of our interconnectedness

---

11. Wendell Berry, "Christianity and the Survival of Creation," *Classical Carousel*, April 8, 2015, http://cleoclassical.blogspot.com/2015/04/christianity-and-survival-of-creation.html.

with all creatures and has galvanized people around the interrelated issues of climate change, justice for the poor, the evils of capitalism, and the need for systemic change. His influential Encyclical, *Laudato Si: On Care for Our Common Home*, which begins with words of St. Francis, provides a corrective to the anthropocentric views of many Christians.[13] Lynn White himself suggested learning from the teachings and example of Saint Francis, and proposed Francis as "a patron saint for ecologists."

In the thirteenth century, Thomas Aquinas celebrated the value of creation in all its diversity and claimed that all creatures together represent and glorify God. In *Summa Theologica*, he wrote:

> The divine goodness could not be adequately represented by one creature alone. He produced many and diverse creatures, that what was wanting to one in the representation of the divine goodness might be supplied by another. For goodness, which in God is simple and uniform, in creatures is manifold and divided; and hence the whole universe together participates in the divine goodness more perfectly, and represents it better than any single creature whatever.[14]

The idea that the multitude of God's creatures reveal the "divine goodness" more completely than any individual creature is profound. If this is so, the extinction of species at the current greatly accelerated rate diminishes creation's ability to represent the goodness of God. This understanding has been expanded in our day by the late Passionist priest Thomas Berry, who spoke of the earth as the "primary revelation" of the divine. He wrote: "The natural world is the life-giving nourishment of our physical, emotional, aesthetic, moral, and religious existence. The natural world is the larger sacred community to which we belong. To be alienated from this community is to become destitute in all that makes us human. To damage this community is to diminish our own existence."[15] We will explore the implications of this understanding in a later chapter.

Martin Luther, whose teachings about human salvation were the

---

12. The Hymnal Revision Committee, Rueben P. Job, Chair, *The United Methodist Hymnal* (Nashville: United Methodist Publishing, 1989), 62.

13. Pope Francis, *Laudato Si: On Care for Our Common Home* (Rome: Libreria Editrice Vaticana, 2015), http://w2.vatican.va/content/francesco/en/encyclicals/documents/papa-francesco_20150524 _enciclica-laudato-si.html.

14. Thomas Berry, "Economics: Its Effects on the Life Systems of the Earth," in *Thomas Berry and the New Cosmology*, ed. Anne Lonergan and Caroline Richards (Mystic, CT: Twenty-Third Publications, 1988), 14.

15. Thomas Berry, *The Dream of the Earth* (San Francisco: Sierra Club Books, 1990), 81.

foundation of the Protestant Reformation, taught that God is present throughout creation. He wrote, "God's entire divine nature is wholly and entirely in all creatures, more deeply, more inwardly, more present than the creature is to itself."[16] Contemporary Lutheran theologian Cynthia D. Moe-Lobeda speaks of this divine presence as *Love*. In *Resisting Structural Evil: Love as Ecological-Economic Vocation*, she writes, "All of creation is loved by a Love that will not cease and is more powerful than any force on earth or beyond." She goes on to speak of the implications of this universal Love: "Love that seeks justice is the counterpoint to structural evil."[17] Moe-Lobeda's book links creation and justice and points toward abundant life for the whole community of life, as this present volume seeks to do.

Teachings that uphold the value of creation are present throughout Christian tradition, reminding us of our responsibility to honor, care for, protect, and seek justice for creation in all its interrelatedness and diversity. These responsibilities become even clearer as we turn to John Wesley as a source for thinking theologically about creation in the context of climate change.

Grace: God's Love at Work in the World

Although John Wesley's primary focus was on salvation, his creation theology was amazingly rich and varied. He saw the wisdom, glory, and goodness of God as revealed through the created universe in all its splendor and diversity. The "book of nature," according to Wesley, is available for all to read:

> The world around us is the mighty volume wherein God hath declared himself. Human languages and characters are different in different nations. And those of one nation are not understood by the rest. But the book of nature is written in a universal character, which everyone may read in his own language. It consists not of words, but things which picture out the Divine perfection. The firmament everywhere expanded, with all its starry host, declares the immensity and magnificence, the power and wisdom of its Creator.[18]

16. Martin Luther, *Luther's Works on CD ROM: 55 Volume American Edition*, ed. Jaroslav Pelikan and Helmut T. Lehman (Minneapolis: Fortress Press, 1957), 37:60.
17. Cynthia D. Moe-Lobeda, *Resisting Structural Evil: Love as Ecological-Economic Vocation*, (Minneapolis: Fortress Press, 2013), xviii.
18. John Wesley, *A Survey of the Wisdom of God in the Creation: A Compendium of Natural Philosophy* (Lancaster, PA: William Hamilton, 1810), 229–30.

God's love is communicated to us through creation generally, but in specific ways as well. Wesley wrote: "Even the actions of animals are an eloquent and a pathetic language. [They] have a thousand engaging ways, which, like the voice of God speaking to our hearts, command us to preserve and cherish them."[19] Animals speak to us of God, reminding us that our responsibility extends to preserving and cherishing them.

Wesley's creation theology provides an expansive and cosmic context to his other theological themes, including some for which he is most well known: prevenient grace, the experience of assurance, and Christian perfection. These themes all relate to grace—a primary emphasis throughout Wesleyan thought.

For Wesley, grace is God's love at work in the world. He identified three aspects of grace: prevenient grace, justifying grace, and sanctifying grace. *Prevenient grace* is grace that is present and active in our lives before we know it, touching us with spiritual inclinations and inviting us into a conscious relationship with God. *Justifying grace* is grace at work in our hearts as we say yes to God's forgiveness and love as revealed in Jesus, and as we experience the assurance of God's unconditional acceptance and love. *Sanctifying grace* is grace that transforms us as we respond to the ongoing activity of the Holy Spirit in our hearts and lives.[20] Wesley used the image of a house to illustrate these three aspects of grace: prevenient grace is the porch, justifying grace is the doorway, and sanctifying grace is the whole inside of the house.[21]

These concepts regarding the workings of grace are familiar in Wesleyan studies. What is less well known is the way that Wesley, especially in his later years, expanded these ideas to encompass salvation within a cosmic view of creation. This is clearest in his sermon "The General Deliverance," which we discussed in the previous chapter. But this all-encompassing view of grace is found in many of Wesley's other writings, interspersed with other themes, as described below.

19. Ibid.
20. "Our Wesleyan Heritage: Distinctive Emphases," What We Believe: The Basics of Our Faith, United Methodist Church, http://www.umc.org/what-we-believe/our-wesleyan-heritage.
21. "Opening Ourselves to Grace: The Basics of Christian Discipleship," The General Board of Discipleship of the United Methodist Church, http://www.umcdiscipleship.org/resources/opening-our-selves-to-grace-the-basics-of-christian-discipleship.

Prevenient Grace

In weighing in on a theological issue that was debated in his day, John Wesley opposed the concept of predestination, which teaches that the elect are destined to be saved while all others will be damned. He insisted that all people everywhere are invited into the blessings of a conscious relationship with the God of love. No one is excluded. He called this inclusive love *prevenient grace*, an archaic term that means "the divine love that surrounds all humanity and precedes any and all of our conscious impulses" and that "awakens in us an earnest longing for deliverance from sin and death and moves us toward repentance and faith."[22] Wesley said, "No man living is entirely destitute of what is vulgarly called 'natural conscience.' But this is not natural; it is more properly termed *prevenient grace*. . . . Everyone has some measure of that light, some faint glimmering ray, which sooner or later, more or less, enlightens every man that cometh into the world. . . . So that no man sins because he has not grace, but because he does not use the grace which he hath."[23]

But for Wesley, God's grace goes even further, encompassing all creation. He saw all people and even "brute creatures"[24] as included in God's loving intentions. Every creature, for Wesley, is a reflection of the Creator. He wrote, "But the great lesson . . . is that God is in all things, and that we are to see the Creator in the [looking] glass of every creature."[25] Animals are to be valued in their own right as fellow creatures who reflect the God of love.

Prevenient grace, the grace at work in our lives even before we are consciously aware of it, is at work throughout the universe, sustaining creatures and enabling them to flourish "as they are capable" and to share in the divine glory.[26] According to Wesley, "God acts everywhere, and therefore is everywhere. . . . God acts in heaven, in earth, and under the earth, throughout the whole compass of his creation; by sustaining all things, without which everything would in an instant sink into its primitive nothing; by governing all, every moment superintending everything that he has made; strongly and sweetly influencing all, and yet without destroying the liberty of his rational creatures."[27] God's

---

22. From *The Book of Discipline of the United Methodist Church*, 2012 (Nashville: United Methodist Publishing, 2012), 50.
23. Sermon 85, "On Working Out Our Own Salvation," *Works*, 3:199.
24. Sermon 60, "The General Deliverance," *Works*, 2:440.
25. Sermon 23, "Upon Our Lord's Sermon on the Mount, III," *Works*, 1:516–17.
26. Sermon 60, "The General Deliverance," *Works*, 2:445.

grace pervades and encompasses the whole universe, as expressed by Paul in Acts 17:28: "In God we live and move and have our being."

Sin and Justifying Grace

These ideas of universal grace offered to all people and to all parts of creation bring to mind the goodness of God's creation and the blessings of life on earth. Tragically, however, sin is pervasive and has taken its toll not only on individual human lives and relationships but on creation as a whole. Wesley, like most biblical scholars of his day, understood the *fall* of humanity as a historical event. Humans and all other creatures lived in an idyllic Garden of Eden and were cast out by God as a consequence for human disobedience. But Wesley also based his belief in the "utter degeneracy" of humanity on the evidence that he saw all around him, especially the universality of war. He said, "If then, all nations, Pagan, Mohammedan, and Christian, do, in fact, make [war] their last resort, what further proof of do we need of the utter degeneracy of all nations from the plainest principles of reason and virtue? Of the absolute want, both of common sense and common humanity, which runs through the whole race of mankind?"[28]

If the carnage of war was so convincing to Wesley of the universality of human sin, what can we say about climate change and the extent of its ongoing harm? Sin cannot be viewed simply as an isolated, individual matter, for its effects on others cannot be measured. Even if we seek to be faithful and lead moral lives, we are enmeshed in institutions and systems that are at cross-purposes with the loving will of God.

Even when we become aware of destructive patterns in our lives that harm God's good creation, we may find it impossible to change simply by exerting our willpower. Paul's dilemma, the lack of power to change ourselves, becomes our dilemma: "For I do not do the good I want, but the evil I do not want is what I do . . ." (Rom 7:19). Justifying grace is God's action that rescues us from this dilemma. By accepting Jesus's invitation into conscious relationship with God, we are offered the gifts of repentance, forgiveness, assurance, reconciliation, and the ability to start anew. The experience of assurance is a central theme of Wesley's theology. He described it by saying, "The testimony of the Spirit is an inward impression on the soul, whereby the Spirit of God directly

---

27. Sermon 118, "On the Omnipresence of God," *Works*, 4:42.
28. John Wesley, "Treatise on Original Sin," 1756, as quoted, Newbiggin Methodist Chapel, http://www.newbigginchapel.co.uk/john-wesley-on-war.html.

'witnesses to my spirit that I am a child of God'; that Jesus Christ hath loved me, and given himself for me; that all my sins are blotted out, and I, even I, am reconciled to God."[29]

Not only is God present throughout creation, we can experience that presence and the assurance of God's forgiveness and love. As we accept and respond to God's justifying grace as revealed in Jesus, a process of spiritual transformation is initiated through which we are offered the power to overcome old and harmful patterns and grow into the people God created and is creating us to be. This process of ongoing spiritual growth has traditionally been called *sanctification*.

Sanctifying Grace: Perfection in Love

For Wesley, sanctification is ongoing growth in love for God and neighbor. It was in this sense that he taught that *entire sanctification or perfection in love* in this life is possible. He said, "By perfection I mean the humble, gentle, patient love of God, and our neighbor, ruling our tempers, words, and actions."[30] Elsewhere he said, "Scripture perfection is pure love filling the heart, and governing all the words and actions."[31]

The idea that believers can become *perfected in love* was controversial even in Wesley's day. But for Wesley this concept did not mean that people arrive at a static state of absolute perfection. Rather, he held out hope that it is possible to grow in the ability to love God and neighbor in an ongoing process without inevitably succumbing to sin. This process of ongoing spiritual renewal does not prevent a person from making mistakes or acting in ignorance, but imparts power over sin. In other words, willfully turning away from God is not inevitable, because God gives us all the power we need to choose love on a moment-by-moment basis. We are given *moral agency*, that is, the ability to take right action, as we grow in love. Wesley said, "By justification we are saved from the guilt of sin, and restored to the favour of God; by sanctification we are saved from the power and root of sin, and restored to the image of God."[32]

This concept of *perfection in love* is not unique to Wesley, but he places it in a cosmic context beyond any of his predecessors. For Wesley, God's sanctifying grace is not solely at work in individual human

---

29. John Wesley, Sermon 10, "The Witness of the Spirit I," in *John Wesley's Sermons: An Anthology*, ed. Albert C. Outler and Richard P. Heitzenrater (Nashville: Abingdon, 1991), 149.
30. John Wesley, *A Plain Account of Christian Perfection*, print version (ReadaClassic.com), 76.
31. Ibid., 37.
32. Sermon 85, "On Working Out Our Own Salvation," *An Anthology*, 488–89.

beings, but in the context of our relationships, situations, and inter-connectedness with other beings and the rest of creation. Growth in love is an ongoing process—one never arrives. It is not absolute or irreversible, nor does it take place in a vacuum, because we are "hedged in by outward circumstances."[33] But as we open ourselves to sanctifying grace and allow ourselves to be transformed and restored to the image of God, all those with whom we are in relationship and creation itself are affected for the better. Michael Lodahl, author of *God of Nature and Grace: Reading the World in a Wesleyan Way*, explains, "This much is certain: for Wesley, to be entirely sanctified is to live in a quality of relationship to God and neighbor characterized by love, and to live in such love is to be restored to the image of God."[34]

As we progress in love and in our ability to "image" God to the rest of creation, grace works with, in, and through us to help move creation toward renewal. Wesley holds out hope that the earth itself will be renewed as humans assume their rightful place in creation, in humility and true holiness of heart and life: "And, to crown all, there will be a deep, an intimate, and uninterrupted union with God; a constant communion with the Father and his Son Jesus Christ, through the Spirit; a continual enjoyment of the Three-One God, and of all the creatures in him."[35]

Contemporary Manifestations of Christian Tradition

Contemporary manifestations of Christian theology keep the tradition alive as it develops in an ongoing way. Several renowned Wesleyan theologians incorporate process theology into their work. Process theology is an evolving line of Christian thought initially developed by Charles Hartshorne, based on the process philosophy of Alfred North Whitehead. Process theologians are influenced by contemporary scientific discoveries about the nature of the universe, including quantum physics and the theory of relativity. Rather than holding to a fixed or static worldview, they see events, energy, and processes as foundational to reality. Likewise, process theologians understand human beings not simply as isolated entities but as inseparable from countless interrelationships and events shared with other beings and with all other parts of the cosmos.[36]

33. Wesley, *A Plain Account of Christian Perfection*, 36.
34. Lodahl, *God of Nature and of Grace*, 203.
35. Sermon 64, "The New Creation," *An Anthology*, 500.
36. This brief description barely touches on a few of the key concepts of process theology. Wesleyan

A process view rejects the concept of God as a dominating or intrusive force acting unilaterally to determine the outcome of events, but instead sees God as the creative power drawing creation toward the fulfillment of divine Love. Human beings have freedom to accept or reject God's loving invitation. This understanding of the nature of God is consistent with Wesleyan thought. In Wesley's words: "God commands all things both in heaven and earth to assist man in attaining the end of his being, in working out his own salvation—so far as it can be done without compulsion, without overruling his liberty . . . without turning man into a machine."[37] God draws us forward for the good of all without taking away our ability to choose, for that would be contrary to the divine nature.

Like Wesley, process theologians point to spiritual experience as evidence of God's pervasive presence and activity throughout the universe. Through deep and sometimes barely perceptible spiritual inclinations, God draws us and all parts of creation toward fulfillment. Michael Lodahl relates Wesley's teachings on sanctification to the hoped-for fulfillment of creation and the realization of God's intended world:

> This biblical theology of creation goes hand in hand with Wesley's optimism of grace, which insists . . . that it is possible in this life (and hence, in this world) to love God and neighbor with all of our being. . . . This perspective has obvious implications for developing a Christian, and particularly a Wesleyan, commitment to social and economic justice as well as to the ecological well-being of our planet. Good stewardship of God's world, entrusted to the creatures called upon to image or reflect God, is stewardship for the long haul![38]

God as love works in, with, and through creation to bring about the best possible outcome for each individual being and for creation as a whole, based on what is possible in our actual, concrete circumstances. Marjorie Hewitt Suchocki says: "Wesley's awesome audacity is to dare to assume that God can accomplish the divine intention for creation within creation and through creation. That intention is simply that creation shall be a living image of God's own love."[39]

scholars John E. Cobb Jr., Bryan P. Stone, Randy L. Maddox, Marjorie Hewitt Suchocki, Michael E. Lodahl, Randy Maddox, Schubert M. Ogdon, Thomas Jay Oord, and others have written extensively about the implications of process theology for understanding the contemporary relevance of John Wesley's theology, including his theology of creation.

37. Sermon 67, "On Divine Providence," *Works*, 2:540–41.
38. Lodahl, *God of Nature and of Grace*, 184–85.

But Lodahl points out that there is an underside to God's non-coercive way of acting in the world and to the freedom and responsibility we human beings have been given. Even if God's intention is the healing of the world, it is not guaranteed.

> Even if our Maker and Molder truly is invested in the venture and risk of freedom exercised by the creature, there is no guarantee that this great labor of God will end successfully. Our mending is not guaranteed, not simply a matter of course. While the prevenient grace of God's presence in the world is faithful and true (Ps 146:6–9), the nature of this grace is persuasive rather than coercive in nature. But if indeed divine grace is persuasive, then the underside is that we may yet enact our own apocalypse.[40]

The stakes are high. Scripture and tradition uphold the inherent value of creation, but human activity is unraveling the web of life and bringing peril to God's creation. This is a spiritual and moral issue. God's will is for creation to flourish, but human choices greatly influence and in some ways determine whether life will flourish or continue to be degraded. Which direction will we choose?

As we have seen, John Wesley agreed with the biblical view that humanity's fall impacted the whole created order. John Cobb suggests that when we speak of the salvation of the world today, in the context of ecological destruction, we should give it "a fullness of meaning that is only hinted at in scripture." He said:

> The forgiveness of sins, the healing of personal brokenness, and liberation from social oppression are all essential ingredients in the fullness of salvation. But if all of that happens, and the natural world continues to decay, that will be a very limited salvation indeed. If famine and disease are decimating the human population, and if our basic stance continues to be one that ignores the causes of these evils, we will hardly be able to claim to have served God's great cause of salvation.[41]

Wesley's view of salvation in the context of creation reminds us that we don't make choices in a vacuum, but in the context of countless interrelationships, events, and processes that connect us with our human family and with the fabric of life. Our actions are in many ways "hedged

---

39. Marjorie Hewitt Suchocki, "Coming Home: Wesley, Whitehead, and Women," in *Thy Nature and Thy Name Is Love*, 57.
40. Ibid.
41. John B. Cobb Jr., *Grace & Responsibility: A Wesleyan Theology for Today* (Nashville: Abingdon, 1995), 133.

in by outward circumstances."[42] Likewise, our actions do not just affect us as individuals, but have consequences for others. Understanding our interrelatedness with the rest of creation provides a foundation that carries us forward as we make decisions not based solely on selfish motives but on the well-being of the whole community of life.

Informed by Tradition: Nurturing Creation

Responding in faith to climate change does not distract us from growing in love of God and neighbor, but takes us deeper in our journey of faith. When considering ways to nurture creation, seeking guidance and empowerment from the Spirit is a good place to start. One way to do so is through the *means of grace*. The means of grace are practices (means) through which we open our hearts and lives to God's grace. These include scripture study, public worship, family and private prayer, meditation, fasting or abstinence, the sacraments of Baptism and Holy Communion, acts of charity, service to others. God's grace works through these and other spiritual practices to increase our faith and transform our lives in the direction of love.

There are many ways that individuals and congregational groups can nurture creation in practical ways, but actions are magnified if they are taken in light of their contribution to the larger cultural shift that is needed. One challenge is to incorporate creation-nurturing activities into the life of the church. In this way, they become part of the larger Christian tradition and inform decision-making about a variety of issues, including climate change. Sunday worship services can incorporate scripture passages, liturgies, hymns, and symbols that honor creation. Adult education classes and Bible studies, children's Sunday school, youth groups, church camps, all-church picnics, and other congregational activities can raise awareness and sensitize people to the value of creation.

Landscaping with native plants minimizes water use while supporting birds, butterflies, and other wildlife. Permaculture gardening mimics nature and builds healthy soil that sequesters carbon. Planting a home, church, or community organic garden brings satisfaction, feeds people, and connects us with the fruitfulness of the earth. Shopping at farmers' markets and buying foods grown regionally support nearby small farms. These practices remind us that we are sustained through the earth and human labor, and save the fossil fuels required to fer-

---

42. Wesley, *A Plain Account of Christian Perfection*, 36.

tilize, package, and ship industrialized food around the world. By promoting such activities, the church provides a witness to the larger community about the necessity of honoring creation and working to establish climate justice.

Eating lower on the food chain by going vegetarian or vegan, or by using meat as a condiment, reduces the environmental impact of meat production and feeds more people per acre. Boycotting factory-farmed animal products expresses sensitivity toward farm animals and is a form of resistance to their cruel and inhumane treatment. These earth-friendly practices express integrity and contribute to changing the culture of self-seeking, overconsumption, and greed.

These kinds of choices may seem to some like a luxury. Many people live in cities, some in dangerous neighborhoods. Not everyone has a safe place outside where they can walk, sit, or plant vegetables. Many people live in *food deserts*—impoverished areas that lack fresh fruit, vegetables, and other healthful whole foods because grocery stores and healthy food providers are miles away.[43] Not everyone can afford high-quality foods. Many families are strapped financially with student loans, low wages, high rents or mortgages, rising food prices, or unpaid medical bills. For parents, the primary challenge is to meet the immediate needs of their children.

These realities highlight the need to both honor creation and establish justice. While finding ways to nurture creation, we must join together in solidarity to work for social and economic justice for all. We will explore this responsibility further when we turn our attention to justice in the second half of this book.

As we seek to nurture God's creation in this time of climate change, of this we can be sure: God is faithful, extending steadfast love to all generations (Ps 100:5). Our tears and prayers do not go unheard, and our small, finite actions are incorporated into God's work of renewing creation. We are called to live in hope as long as God's prevenient grace moves through creation, God's justifying grace enables people to start over, and God's sanctifying grace transforms people's lives and renews the world through love.

---

43. "USDA Defines Food Deserts," *Nutrition Digest*, Vol. 38, no. 2, American Nutrition Association, http://americannutritionassociation.org/newsletter/usda-defines-food-deserts.

6

———

Reason: The New Creation Story

In other words, it is always easier to deny reality than to watch your worldview get shattered, a fact that was as true of die-hard Stalinists at the height of the purges as it is of libertarian climate deniers today.[1]

—Naomi Klein

Although there is overwhelming consensus among climate scientists that anthropogenic climate change is real, the general public is confused about its reality and the extent of the problem. Reasons for this confusion abound.

In *Don't Even Think About It: Why Our Brains Are Wired to Ignore Climate Change*, George Marshall asks, "What explains our ability to separate what we know from what we believe, to put aside the things that seem too painful to accept? How is it possible, when presented with overwhelming evidence, even the evidence of our own eyes, that we can deliberately ignore something—while being entirely aware that this is what we are doing?"[2]

Marshall points to studies that show why our brains avoid or don't reason well about climate change. Many things get in the way of our

1. Naomi Klein, "Capitalism vs. the Climate," in *The Nation*, November 9, 2011. https://www.thenation.com/article/capitalism-vs-climate/.
2. George Marshall, *Don't Even Think About It: Why Our Brains Are Wired to Ignore Climate Change* (New York: Bloomsbury, 2014), 1.

thinking clearly about it, including: 1) denial that it is real or that there is anything we can do to stop it; 2) the magnitude and complexity of the issue; 3) confusion because of how it is framed; 4) perceived distance from its consequences in time and space; 5) fear of taking an unpopular stand on politically controversial or emotionally charged issues; and 6) unwillingness to consider lowering our standard of living for uncertain future benefits. In addition to these psychological blocks, socially constructed codes of silence and moral confusion may prevent open discussion of the topic, including in churches.[3]

There are also powerful special interests that deliberately spread confusion in order to control the dialogue about climate change for economic, political, or ideological reasons. The funders of these organized campaigns to sow doubt about planetary warming include Exxon Mobil, Shell, and other fossil-fuel corporations, free-market think tanks like the Heartland Institute, and the Koch brothers and other wealthy individuals who pool their vast wealth as *dark money* in tax deductible "philanthropic" organizations like Americans for Prosperity. These behind-the-scenes moneyed interests spend millions to sow doubt about the issue, attack climate science (and scientists), determine how the topic is framed in the media, and prevent strong governmental action to mitigate its dangers. They fund misleading industry studies, produce position papers that refute mainstream climate science, hire spokespersons to debate climate scientists, and create advertisements that downplay or deny the dangers of climate change. These tactics create a sense of confusion and paralysis about the issue.[4]

Another powerful constituency that influences the climate debate in the United States is the Religious Right. This primarily Christian constituency is aligned with conservative social, political, and economic interests and is a powerful and organized force in the Republican Party.

This conservative religious lobby's talking points and policy proposals on energy and climate are largely indistinguishable from those of the fossil-fuel industry. Recent initiatives have focused on "Academic Freedom" legislation designed to "teach the controversy" about climate change in public schools.[5] Legislation to this effect has been drafted by the American Legislative Exchange Council (ALEC)—a conservative secular organization that brings corporate leaders together

---

3. Ibid., 1–3.
4. Naomi Oreskes and Erik M. Conway, *Merchants of Doubt* (New York: Bloomsbury, 2010), 247.
5. Devin Powell, "See Where Climate Science Conflict Has Invaded U.S. Classrooms," *Smithsonian.com* (September 23, 2015), http://www.smithsonianmag.com/science-nature/see-where-climate-science-conflict-has-invaded-us-classrooms-180956707/?no-ist.

with conservative lawmakers to draft model legislation on various issues to be presented around the country in state legislatures. *Teach the controversy* legislation has also been supported by the Alliance for Defending Freedom, a conservative Christian advocacy group, and the Discovery Institute—a creationist think tank.[6] This uninformed and deliberately confusing approach to climate change was reflected by then-candidate Donald Trump in a 2016 *New York Times* interview, when he said, "You know the hottest day ever was in 1890-something, 98. You know, you can make lots of cases for different views. I have a totally open mind. . . . It's a very complex subject. I'm not sure anybody is ever going to really know."[7]

Right-wing Christian groups deny climate science and evolutionary science on the basis that they are unbiblical. The Cornwall Alliance's website hosts a sign-on declaration, "An Evangelical Declaration on Global Warming," stating that "there is no convincing scientific evidence that human contribution to greenhouse gases is causing dangerous global warming." The Cornwall Alliance also offers a DVD called "Resisting the Green Dragon: A Biblical Response to One of the Greatest Deceptions of Our Day," which outlines the dangers of the new and false "religion" of environmentalism. Not surprisingly, the organization also works to prevent the teaching of evolution in public schools.[8]

Although political and economic interests help fund and influence the Christian Right's opposition to climate science, there are also theological factors at work. An analysis of anti-environmental sentiment within the Religious Right reveals that some are convinced that concern for the environment is based on the worship of nature. Others, who believe in apocalyptic prophecies about the coming end times, feel that it is pointless to worry about climate change.[9] What they hold in common, however, is their insistence that the creation stories in the book of Genesis must be taken literally.

Creationism, the belief that the creation stories of Genesis are scien-

6. Katherine Stewart, "America's theologians of climate science denial," *The Guardian* (November 4, 2012), https://www.theguardian.com/commentisfree/2012/nov/04/america-theologians-climate-science-denial.
7. "Donald Trump's New York Times Interview: Full Transcript," *New York Times*, November 23, 2016, http://www.nytimes.com/2016/11/23/us/politics/trump-new-york-times-interview-transcript.html?_r=0.
8. "Evangelical Declaration on Global Warming," *The Cornwall Alliance for the Stewardship of Creation*, http://cornwallalliance.org/landmark-documents/evangelical-declaration-on-global-warming-2/.
9. B. D. Zaleha A. Szasz, "Why Conservative Christians Don't Believe in Climate Change," *Bulletin of the Atomic Scientists* (September 1, 2015), http://thebulletin.org/2015/september/why-conservative-christians-dont-believe-climate-change8722.

tific fact, is widespread among conservative Christians, who seek to introduce this doctrine even in public schools. This sets the creation stories in scripture in opposition to the scientific story of the origins and nature of the universe. Was the universe created in fifteen billion years or in seven days? In pre-scientific times, Christians did take the creation stories in Genesis literally, but times have changed. Scientific discoveries have revealed aspects of the universe unknown in ancient times.

One form of denial at work in these and other conversations about climate change is people's refusal to consider evidence that contradicts their worldview. Science is continually revealing new information about the natural world, its origins and interconnectedness, and the causes and impacts of planetary warming. Reason enables us to weigh the evidence, reflect on its implications, form rational conclusions, and make informed decisions as we consider how to respond to the earth's changing climate in a reasonable way. But in the words of Naomi Klein, "it is always easier to deny reality than to watch your worldview get shattered. . . ."[10]

None of these pitfalls need confuse us or hold us back. Faith in God's goodness enables us to overcome denial, fear, and confusion as we seek truth about these issues.

John Wesley on Science and Creation

John Wesley lived during the scientific revolution. He valued reason and studied evidence acquired through science in order to gain knowledge about creation. Although he understood the creation stories in Genesis as historical—as did most people of his time—he did not interpret them as presenting a *scientific* account of the origins of the universe. He wrote, "The inspired penman in this history [Genesis] . . . describes things by their outward sensible appearances, and leaves us, by further discoveries of the divine light, to be led into the understanding of the mysteries couched under them."[11] Wesley accepted the Copernican view of the universe, which directly challenged the ancient worldview as presented in Genesis. Like other Enlightenment figures, he accepted that the earth and other planets orbited the sun, because this view was based on empirical evidence gained through the scientific method.

10. Naomi Klein, "Capitalism vs. the Climate."
11. John Wesley, *Wesley's Notes on the Bible* (Grand Rapids: Francis Asbury, 1987), 25.

Wesley had no way of knowing about the science of ecology, with its understanding of the complex interrelationships that species have with each other and with the living systems of the earth. But he was aware of the interconnectedness of the varied aspects of creation. He even borrowed from the writings of biologists of his day who anticipated the discoveries of Charles Darwin by stressing the progressive development that was going on in nature. He wrote,

> The whole progress of nature is so gradual, that the entire chasm from a plant to a man, is filled up with diverse kinds of creatures, rising one above another, by so gentle an ascent, that the transitions from one species to another are almost insensible. And the intermediate space is so well husbanded, that there is scarce a degree of perfection which does not appear to some.[12]

Scientific theories about the universe did not threaten Wesley's faith. He was committed enough to scientific understandings to publish a two-volume "compendium of natural philosophy" in 1763 called *A Survey of the Wisdom of God in Creation*, adapted from writings of natural scientists and held together with his theological commentaries. Wesley summarized his reasons for writing this compendium, which demonstrated an understanding of God's creation based on the science of his day:

> How small a part do we know even of the things that encompass us on every side? I mean, as to the very facts! But as to the reasons for almost everything which we see, hear, or feel, after all our researches and inquisitions, they are hid in impenetrable darkness. I trust, therefore, the following tract may, in some degree, answer both those important purposes. It may be a means, on the one hand, of humbling the pride of man, by showing that which is surrounded on every side, with things which we can no more account for, than for Immensity or Eternity. And it may serve, on the other, to display the amazing Power, Wisdom, and Goodness of the great Creator; to warm our hearts, and to fill our mouths with wonder, love, and praise![13]

To reject scientific theories on the grounds that we should take the Genesis creation stories literally would greatly impoverish our understanding of the universe. Ongoing scientific discoveries reveal to us a

---

12. John Wesley, *A Survey of the Wisdom of God in the Creation or a Compendium of Natural Philosophy* (Bristol: William Pine, 1763), 1:234.
13. Ibid., I:vi.

universe far more amazing and mysterious than previous generations could have imagined. Some call this the "New Creation Story."[14]

The New Creation Story

We live in an incredible time. Scientists are continually making new discoveries that point out the limitations of earlier theories and shed further light on the nature and origins of the universe. We know now that the size of the universe is far greater than our ancestors in biblical times could have dreamed. Our sun is one of two hundred billion stars that make up the Milky Way Galaxy, yet the *observable universe* contains over a hundred thousand million galaxies.[15]

Scientific discoveries about the vastness of outer space have their counterpart in discoveries about the inner dimensions of matter. Quantum physics reveals that atoms are not physical building blocks at all.[16] In scientific experiments, the smallest sub-atomic "particles" sometimes act as particles and sometimes as waves, depending on what scientists are looking for.[17]

Our awareness of the dimensions of both outer and inner space is matched by an incredibly expanded understanding of time. Generally accepted scientific theories point to a vast, complex, and interrelated universe, which has been evolving for approximately fifteen billion years. The earth formed about four and a half billion years ago. Life emerged approximately 3.8 billion years ago and developed as bacteria and other single-celled organisms. A billion years later, multi-cellular life began to evolve in diverse and complex ways, with each creature developing together with its unique habitat. Symbiotic relationships formed among creatures and food chains developed, bringing about an interconnected web of life. The earliest modern humans (*Homo sapiens*) appeared in Africa some 200,000 years ago.[18]

We are also learning about how interconnected we are with other species and how dependent we are on the earth for life itself. Our cells contain between 70 and 90 percent water and our bodies are made up of the same elements that make up the earth's crust.[19] Our DNA shows

---

14. Marjorie Hope and James Young, "Thomas Berry and a New Creation Story," *Christian Century* (August 16–23, 1989), http://www.religion-online.org/showarticle.asp?title=852.

15. Edward Denis, *Jesus and the Cosmos* (Mahwah, NJ: Paulist, 1991), 12.

16. Denis Postele, *Fabric of the Universe* (New York: Crown, 1976), 74–77.

17. Fritjof Capra and David Steindl-Rast, *Belonging to the Universe: Explorations on the Frontiers of Science and Spirituality* (San Francisco: HarperSanFrancisco, 1992), 38.

18. "What does it mean to be human? Homo Sapiens," Smithsonian National Museum of Natural History, http://humanorigins.si.edu/evidence/human-fossils/species/homo-sapiens.

how closely related we are to other creatures. For instance, only 1.6 percent of the DNA of human beings is different than that of pygmy or common chimpanzees. That is, 98.4 percent of our DNA has the exact same makeup as the DNA of chimps. The *genetic distance* (1.6 percent) between chimps and humans is less than that between such closely related bird species as red-eyed vireos and white-eyed vireos (2.9 percent) or even between two species of gibbon (2.2 percent).[20] Yet, amazingly, we human beings have been blessed with the ability to reflect on ourselves, the universe, and the divine.

As Larry Rasmussen said, science offers us "the stunning portrayal of a common creation in which we are radically united with all things living and non-living, here and into endless reaches of space, and at the same time radically diverse and individuated. . . . And all of it is not only profoundly inter-related and inseparably interdependent but highly fine-tuned so as to evolve together. We are all—the living and not living, organic and inorganic—the outcome of the same primal explosion and same evolutionary history. All internally related from the very beginning, we are the varied forms of stardust in the hands of the creator God. This reality is the most basic text and context of life—and a theology of life."[21]

This "stunning portrayal of a common creation" strengthens John Wesley's claim that scientific revelations of the universe can humble our hearts and inspire us to "wonder, love, and praise." Amazingly, this vision of the universe also confirms ancient and contemporary Indigenous worldviews about the radical interrelatedness of all parts of creation.

Today, many people in the climate justice movement are looking to Indigenous communities as leaders in struggles to protect the land, air, and water and as mentors in the search for creation-honoring worldviews with power to motivate action for systemic change. Most people in the industrialized world, however, are steeped in a worldview based on the dominant economic and development model. But as impacts of the earth's changing weather patterns become ever-more frequent and extreme, people may start questioning the conventional wisdom. Will technological innovation solve the problem of climate change? Will free-market capitalism and economic growth finally bring about the

19. Dr. Neil A. Campbell, *Biology: Third Edition* (Redwood City, CA: Benjamin/Cummings, Inc., 1987), 41.
20. Jared Diamond, *The Third Chimpanzee: The Evolution and Future of the Human Animal* (New York: HarperCollins, 1992), 23.
21. Larry Rasmussen, "Theology of Life and Ecumenical Ethics," *Ecotheology: Voices from North and South*, ed. David G. Hallman (Eugene, OR: Wipf & Stock, 2009), 120.

common good? Even for people who accept the reality of global warming, our worldview informs our response. We move now to a discussion of competing worldviews and varied ways of relating to creation.

Competing Worldviews

Although the burning of fossil fuels is the primary cause of climate change, deforestation also contributes to the problem. Intact tropical and temperate forests absorb carbon dioxide from the atmosphere through photosynthesis and store it in tree trunks, foliage, and soil. When forests are cut down this stored carbon is released into the atmosphere.

Healthy forests absorb carbon that has been released through industrial processes. They sequester carbon so efficiently that scientists and climate negotiators call them "carbon sinks." The Amazon Rain Forest has been called "the lungs of the planet" because of the rate at which it draws in carbon dioxide and releases oxygen into the atmosphere. In addition to sequestering carbon, tropical forests are the most diverse ecosystems on the planet, containing half of the earth's species. As these ecosystems are destroyed, animal and plant species are going extinct, many before they have been identified.[22]

When environmental awareness was growing in the 1970s, it became popular to purchase individual plots of rainforest in the Amazon to preserve in perpetuity. People bought certificates declaring ownership of an acre of rainforest and gave them to children as birthday gifts. A quick Internet search reveals that these sales are still taking place, often in partnership with conservation groups. This individualistic approach may have preserved some individual plots of rainforest. It may assuage the guilt of individuals in industrialized nations over damage caused by our way of life. But it has not slowed the overall rate of tropical deforestation, species loss, or climate change. It does not require a change in the dominant development model or worldview. These sales will not bring ecosystem regeneration or preserve the lives and cultural diversity of people who live there.

Meanwhile, Indigenous tribes have been working for decades to protect the Amazon. Tropical forest defenders are often targeted by large landowners, developers, loggers, and ranchers who profit by converting tropical forests into agricultural and grazing lands in order to

22. "Amazon: Lungs of the Planet," British Broadcasting Company (November 18, 2014), http://www.bbc.com/future/story/20130226-amazon-lungs-of-the-planet.

produce export commodities for the global market. In 1988, Brazilian union leader Chico Mendez was martyred while defending the Amazon and supporting the rights of rubber tappers to sustainably harvest nuts and rubber in the forest.[23] More recently, in 2015, several Amazonian environmental activists were murdered in Honduras, including the renowned Indigenous Lenca leader, Berta Caceres. In 2015 alone, 185 environmental activists were killed in sixteen countries, including Brazil, Colombia, Honduras, and the Philippines. People from Indigenous groups represent 40 percent of the total victims.[24]

Similar conflicts are taking place around the world, reminding us that working for justice is an essential part of caring for creation. Mangrove forests in Southeast Asia protect coastlines, sustain a diversity of sea life, provide a livelihood for traditional fisherfolk, and help slow climate change, but they are being destroyed and displaced by shrimp farms to provide shrimp for the global seafood market.[25] Lush tropical forests in Indonesia and Malaysia are home to Indigenous tribes and provide the habitat for many species, including endangered Orangutans. These forests are being replaced by vast palm plantations to provide palm oil, which is found in many processed foods and household products sold in the United States.[26]

There are two opposing worldviews at work in these conflicts over the use of traditionally shared forests, lands, waters, and other common resources. One is based on the dominant economic and development model, which promotes exports and turns the gifts of the earth into for-profit commodities to be incorporated into the global marketplace. The other is based on the worldview of Indigenous peoples who have lived sustainably on the earth for centuries, and who honor all the interrelated parts of creation as essential. This worldview is described by Chief Seattle, who said, "Humankind has not woven the web of life. We are but one thread within it. Whatever we do to the web, we do to ourselves. All things are bound together. All things connect."[27]

Industrial agriculture also contributes to our changing climate. In

23. Andrew Revkin, *The Burning Season: The Murder of Chico Mendes and the Fight for the Amazon Rain Forest*, Reprint Edition (Washington, DC: First Island, 2004), 12.
24. Rachel Nuwer, "The Rising Murder Count of Environmental Activists," *New York Times* (June 20, 2016).
25. Alister Doyle, "Mangroves under threat from shrimp farms: U.N.," Reuters (November 14, 2012), http://www.reuters.com/article/us-mangroves-idUSBRE8AD1EG20121114.
26. "Palm Oil and Tropical Deforestation," Fact Sheet, Union of Concerned Scientists, http://www.ucsusa.org/global_warming/solutions/stop-deforestation/palm-oil-and-forests.html#.V4ltwr-grKUl.
27. "Chief Seattle, Duwamish, 1780–886," California Indian Education, http://www.californiaindianeducation.org/famous_indian_chiefs/chief_seattle/.

many instances this is related to deforestation, as forests are cleared to make way for grazing land for cattle, soy plantations for animal feed, and other export crops. Corporations engage in *biopiracy* by exploring, extracting, appropriating, and patenting biologically diverse resources and Indigenous knowledge.[28] The monopoly of corporations like Monsanto over our food supply makes food crops more uniform and requires large amounts of fossil-fuel-based fertilizers and pesticides. Many monoculture crops are genetically modified to tolerate high doses of herbicides or to carry toxic pesticide genes. Industrialized farming ignores traditional wisdom and creates its own problems, including the killing of beneficial insects and other organisms that are naturally present in healthy soil. Healthy soils sequester large amounts of carbon. When soil is stripped, tilled, treated with conventional herbicides and pesticides, and planted with monoculture crops year after year, it loses its fertility as well as its ability to sequester carbon. This creates a vicious cycle requiring ever-more artificial inputs to grow crops on depleted soils.

The foods that we access from the global supply chain are covered with the sheen of oil. Crops grown for export to the global market do not feed the people who live nearby but are shipped around the world in order to provide processed and out-of-season foods for those who can afford them. In the United States food travels an average of over 1,500 miles to get from producer to consumer.[29] This contributes to planetary warming because of the vast amounts of fossil fuels used to transport foods around the world.

Meanwhile, Indigenous groups are calling for food sovereignty, food security, and an end to biopiracy. The Indigenous Food Sovereignty Network states: "Food is a right from the Creator; in this respect the right to food is sacred and cannot be constrained or recalled by colonial laws, policies and institutions. Indigenous food sovereignty is fundamentally achieved by upholding our sacred responsibility to nurture healthy, interdependent relationships with the land, plants, and animals that provide us with our food."[30]

For Christians, attitudes and actions toward Indigenous peoples that express repentance, humility, and openness to incorporating creation-honoring attitudes provide a corrective to dominating forms of Chris-

---

28. "Indigenous Seed Sovereignty," Sierra Seeds, http://sierraseeds.org/indigenous-seed-sovereignty/.

29. "Globetrotting Food Will Travel Farther Than Ever This Thanksgiving," Worldwatch Institute, http://www.worldwatch.org/globetrotting-food-will-travel-farther-ever-thanksgiving.

30. Ibid.

tianity, which have facilitated colonization in the past and continue to justify continued exploitation of Indigenous cultures and lands. Pope Francis, in *Laudito Si*, said that "it is essential to show special care for indigenous communities and their cultural traditions. They are not merely one minority among others, but should be the principal dialogue partners, especially when large projects affecting their land are proposed. For them, land is not a commodity but rather a gift from God and from their ancestors who rest there, a sacred space with which they need to interact if they are to maintain their identity and value." The pope adds that while Indigenous peoples around the world are being pressured to leave their homelands, "When they remain on their land, they themselves care for it best."[31]

Indigenous worldviews provide something important that is missing in the mainstream climate debate. New understandings that we are gaining from science uphold ancient Indigenous wisdom about the inherent value and intricate interrelatedness of all parts of creation. Our challenge is to learn from and incorporate this wisdom, which is based in a deep understanding of creation. All things really are connected.

The Great Irony

The great irony we are faced with is that the same science that enables us to delve deeply into the mysteries of the universe also enables us to create technologies by which we are damaging the earth's ecosystems and wreaking havoc on its creatures. Understanding sub-atomic particles has given people the ability to create nuclear medicine, but also nuclear weapons. Nuclear power, which some promote as an alternative to fossil fuels, carries the risk of contamination from radioactive waste, as evidenced by the ongoing Fukushima disaster. Knowledge about DNA has given people the ability to treat genetic diseases, but also to engage in profit-based genetic engineering of plants, animals, and people.

Various technologies have combined to make possible the widespread extraction and burning of fossil fuels, resulting in the release of greenhouse gases into the atmosphere on a massive scale. Other technologies in widespread use make possible large-scale manufacturing, heavily polluting industries, highly mechanized deforestation practices, and industrial agriculture, including factory farming. Many

31. Pope Francis, *Laudato Si: On Care for Our Common Home* (Rome: Libreria Editrice Vaticana, 2015), 91.

of these technologies have been put into use without public debate, precaution, or regard for their impacts on the human community or the natural world.

Although we all face the consequences, decisions about what technologies to develop and implement are made by a small group of powerful people based on what is profitable and will further their ends. This lack of public input into decision-making about technology, as well as disproportionate access to technologies, is fueling calls for public debate and a more democratic decision-making process. Many are also calling for use of the *Precautionary Principle*, a strategy to prevent potentially dangerous technologies, processes, or chemicals from being released for general use unless they are proven safe.

Many technological solutions are being proposed for solving the climate crisis, including geoengineering of the planet. Research and preliminary projects are underway to develop so-called *Plan B* technologies, which would intervene in the climate system to counter the harmful effects of global warming.[32] Most of these technologies involve releasing particles into the atmosphere that would reflect sunlight back into space in order to reduce atmospheric warming. The most frequently discussed option, *Solar Radiation Management*, involves the spraying of sulfate aerosols into the atmosphere. Other options include space mirrors, "cloud brightening," or spraying seawater into the sky to increase cloud cover.[33] Scientists, engineers, entrepreneurs, and government agencies are spending millions on plans for such projects to try to engineer our way out of planetary warming, using the same mindset that brought us the problem in the first place. These projects would not treat the underlying causes of climate change, but only mask symptoms. None of these high-tech solutions have been proven and many have potentially catastrophic unintended effects.

How ironic it is that proponents of these technological fixes think that they are more reasonable than doing what is necessary to institute *Plan A*, which would require us to strictly regulate and limit greenhouse gas emissions and quickly transition to renewable power. Slowing climate change is not what these planners have in mind. There is no talk of climate justice or reverence for the earth at conferences where plans and prototypes for these geoengineering projects are displayed.

---

32. Olive Hamilton, "Geoengineering Is Not a Solution to Climate Change," *Scientific American* (March 10, 2015).
33. Klein, *This Changes Everything*, 258.

These high-tech approaches fit perfectly into the dominant market-based development model and worldview.

In contrast, many technologies do work with the earth's natural processes and reduce the amount of carbon flowing into the atmosphere. Solar, wind, thermal, and hydroelectric power-generating systems are becoming more common and affordable. Low-impact and energy-efficient products are widely available. Transitioning to 100 percent renewable power is technologically possible. What we need is the political will to make a "clean energy revolution" happen now.[34]

Still, all technologies come with greater or lesser environmental and social costs. Some attempts to replace coal, oil, and natural gas with renewable sources of power have unintended negative impacts. For instance, industrial biofuel plants may burn trees to generate power, destroying forests and releasing stored carbon.[35] Corn grown for ethanol competes with corn grown for food, causing food prices to rise. The production of electric and hybrid vehicles requires heavy metals for batteries and significant amounts of fossil fuels to ship parts around the world through global supply and assembly lines. Fossil fuels (often coal) and other toxic chemicals are used even in the production of solar panels.[36]

It is unrealistic to think that climate change will be resolved simply by transitioning to alternative technologies, while maintaining high levels of consumption and expanding the global economy indefinitely. From the perspective of a worldview in which all things are connected, a responsible approach to climate change also means conserving resources, focusing on simpler alternative technologies, and rejecting excessive consumption.

Reducing the atmospheric burden of persistent greenhouse gases requires us to understand and facilitate the earth's natural regenerative processes. Photosynthesis is a proven method that could sequester carbon on a large scale and begin the process of reducing the burden of carbon in the atmosphere. Reforestation effectively draws down atmospheric carbon and stores it in the trees, plants, and soil of tropical and temperate forests. Restoring native grasslands and meadow

34. "The World Can Transition to 100% Clean, Renewable Energy," The Solutions Project, http://thesolutionsproject.org/.
35. "Our Forests Aren't Fuel," Natural Resources Defense Council, March 7, 2016, https://www.nrdc.org/resources/our-forests-arent-fuel.
36. Christina Nunez, "How Green Are Those Solar Panels, Anyway?" *National Geographic*, November 11, 2014, http://news.nationalgeographic.com/news/energy/2014/11/141111-solar-panel-manufacturing-sustainability-ranking/.

ecosystems builds soil that is alive with healthy bacteria and other organisms that preserve soil health while sequestering carbon. Widespread conversion of industrialized agriculture to small regional farms that use regenerative methods of organic and low-till agriculture to restore healthy soil would significantly reduce agricultural emissions, sequester substantial amounts of carbon, and cut down on long-distance shipping of foods around the world. This could be done on a large scale—if there were political will.

The global marketplace with its utilitarian worldview encourages engineered solutions that establish dominance over nature. In contrast, policies based on a worldview that sees all things as connected might institute a mix of approaches, including a change in consumption patterns among the wealthy, strong regulations limiting fossil-fuel extraction, subsidies for renewable technologies, development of public transportation, regeneration programs that sequester carbon through reforestation and meadow restoration, support for permaculture and small organic farms, incentives for energy conservation, and other shifts in the system that perpetuates climate change.

The Story of the Universe Is Our Story

Science and technology have dramatically altered the human relationship to the natural world. Harmful technologies threaten life on earth. Yet some of the same discoveries about the nature of the universe that have made such technologies possible also have positive implications, which may be significant for every area of human life and thought, including theology. Indeed, many believe that incorporating the new story of the universe being revealed through science into our way of seeing reality may be a critical step in making the paradigm shift in human consciousness that is necessary for us to make it through this crisis.

The idea of a *paradigm shift* was introduced by Thomas Kuhn in reference to times of major revolutions in scientific worldview.[37] Such shifts affect concepts, values, and cultural perspectives. The paradigm shift that is going on in science today has implications for our understanding of the universe. Indeed, part of our problem is that our dominant institutions are based in an old paradigm. Fritjof Capra said, "The old scientific paradigm may be called Cartesian, Newtonian, or Baconian, since its main characteristics were formulated by Descartes, Newton,

37. Capra and Steindl-Rast, *Belonging to the Universe*, 34.

and Bacon. The new paradigm may be called holistic, ecological, or systemic, but none of these adjectives characterizes it completely."[38]

One significant implication of the paradigm shift in science is a new understanding of knowledge itself. The empiricism that was so highly valued in John Wesley's day is itself being brought into question, with the realization that the idea of an *objective viewpoint* is illusory. This realization comes to us from science, but is true in theology as well. As David Steindl-Rast said, "You realize that your clean concept, your clean observation, is impoverished in that it artificially abstracts you from the complicated truth of your being caught in a web of interconnections."[39] We are not outside observers of the phenomena taking place in the universe. We do not understand the whole. We are not objective because we see things from the perspective of our own particular human context.

Thomas Matus said, "The shift . . . involves the realization that I belong to the whole universe, not as if I were a negligible phenomenon on a small planet in a minor solar system but as a vital participant in the living cosmos. This realization is both the context and the condition of God's self-disclosure."[40] When considering the story of the nature and origins of the universe, the story of creation, *it is our story that is being told.* We are part of it!

Our worldview is relevant to how we address the challenge of climate change. Our scientific understandings and advanced technologies—combined with the dominant utilitarian worldview—present us with a profound choice, as made clear by the progressive threat of climate chaos. Will we use our rational powers for good or ill, to enhance life or destroy it? Common sense tells us that the choices we make now have a bearing on how this story (our story!) turns out. Will life on earth continue to be diminished as we imagine that we have no power to change direction? It is time to awaken to who we are: children of God and children of the earth, active participants in the universe story and key players in the story of life on Planet Earth.

Utilizing Reason: Awakening to Who We Are

Awakening to who we are means opening our mind to learning about the origins and nature of the universe of which we are a part. Astron-

---

38. Ibid., xi.
39. Ibid., 160.
40. Ibid., 161.

omy, quantum physics, evolutionary biology, and other scientific fields illuminate the mysteries of creation. Natural history museums, planetariums, and nature documentaries bring scientific discoveries to life, as do birdwatching and stargazing excursions. These kinds of trips are especially enriching for children. They put who we are and our place in the universe into perspective.

Utilizing reason also means educating ourselves about climate change, weighing the scientific evidence, and sharing what we learn with others. There are many ways to raise awareness and expose the myths of denial. Hosting a speaker or showing a film initiates discussion. Starting a book study takes the conversation deeper.

When considering individual actions, reason will guide us toward commonsense approaches that respect a holistic worldview and cooperate with the earth's regenerative powers. Those who can afford to may purchase renewable and energy-efficient products, but this can't be our sole response to climate change. Research will help us know which purchases make sense, but we cannot buy our way out of this dilemma. Rather, those of us who have enough to live on can *reduce, reuse, and recycle,* and even *resist and refuse* to purchase unnecessary products that will end up in landfills. We can cut energy use by adjusting our thermostats, insulating our homes, driving less, turning off lights, and using simpler alternative technologies such as bicycles, clotheslines, drying racks, and evaporative coolers. We can organize errands into fewer trips, carpool with neighbors, ride the bus, or walk.

Individual lifestyle choices, however, will not be enough to effectively combat climate change. We can work with others to learn where products originate and act on that knowledge by boycotting products such as shrimp, palm oil, fast food burgers, and other products that destroy critical habitat or people's lives or livelihoods. Even more important is advocating for trade and development policies that protect against the exploitation of people and the earth, and demanding an end to the persecution of activists for defending the ecosystems that they call home.

We are likely, at some time, to find development decisions being made in our own regions that impact the climate. Working with a local group to expand public transportation, create bike paths, protect a public water system, create a community solar installation, or stop an environmentally harmful development can be effective and worthwhile. Campaigns such as these honor creation, build community, strengthen participatory democracy, and demonstrate the rejection of a utilitarian worldview. Joining with local, statewide, nationwide, or international campaigns demonstrates solidarity, builds momentum, helps shape public opinion, and pressures lawmakers to take positive climate action.

The extent of damage due to climate change still depends to a large degree on what actions we take. What is at stake is the ability of our earthly home to nurture life, including human life. The phrase *near-term human extinction* is becoming more common as warming accelerates.[41] This term highlights the urgent question of whether humanity will honor creation by taking the strong collective action necessary to mitigate the worst effects of climate change and heal the earth's regenerative systems or whether we will continue on the present course toward runaway climate change.

Still, we have been given a great gift at this time in history—a creation story that can help us rise together to address the great challenges of our time. Now, with the help of science, people all over the world are learning *through empirical evidence* the incredible story of the origin and nature of the universe. Whether we call it the "new creation story," the new "scientific paradigm," or the resurgence and confirmation of ancient Indigenous worldviews, the story of creation now being revealed through science has profound implications for our theological understanding. Here on earth we are radically united and inseparably interdependent with each other and with the ecosystems and other species with whom we have evolved. The story of the universe is our story, and we are a part of the whole.

---

41. Sam Carana, "The Threat of Global Warming Causing Near-Term Human Extinction," *Arctic News*, http://arctic-news.blogspot.com/p/threat.html.

7

Experience: Creation as Sacrament

Learning from religions, I suggest that we could find a different approach to climate change that recognizes the importance of conviction: the point at which the rational crosses into the emotional, the head into the heart, and we can say, I've heard enough, I've seen enough—now I am convinced.[1]

—George Marshall

As we saw in the previous chapter on reason, human knowledge is partial and limited. Reason only goes so far, and a completely objective perspective is illusory. Our observations are affected by our personal experiences and the context of our lives. Yet this does not diminish the value of our observations. In fact, our experiences add yet another dimension to our knowledge. Although convictions based on direct experience cannot be proven, such experiences can be more convincing than any presentation of facts. As John Wesley said, "Experience is worth a thousand reasons."[2]

Rational arguments alone do not have the power to motivate people to face and respond to climate change. Being engaged at the level of

---

1. George Marshall, *Don't Even Think About It: Why Our Brains Are Wired to Ignore Climate Change* (New York: Bloomsbury, 2014), 225.
2. Donald A. D. Thorsen, *The Wesleyan Quadrilateral: Scripture, Tradition, Reason, & Experience as a Model of Evangelical Theology* (Grand Rapids: Zondervan, 1990), 217.

personal experience is necessary for us to fully grasp the implications of a warming world and to follow up with action.

In December 2015, on the eve of the Paris climate summit, our local Climate Change Coalition organized an Interfaith Prayers for the Climate service in the sanctuary of the Nevada City United Methodist Church. Candles were lit as people gathered to the sounds of a Native American flute. We honored early Indigenous inhabitants and their descendants, then read the words of Chief Seattle reminding us that we are all part of the web of life. Different people read scriptures, statements, and prayers from the world's faith traditions. Someone sang a Christian hymn lifting up the beauty of creation and the joy of life. A space was created for a time of silent reflection, Quaker-style, and for people to share what was in their hearts. Participants voiced their joys and concerns, which included gratitude for the beauty of the earth, blessings for the victims of the terrorist attacks that had taken place in Paris just a few days earlier, desire for peace in the world, and hope for the success of the climate talks. These heartfelt expressions culminated in a formal prayer incorporating the spoken and unspoken yearnings of the people present. We closed by singing an energetic song from the earth-centered Pagan tradition, which had spiritual but not religious lyrics that repeated with rising intensity, calling us to action:

> And let it begin with each step we take
> And let it begin with each change we make
> And let it begin with each chain we break
> And let it begin every time we awake
> We are alive! We are alive! We are alive! We are alive!

This service brought together facts and concerns about climate change, despair about terrorism, hopes for the climate talks, prayers for world leaders, and love for the earth. Those of us who participated connected at the level of spiritual experience with people from different faith and philosophical traditions. We faced our griefs and shared our hopes, supported each other, and in the process, we experienced for a brief time the world as we yearn for it to be. Many of us who attended the service were inspired to join the local climate march the next day, in solidarity with demonstrators who gathered in communities around the world to call for strong action at the Paris climate talks.

The Rational Brain and the Emotional Brain

Even if we fully accept the evidence of planetary warming presented by science, it may not move us to action. In *Don't Even Think About It*, George Marshall cites research showing that our brains are not wired to respond to distant and vague threats (such as climate change), but to more immediate and obvious ones. People who don't identify as environmentalists won't respond if they perceive our changing climate solely as an environmental issue that threatens penguins, polar bears, and coral reefs. Relatively few people will be motivated to act if they see it as something affecting other people who are not like them, or who are far away, or who only exist in the future. Even people who are convinced by the science that climate change is real can distance themselves emotionally and take cues for action or inaction from their social group.[3] In some settings it can feel awkward or even rude to bring up the topic. Psychic distancing, social conformity, and culturally imposed silence can happen anywhere, especially in churches that promote uniformity in thinking.

In a chapter titled "The Two Brains," Marshall draws on the thinking of evolutionary psychologists and other scientists to explain that human beings have developed two distinct systems for processing information. He identifies these two systems as the *rational brain* and the *emotional brain*. He writes: "One is analytical, logical, and encodes reality in abstract symbols, words, and numbers. The other is driven by emotions . . . , images, intuition, and experience. Language operates in both processes, but in the analytic system, it is used to describe and define; in the emotional system, it is used to communicate meaning, especially in the form of stories."[4]

Scientific facts, theories, and logical arguments about global warming speak to the rational brain and enable us to evaluate its realities and dangers, but they do not engage the emotional brain, which dominates our perception of risk and motivates us to respond to nearby or short-term opportunities or dangers. Scientific graphs, charts, and measurements may appeal to the rational brain, but they aren't enough to engage people at a deep level. The emotional brain is engaged by images, poems, songs, and stories that evoke emotion and appeal to intuitive ways of knowing. The challenge, then, is to engage the emotional brain by translating scientific data on climate change

3. Marshall, *Don't Even Think About It*, 24.
4. Ibid., 48.

into stories and metaphors that draw on experience and provide meaning, making the information relevant at a deep level.

Marshall points out that religious faith and spiritual connection have the power to draw people together in a common purpose and inspire them to a higher calling. A faith approach to climate change helps bring the rational brain and the emotional brain together, so that we move to "the point at which the rational crosses into the emotional, the head into the heart."[5] Our faith communities have the potential to help us find the spiritual resources we need to overcome despair, face the challenges of climate change, and reach out in loving actions that honor creation. For this to happen, faith must become real at the level of our own spiritual experience.

The whole range of human experience contributes to our understanding of reality, but John Wesley emphasized the value of *spiritual experience*. He spoke about *experiential knowing* based on direct insight and about *spiritual senses*[6] through which we experience the reality of God.

Wesley focused primarily on the experience of the assurance of God's love for us and the resulting love we have for others. But he also spoke about the experience of God in creation.

When he wrote that "The world around us is a mighty volume in which God hath declared himself . . . to people of all nations," he expected people to be able to read that "mighty volume" and to experience the "immensity and magnificence, the power and wisdom of its Creator." When he wrote "Even the actions of animals . . . have a thousand engaging ways, which, like the voice of God speaking to our hearts, command us to preserve and cherish them," he hoped that people would hear God's command and respond. Wesley upheld the biblical view that God is revealed and can be experienced through creation.

The Experience of God in Creation

As we have seen, Christian tradition is complex and multi-faceted. Traditional Christian teachings have often emphasized God's *transcendence*, that is, the aspect of God's nature that *transcends* creation. Solely focusing on God's transcendence can lead to the devaluing and

---

5. Ibid., 225.
6. John Wesley, Sermon 130, "On Living without God," *The Works of John Wesley*, ed. Albert C. Outler (Nashville: Abingdon, 1986), 4:168.

exploitation of the natural world, or it can support the concept of *stewardship* of creation on behalf of the Creator God.

Traditional Christian teachings have also acknowledged God's *immanence*, that is, God's presence and activity in, with, and through creation. This concept is based on biblical passages about the action of the Holy Spirit in creation (Gen 1:2; Rom 8:26) and on the divinizing presence of Christ in creation through the Incarnation (John 1:14; Heb 1:2–3a) and Resurrection (Rom 1:4; Eph 1:20). The biblical concept of *immanence* is confirmed by people's experiences of the divine through the natural world. The emphasis on God's immanence has been kept alive through the past two thousand years, especially by Catholic monastic orders, the Eastern Orthodox Church, and other contemplative traditions. The doctrine of God as both immanent and transcendent, however, has been generally accepted throughout the history of Christianity. Today, the focus on God's immanence within creation is especially important as a corrective to Christian views on human domination. It highlights what is at stake with the monumental challenge of climate change and other threats to God's creation, and may motivate us to action. In *God in Creation*, Jürgen Moltmann explains:

> An ecological doctrine of creation today must perceive and teach God's *immanence* in the world. This does not mean departing from the biblical traditions. On the contrary, it means a return to their original truth: through his cosmic spirit, God the Creator of heaven and earth is present *in* each of his creatures and *in* the fellowship of creation in which they share. God is not merely the Creator of the world. He is also the Spirit of the universe. Through the powers and potentialities of the Spirit, the Creator indwells the creatures he has made, animates them, holds them in life, and leads them into the future of his kingdom.[7]

Moltmann's statement that God is "the Spirit of the universe" is similar to John Wesley's claim that God is "the soul of the universe." Wesley spoke of God's presence and activity in, with, and through creation as God's *omnipresence*. Most importantly, he insisted that God's presence and activity can be discerned in human experience. He said that "we should use and look upon nothing as separate from God, which indeed is a kind of practical atheism; but, with a true magnificence of thought, survey heaven and earth, and all that is therein, as contained by God in the hollow of his hand, who by his intimate presence holds them all in

---

7. Jürgen Moltmann, *God in Creation* (Minneapolis: Fortress Press, 1993), 13.

being, who pervades and actuates the whole created frame, and is, in a true sense, the soul of universe."[8]

Michael Lodahl expands on this thought: "To look upon nothing as separate from God is to read each and every thing as filled with God. . . . To use nothing as separate from God is to live lightly and carefully in the world, in the conviction that nothing exists simply in itself or simply for me and my use or consumption. Instead, each and every thing exists as a mode and means of divine presence."[9]

These reflections on God as immanent and omnipresent bring us to a view of creation as sacrament. In Christian tradition, sacraments are "outward and visible signs of inward and spiritual grace."[10] In the sacraments of Baptism and Holy Communion, the common everyday elements of water, bread, and wine represent and mediate the sacred reality of the divine. These basic visible elements represent and mediate the invisible, spiritual reality of God's grace to those who are open to this experience. At the same time, these elements remind us of the sacredness that pervades all parts of physical reality, including things we have taken for granted as ordinary. Creation itself is a sacrament—an outward and visible manifestation of a spiritual reality that can be known through personal experience.

The concept of a sacramental universe has been affirmed by varied Christian communions. In a 1991 pastoral letter called "Renewing the Earth," the United States Conference of Catholic Bishops spoke of "a sacramental universe." The bishops wrote, "The whole universe is God's dwelling. Earth, a very small, uniquely blessed corner of that universe, gifted with unique natural blessings, is humanity's home, and humans are never so much at home as when God dwells with them."[11]

Likewise, the Ecumenical Patriarch Bartholomew of the Orthodox Church has called on Christians to "accept the world as a sacrament of communion, as a way of sharing with God and our neighbors on a global scale. It is our humble conviction that the divine and the human meet in the slightest detail in the seamless garment of God's creation, in the last speck of dust of our planet."[12]

Latin American liberation theologian Leonardo Boff has proposed

8. Wesley, Sermon 23, "Upon our Lord's Sermon on the Mount, III," *Works*, 1:516–17.

9. Michael Lodahl, *God of Nature and of Grace: Reading the World in a Wesleyan Way* (Nashville: Abingdon, 2003), 124.

10. What We Believe: The Sacraments, The Episcopal Church, http://www.episcopalchurch.org/page/sacraments.

11. "Renewing the Earth," United States Conference of Catholic Bishops (November 14, 1991), http://www.usccb.org/issues-and-action/human-life-and-dignity/environment/renewing-the-earth.cfm.

that in the context of global capitalism, with its destruction of the earth and oppression of the poor, theology must include a sacramental view of creation. He said, "To reach the root of the evils that confront us as well as to find a solution for them, we need a new theological worldview that sees this planet as a great sacrament of God, the temple of the Spirit, the place of creative responsibility for human beings, a dwelling place for all beings created in love."[13] For Boff, a sacramental view of creation has power to motivate transformational social struggle.

The Experience of an "Industrially Despoiled Planet"

In relating this sacramental understanding of creation to the climate crisis, one serious implication is this: if God is revealed through the natural world, experiences of the divine through creation will be less likely if the natural world is despoiled. A degraded creation will be less able to mediate the glory of God. As Thomas Berry said,

> Our exalted sense of the divine comes from the grandeur of the universe, especially from the earth in all the splendid modes of its expression. Without such experience, we would be terribly impoverished in our religious and spiritual development. If we lived on the moon, our sense of the divine would reflect the lunar landscape, our imagination would be as desolate as the moon, our emotions lacking in the sensitivity developed in our experience of the sensuous variety of the luxuriant earth. If a beautiful earth gives us an exalted idea of the divine, an industrially despoiled planet will give us a corresponding idea of God.[14]

The experience of an industrially despoiled planet is becoming more and more common today. Probably each person reading this book could recount their own story of an area they love that has been threatened, degraded, or destroyed. People around the world are experiencing the degradation of their local ecosystems, and as we have seen, climate change is outpacing all other environmental harms.

An implication of God being truly present within creation is that the harm human beings are doing to creation must also be impacting God.

12. The Ecumenical Patriarch Bartholomew, "Global Responsibility and Ecological Sustainability," Halki Summit I, Istanbul (June 20, 2012).
13. Leonardo Boff, "Social Ecology: Poverty and Misery," in *Ecotheology: Voices from North and South*, ed. David G. Hallman (Eugene, OR: Wipf & Stock, 1994), 245.
14. Thomas Berry, "Economics: Its Effects on the Life Systems of the World," in *Thomas Berry and the New Cosmology*, ed. Anne Lonergan and Caroline Richards (New London, CT: Twenty-Third, 1987), 17.

Could it be that the immanent and omnipresent God suffers loss and pain when creation is despoiled?

In a 2000 essay, "The Green Face of God: Christianity in an Age of Ecocide," Mark I. Wallace makes the case that this is so. He proposes an earth-centered model of the Holy Spirit as the "green face of God," indwelling and sustaining all creation. He writes, "Because God as Spirit is enfleshed within creation, God experiences within the core of her deepest self the agony and suffering of an earth under siege. *The Spirit, then, as the green face of God, has also become in our time the wounded God.* The Earth Spirit is the wounded God who daily suffers the environmental violence wrought by humankind's unremitting ecocidal attitudes and habits."[15]

The problem, he says, is that this model "places the divine life at risk." He says, "God, then, is so internally related to the universe that the specter of ecocide raises the risk of deicide: to wreak environmental havoc on the earth is to run the risk that we will do irreparable harm to the Love and Mystery we call God. The wager of this model is that while God and world are not identical to one another, their basic unity and common destiny raises the possibility that ongoing assaults against the earth's biotic communities may eventually result in permanent injury to the divine life itself."[16]

The implications of this possibility are staggering. The only response to injury of such magnitude is ongoing repentance, unwavering willingness to be transformed, and prayer "without ceasing" (1 Thess 5:17). For it means that God as Love is so completely invested and so deeply immanent within creation that God shares in the fate of the earth. Certainly, at the very least, God shares the suffering of creation as a parent shares in the suffering of a beloved child. God weeps for the harm we do to ourselves and each other, to the community of life, and to love itself.

For some, the experience of the degradation of the natural world leads to feelings of depression and denial. It is easy to feel hopeless, especially when it is clear that our fossil-fuel intensive way of life is a big part of the problem. Those of us who live in industrialized nations know that we are complicit in the damage being done to God's creation, but the change may seem too costly or even impossible. How can we face the overwhelming suffering that is going on today? How can we

15. Mark I. Wallace, "The Green Face of God: Christianity in an Age of Ecocide," in *Crosscurrents* vol. 50, issue 3 (Fall 2000), http://www.crosscurrents.org/wallacef00.htm.
16. Ibid.

share the grief of our time? How can we face the future? How can we face our children, or ourselves? How can we face our God?

George Marshall points out that one benefit of religion is that it helps people face and cope with moral confusion, guilt, and despair, which are common responses to climate change. He wrote, "Finally we could learn to find ways to address the feelings of blame and guilt that lead people to ignore or deny the issue, by enabling people to admit to their failings, to be forgiven, and to aim higher. By concentrating on universal and non-negotiable 'sacred values,' we could sidestep the arid cost-benefit calculations which encourage us to pass the costs onto future generations."[17]

These reflections bring us to the experience of assurance, which was a primary area of focus in John Wesley's theology. Our sense of assurance of God's forgiveness and love is the essence of justification—it is an experience that comes to us as we say "yes" to the invitation of unconditional love offered by Jesus. In the words of twentieth-century theologian Paul Tillich: "You are accepted. *You are accepted*, accepted by that which is greater than you, and the name of which you do not know. Do not try to do anything now; perhaps later you will do much. Do not seek for anything; do not perform anything; do not intend anything. *Simply accept the fact that you are accepted.*" By simply accepting that we are accepted, we are set free from the guilt, shame, and pre-patterned bondage of the past.

This crucial choice sets us free to start anew, to enter into a new way of living that includes openness to the ongoing transformation of our lives. In traditional Christian terms this process is called sanctification. This process, too, involves spiritual experience as the tangible presence of the Holy Spirit comforts, guides, empowers, transforms, draws us together in love, and inspires us to act in compassion for God's beloved world. In the words of Marjorie Suchocki, "Justification is for the sake of sanctification, clearing away the hindrances, in order that God's creative destiny for the world shall at last have full sway."[18] Surely in our day God's creative destiny for the world includes the healing and regeneration of creation, together with all that this vision entails.

---

17. Marshall, *Don't Even Think About It*, 225.
18. "Coming Home: Wesley, Whitehead, and Women," Marjorie Hewitt Suchocki, in *Thy Nature and Thy Name Is Love: Wesleyan and Process Theologies in Dialogue*, ed. Bryan P. Stone and Thomas Jay Oord (Nashville: Abingdon, 2001), 58.

Engaged by Experience: Practicing the Presence of God

Discerning a faithful response to climate change depends upon seeking and following the guidance of the Spirit. We receive guidance through scripture and traditional church teachings that direct us toward love. Reason enables us to think clearly and points us in the direction of right action. But it is when we experience the Spirit's guidance that our direction becomes clear.

In the context of climate change, such guidance is crucial. There are so many possible ways to honor creation and work for justice. How can we know what actions to take? Regular prayer and other spiritual disciplines attune us to the Spirit's call. In addition to the traditional means of grace, there are many forms of spiritual practice that open us up to the guidance and grace of God. Many find spiritual connection through sitting or walking in a place of natural beauty. In this way we open ourselves to the experience of creation as sacrament. As we open ourselves to creation's suffering, grace enables us to face the pain of this time and to know the assurance of God's unconditional love.

A well-established spiritual practice in Christian tradition is "practicing the presence of God."[19] Wesley called on his listeners to "spare no pains to preserve always a deep, a continual, a lively, and a joyful sense of God's gracious presence."[20] As we cultivate the awareness of God's presence throughout our daily lives, we become more mindful and attuned to the divine will.

There are many ways to incorporate spiritual experience into work on climate change in order to engage people more deeply. Communal worship and shared spiritual experiences engage the emotional brain through symbol, story, ritual, prayer, music, song, poetry, sacrament, and other forms of creative expression that have power to motivate us to take loving action for the sake of God's world. Such events may be centered in a particular faith tradition, designed with an interfaith focus, or based on secular principles that foster inclusivity and mutual understanding. It is important for our morale to connect with others who understand the magnitude of the dangers of climate change and are willing to act. Sometimes these connections can be deeper with people in activist circles than with people in our churches.

Suggestions for action have been presented in this book at the end

19. Brother Lawrence of the Resurrection, *The Practice of the Presence of God,* trans. Donald Attwater (Springfield, IL: Templegate, 1974), 122–26.
20. Sermon 118, "On the Omnipresence of God," *Works,* 4:47.

of each chapter. There are more suggestions to come. This brings us to the question: What, specifically, are we called to do? We can't do everything, nor should we try. Each of us must decide for ourselves how to live our lives and where to put our energy. A spiritual mentor or supportive community can assist us in making such decisions. It helps to consider our gifts, our passions, and what we can uniquely contribute to the movement for climate justice.

The key for making action choices is to seek the Spirit's guidance generally and in each particular situation. Committing ourselves to responding in faith to climate change does not distract us from growing in love of God and neighbor but takes us deeper in our journey of faith.

In the past four chapters, scripture, tradition, reason, and experience have helped us develop the theme of creation in the context of our changing climate. In the next four chapters, we will use these same four sources of authority to help us develop the theme of justice, as we interpret scripture, discern what is valuable in traditional church teachings, use our own common sense, and stay true to our own experience. There is no shortcut. But one thing is certain: a faithful response to climate change involves an experiential shift, a spiritual revolution, an ongoing transformation of the whole person in the direction of love.

PART III

Establishing Justice

8

Scripture: Transforming the Jericho Road

On the one hand, we are called to play the Good Samaritan on life's roadside, but that will be only an initial act. One day we must come to see that the whole Jericho Road must be transformed so that men and women will not be constantly beaten and robbed as they make their journey on life's highway.[1]

—Martin Luther King Jr.

In the previous four chapters, we explored the theme of *creation* from the perspective of scripture, tradition, reason, and experience in the context of the climate crisis. We now shift our focus and employ these same four sources of authority to illuminate our understanding of *justice* as we seek to develop a faithful response to climate change.

We begin with scripture. There are countless passages in the Hebrew Scriptures that emphasize social and economic justice, including the core Jewish liberation story of the Exodus, celebrated during Passover by faithful Jews throughout the centuries. This ancient story about Hebrew slaves demanding justice and escaping from Egypt's Pharaoh has inspired many liberation struggles, including contemporary Latin American liberation movements.

---

1. Martin Luther King Jr., "Beyond Vietnam," in *Martin Luther King Jr. and the Global Freedom Struggle*, The Martin Luther King Jr. Research and Education Institute, Stanford University, http://kingencyclopedia.stanford.edu/encyclopedia/documentsentry/doc_beyond_vietnam/.

The contemporary faith-based Jubilee movement, which works for the debts of poor nations to be canceled, finds its authority in the ancient call in Leviticus for a Jubilee year to be celebrated every fifty years. During the Jubilee, slaves were to be set free, debts canceled, land returned to its original owners to prevent wealthy landowners from accumulating large land holdings, and fields left fallow to restore the fruitfulness of the land (Lev 25:8–13). Immigrant rights groups point to passages that demand protection for sojourners. "The stranger who sojourns with you shall be to you as the native among you, and you shall love him as yourself" (Lev 19:34 RSV) is a biblical mandate that informs our treatment of migrants as climate change makes various regions uninhabitable.

The Hebrew prophets continually urged the people of Israel to repent. They prophesied that disaster would come upon the whole community if they didn't reject idolatry and establish justice in the land. They held the priests particularly responsible for leading the people astray, and challenged the rich because of their oppression of the poor. They admonished the people against idolatry, as when Jeremiah said, "And I will utter my judgments against them, for all their wickedness in forsaking me; they have made offerings to other gods, and worshiped the works of their own hands" (Jer 1:16). This admonition takes on renewed meaning in an age dominated by technologies that many believe are essential. Likewise, the prophetic demand for justice is still relevant today: "He has told you, O mortal, what is good; and what does the Lord require of you but to do justice, and to love kindness, and to walk humbly with your God" (Mic 6:8).

Passages related to justice are also found throughout the New Testament, beginning with the infancy narratives in the gospels of Matthew and Luke, which point to Jesus as one who would raise up the lowly and challenge the powers of this world. Several of Jesus's parables emphasize justice, including the Rich Man and Lazarus (Luke 16:19–31) and the Sheep and the Goats (Matt 25:31–46). According to these stories, God's judgment is based on whether or not we act with compassion and justice toward the poor.

All four gospels portray Jesus as taking a strong stand for justice. The central conflict in his life was strikingly political. He directly challenged the representatives of the Jewish religious establishment and practiced non-cooperation with oppressive laws. Healing was a primary aspect of his ministry, and he broke the Law repeatedly by healing on the Sabbath. Jesus refused to be bound by the *purity codes* that separated so-called "clean" from "unclean" people. He overturned the tables of the moneychangers in the Temple, directly confronting the corrupt economic system of his time. The Sadducees and Pharisees, who collaborated with Rome by keeping order among the Jews, agreed that Jesus's death was necessary for the sake of national security. "If we let him go on like this," argued the high priest Caiaphas, "everyone will believe in him, and the Romans will come and destroy both our holy place and our nation" (John 11:48). Jesus was put to death because he was considered a threat to the interlocking political, economic, and religious institutions that made up the domination system of his day.

The tragic scenes of Jesus's death give way in Acts and the Epistles to a note of triumph, as writers portray a resurrected people living in the presence of the Risen Christ and motivated by the Holy Spirit. These early Christians, too, challenged the governing authorities and refused to submit to the Roman Empire, as willing to face their own death as Jesus was.

Although some New Testament passages were written to maintain order and establish hierarchies in the church, many are liberating. Some include a call to faithfulness in the face of ongoing oppression by the rulers of this world. The spiritual struggle against the powers and principalities is described in Ephesians: "For our struggle is not against enemies of blood and flesh, but against the rulers, against the authorities, against the cosmic powers of this present darkness, against the spiritual forces of evil in the heavenly places" (Eph 6:12). The ruling institutional powers that dominate our world are generally at cross-purposes with the loving will of God. Conventional wisdom often points toward death, not life. Paul said, "Do not be conformed to this world, but be transformed by the renewing of your minds . . ." (Rom 12:2). In spite of the human-constructed systems of this world, the Spirit can be trusted to give us the insight and strength to follow wherever Jesus leads.

The whole scope and tenor of scripture affirms the centrality of compassion and justice as expressions of divine love. Although the above passages and many others shed light on the theme of justice, our primary text in this chapter is the parable of the Good Samaritan, the well-loved story that challenges us to be neighbors to those who are in distress (Luke 10:25–37). All the actors for high drama and intrigue are here: robbers who attack a traveler, an unnamed victim left to die in the road, self-righteous religious leaders who pass him by, and a despised Samaritan who saves the victim and becomes the hero of

Jesus's story. Using scripture, tradition, reason, and experience to explore the theme of justice in this parable will enable us to expand our understanding of what it means to love our neighbors in this time of climate change.[2]

Who Is My Neighbor?

Luke frames this parable in an interaction between Jesus and a lawyer who puts him to the test by asking, "Teacher, what shall I do to inherit eternal life?" (In a parallel story in Mark 10 the question is "What is the greatest commandment?") Here Jesus directs the question back to the lawyer by asking him, "What is written in the Law? How do you read?" The lawyer answers, "You shall love the Lord your God with all your heart, and with all your soul, and with all your strength, and with all your mind; and your neighbor as yourself." Jesus responds, "You have answered right. Do this and you will live." But the lawyer will not leave it at that. Because he desires to justify himself, he asks Jesus, "And who is my neighbor?"

Who is my neighbor? This is a perennial question—whom should I include within my circle of concern? We see images of profound suffering taking place around the world that far surpass our ability to respond. We want to be compassionate, but we also must be realistic. Where do our responsibilities lie? Who is my neighbor? When the lawyer asks the question, Jesus responds by telling the following story.

> A man was going down from Jerusalem to Jericho, and he fell among robbers, who stripped him and beat him, and departed, leaving him half dead. Now by chance a priest was going down that road; and when he saw him he passed by on the other side. So, likewise, a Levite, when he came to the place and saw him, passed by on the other side. But a Samaritan, as he journeyed, came to where he was; and when he saw him, he had compassion, and went to him and bound up his wounds, pouring on oil and wine; then he set him on his own beast and brought him to an inn, and took care of him. And the next day, he took out two denarii and gave them to the innkeeper, saying, "Take care of him; and whatever more you spend, I will repay you when I come back. (Luke 10:30–35, RSV)

2. In chapter 3, I demonstrated the use of scripture, tradition, reason, and experience separately as tools through which to explore the creation-centered passage from Romans 8:18–26. In this chapter, I use these sources of authority less explicitly, in an interactive process that allows the story to flow.

This parable clarifies what love of God and neighbor requires. It is also a call to justice. It contains a critique of people like the priest and Levite who function within respectable roles in unjust systems that oppress others. The story includes a surprising twist, for it is a despised Samaritan who rescues the wounded man. This unlikely hero has compassion on the victim, rescues him, and treats him with extravagant care.

In *The Power of Parable*, John Dominic Crossan claims that the term "good Samaritan" has become a "redundant cliché," as if it simply means one person helping another. People in the first century, however, would have heard "good Samaritan" as a "cultural paradox—a social contradiction in terms."[3] This is "a story that challenges listeners to think long and hard about their social prejudices, their cultural presumptions, and yes, even their most sacred values."[4]

After the robbers ambush the man, a priest and then a Levite see him lying there and pass by. These two figures represent privileged members of the Jewish religious establishment. Crossan wrote, "In the Jewish homeland, the priest and the Levite—think of them as first-level and second-level clergy—represent the culturally given 'good guys.' Priest and Levite versus Samaritan represent the positive and negative cultural polarities of first-century Jewish tradition."[5]

The way Jesus tells this story, the "good guys" don't look so good. By portraying the priest and Levite as hard-hearted and hypocritical, Jesus calls out so-called "good" religious people who ignore and thus perpetuate suffering. By doing so he critiques the religious establishment that provides moral cover and justification for an unjust and oppressive system, as the Hebrew prophets did before him.

After telling the story, Jesus asks the lawyer, "Which of these three was a neighbor to the man who fell among robbers?" The lawyer answers, "The one who showed mercy on him." Jesus says to him, "Go and do likewise" (Luke 10:36–37). As Jesus's followers, we are challenged to demonstrate compassion, as exemplified by the Good Samaritan. As we will see, compassion in our day requires not only acts of mercy, but also acts of justice.

---

3. John Dominic Crossan, *The Power of Parable: How Fiction by Jesus Became Fiction about Jesus* (New York: HarperCollins, 2012), 60.
4. Ibid., 62.
5. Crossan, *Power of Parable*, 60.

Compassion

It is worth taking time here to explore the meaning of compassion as it appears in this parable. The Greek word here interpreted as "compassion" is *splagchnizomai*, which means to "to be moved in the inward parts," that is, to feel sympathy, to pity, or to be moved with compassion. The word comes from *splanxna*, which means "the inward parts, especially the nobler entrails—the heart, lungs, liver, and kidneys. These gradually came to denote the seat of the affections."[6] This word implies a deeply moving, gut-level experience that results in loving action.

The word *splagchnizomai* appears elsewhere in the gospels, including in the story of the Prodigal Son, whose father met him with compassion and gave him an extravagant welcome upon his return. It most often appears when relating Jesus's heartfelt response and loving action toward people in need. Compassion was a distinguishing characteristic of Jesus's ministry.

John Wesley had a heart for the poorest and most vulnerable members of society. He insisted that members of the early Methodist societies visit poor, sick, and imprisoned people in order to keep compassion alive. As we will see in the next chapter, Wesley's compassionate stance toward poor and oppressed members of society also led him to take strong stands on various social justice issues, especially slavery. He also spoke out against the harms of the Industrial Revolution, emerging capitalism, and the great economic and social inequalities of his day. For Wesley, *social holiness* was what love of God and neighbor required.

When considering John Wesley's emphasis on compassion, Michael Lodahl points out that in this time of ecological degradation, compassion must extend to future generations and the non-human creation:

> Wesley generally followed the biblical pattern of focusing on love for God and neighbor—and even here we have not taken seriously enough that a great many of our neighbors are denizens of the future, people yet to be born, whom we are called upon to love by doing all we can to see to it that they inherit a habitable world. Loving our neighbors of the future demands nothing less. However, if indeed God's "compassion is over all that he has made" (Ps 145:9), as Wesley so liked to repeat, then we may legitimately ask whether the category of "neighbor" should stop with

6. #4697 (*splagchnizomai*) in *Strong's Concordance*, Bible Hub, http://biblehub.com/greek/4697.htm.

fellow human beings. What of the animals we befriend? What of those "wilder" creatures of God's good world? What of those creatures for whom we see little or no value?

As we have seen, Wesley recommended developing empathy toward our fellow creatures, including "brute beasts," through the "softening and enlarging of our hearts," which is made possible through grace as we grow in love.[7] Lodahl links this experiential shift with the story of the Good Samaritan:

> The implication here is that, through prayer, meditation, and increasing openness to the working of God's Spirit within us, we may actually begin to *feel God's feelings* for all of God's creatures—for all our fellow earthlings. And if Jesus' famous parable about the compassionate Samaritan is any indication, then feeling compassion is the first and prerequisite step on the road toward healing, mending actions on behalf of the other.[8]

In a Christian approach to climate change, compassion is central. Compassionate action is what love of God and neighbor requires, and love is the essence of eternal life.

In light of the parable of the Good Samaritan, we must seek a model of compassion sufficient for addressing the great challenges of our times, including climate change. How can we serve as neighbors to those who are in distress while also addressing underlying systemic problems in order to prevent others from falling victim along the road?

In *Compassion: Loving Our Neighbor in an Age of Globalization*, Maureen H. O'Connell makes the case that we who are privileged, twenty-first-century Christians must reinterpret what it means to have compassion for our neighbors. Our context has been radically changed by globalization—the globalization of the economy, the globalization of culture, the globalization of climate change. It is making the road itself more dangerous, multiplying victims, and concealing the links of dependence, responsibility, and exploitation that tie us to every person on earth. O'Connell writes:

> In our contemporary reality, defined by dehumanizing suffering, shaped by encounters with others that are increasingly defined by gross inequality and driven by an expanding global market economy, it is not

---

7. John Wesley, Sermon 60, "The General Deliverance," ed. Albert C. Outler, *The Works of John Wesley* (Nashville: Abingdon, 1986), 2:436.
8. Michael Lodahl, *God of Nature and of Grace: Reading the World in a Wesleyan Way* (Nashville: Abingdon, 2003), 206.

enough for individual travelers to step into the ditch and offer emergency aid to the victims of humanly perpetrated violence. There are more victims than travelers, and the road to Jericho is paved with their labor and social deprivation. In addition, the distinction between innocent travelers and guilty robbers is increasingly blurred, and material resources alone cannot provide sufficient healing. We need a new approach to compassion.[9]

The priest and Levite confront us with the fact that our social location may prevent us from seeing how we participate in unjust systems that oppress or victimize people. For example, white people can be blind to *white privilege*, even as they receive all the benefits of whiteness when it is defined as the norm. People who are wealthy may not see how their wealth is structurally related to poverty. The distance and complexity of globalization make it hard for privileged people to see how they contribute to the suffering of people in other parts of the world. According to O'Connell:

> It is no longer possible to absolve ourselves of the sinful conditions of the passage down to Jericho. Globalization has blurred the distinction between those who innocently travel and those who rob others of their dignity along the way. Today, the road grows more and more treacherous for more and more people. Consequently, Samaritanism means we must integrate loving our suffering neighbors with seeking their forgiveness for our participation in the sins of individualism, consumerism, and privilege.[10]

Global realities require us to rethink what it means to be a neighbor.

Ambushed by Climate Change

Human suffering is exacerbated as poor regions and nations find themselves ambushed by climate change. Most greenhouse gases that contribute to global warming have been released by wealthy industrialized nations, while poor and vulnerable nations and regions are at greatest risk. People are facing the loss, pollution, or degradation of the lands upon which their cultures developed and upon which their lives depend. At the same time, wealthy nations and corporations are appropriating access to resources that are needed for life, such as water, as

---

9. Maureen H. O'Connell, *Compassion: Loving Our Neighbor in an Age of Globalization* (Maryknoll, NY: Orbis, 2009), 5.
10. O'Connell, *Compassion*, 205–6.

well as fossil fuels that drive the global economy while emitting greenhouse gases that cause climate change.

As the planet continues to warm, weather disasters will no longer simply be considered acts of God. As islands sink below rising seas, fresh-water supplies disappear, extreme droughts cause crop failures, and tropical diseases spread, victims of these events will understand that certain human beings of our time destabilized the earth's climate through the profligate use of fossil fuels. Future generations will know, too, that climate change could have been mitigated if people had cared enough. This is still possible if we can muster the moral courage and political will to make it so.

But powerful special interests are determined to keep the fossil-fuel party going as long as possible, to keep the economy growing and the money flowing up to the top. Coal, oil, and gas companies plan to sell and burn all their reserves, even though calculations show that doing so would leave the planet largely uninhabitable, thus condemning many to die. To wreck the planet for profit is robbery of the worst kind. To knowingly profit by disrupting the integrity of the earth's natural systems robs creation of the abundance that God alone provides.

Of course, coal, oil, and gas companies can't do this alone. Those of us who are privileged enough to be able to travel freely along the Jericho Road of our time need to consider how we contribute to this thievery. We, too, participate in the fossil-fuel economy. Are we indentured servants, willing to serve the system as long as it will maintain us at a comfortable level? Are we allowing ourselves to be bribed by the comforts we have come to consider essential? We may benefit in some ways, but at what cost? At what cost to our children, to our human family, to the future, to the community of life? At what cost to our souls? Are we travelers or are we robbers along the Jericho Road? This moral blurring is part of the agony of our time.

In a sense, all of us have been ambushed by climate change. While people in poor and vulnerable regions are experiencing its effects most severely, ultimately, we will all be impacted. The human family, the community of life, our children's future—all have been overtaken by thieves. Many of us realize our complicity, but we are enmeshed in a way of life that depends upon the use of fossil fuels. Some are paralyzed by a sense of powerlessness, thinking that we are victims of anonymous forces beyond our control.

It is easy for people to get bogged down thinking about climate change, to feel paralyzed, and to end up doing nothing. First, there is the dilemma of feeling like a hypocrite for wanting to stop climate change, but continuing to use fossil fuels. Second, most of us would like to cut down on our use of fossil fuels (for instance, gas), but many of the alternatives (for instance, electric cars) are too expensive. In the United States, as wages stagnate and prices rise, working people struggle to pay their bills. This brings us to the third dilemma: time. Many families have serious time constraints, often related to the need for more than one paycheck or the need to work extra hours. When people are already strapped, it is hard to take on something as big as climate change.

These very challenges demonstrate why we must work for justice for poor and working people if we want climate justice. In the United States, the bottom has been dropping out from under the middle class for decades. Standards of living for the majority have been falling. The tax code favors large corporations, financial institutions, and the rich. Climate justice must include policies that make life more manageable for people trying to support their families and those who struggle to make ends meet.

None of us alone can stop climate change, but together we can contribute to the growth of a movement that can. Fortunately, the demand for climate justice is part of the movement for global justice, which is growing stronger and gaining momentum. This movement has been called a "peoples' globalization" and "globalization from below." Only "people power" will be able to build a movement strong enough to bring systemic change.

Compassion in our time means identifying and changing the institutions and systems that perpetuate climate change and other forms of injustice. Now more than ever, Martin Luther King Jr.'s call to systemic transformation must be heard:

> A true revolution of values will soon cause us to question the fairness and justice of many of our past and present policies. On the one hand we are called to play the Good Samaritan on life's roadside, but that will be only an initial act. One day we must come to see that the whole Jericho Road must be transformed so that men and women will not be constantly beaten and robbed as they make their journey on life's highway. True compassion is more than flinging a coin to a beggar. It comes to see that an edifice which produces beggars needs restructuring.[11]

11. King, "Beyond Vietnam."

Challenged by Scripture: Compassion in Action

As followers of Jesus, the compassionate one, we are called to honor creation and establish justice, which in our day includes working to transform the whole Jericho Road. For some of us this may take a change in perspective, away from a self-centered focus. Even if we have been blinded by privilege, pride, greed, or complacency, we can regain our sight.

Maureen O'Connell makes three suggestions for living out Good Samaritan values amid the complexities of our time. First, we must seek to understand our connections to the causes of the suffering of others, both in our communities and around the world. Second, we must listen to those who experience oppression in order to understand varied perspectives and social contexts. Third, we must move away from a self-centered view of human well-being by seeing ourselves as part of a global community seeking the common good. By applying these principles we adopt a model of compassion sufficient for our time.

Understanding our connections to the causes of the sufferings of others means recognizing the effects upon others of privileges, unconscious attitudes, or behaviors that we take for granted. By developing self-awareness, we break through unconscious patterns, which may include white privilege, male privilege, class privilege, a sense of national superiority, homophobia, ageism, bias against people with disabilities, self-righteousness, or the idolatry of money. Many activist groups offer anti-oppression trainings, which sensitize people to social location, privilege, attitudes, and behaviors that prevent full and equal participation of all people. People who have traditionally identified with the dominant culture can learn by working with and taking direction from these groups, which may also establish protocols to ensure diverse and egalitarian leadership. Humbling ourselves and acknowledging our need to grow in diversity awareness enables us to break through layers of cultural conditioning and to ground ourselves in God's inclusive love.

Churches that traditionally support ministries of mercy may join with local groups that advocate for justice. By doing so, we join with others to create a more compassionate community. As we move toward climate justice, listening to those whose lands and cultures are being lost to rising seas or extreme drought helps us see through their eyes. Hearing stories of people working to protect their air, land, and water from fossil-fuel contamination exposes us to their plight and may move us to compassion. Listening to first-hand accounts, seeing films, or reading stories from our neighbors working for climate justice gives us new insights, shows us moral courage, and may motivate us to move to the front lines of climate action.

Finally, a self-centered view of life must be abandoned. We do not flourish as individual entities, but as a global community of neighbors. By standing with people who are or have historically been oppressed, we participate in inclusive community, link various issues, and build the foundation for a broad coalition working for justice that includes climate justice. By working together as diverse people in relationships of mutual respect, we envision new ways of creating communities that protect people and sustain life.

If we model ourselves on Jesus and let the Holy Spirit guide, transform, and empower us, we will "go and do likewise" ourselves, serving as neighbors and learning from those who know what it is like to be abandoned along the Jericho Road. As we join in exploring new ways of being in community together, we demonstrate an alternative future now. As we work with others to create a world of mercy and justice, we grow in love in our relationships with God, with our neighbors around the world, with future generations, and with all creation.

Who Will Rescue Us?

As we consider the story of the Good Samaritan in the context of a warming world, the question arises: Who will rescue us from the grim prospect of runaway climate change? Who are the Samaritans of our day? We will probably not find them among those who maintain wealth, status, and respectability at the centers of power. We must look elsewhere.

The global struggle for climate justice is being led not by politicians or CEOs or entrepreneurs or big green environmental groups, but by the very people who are perceived by the privileged as having no power. Many people who feel excluded from the benefits of the present system are organizing across issues and across regions, and action for climate justice is gaining momentum. Climate justice activists in poor nations most vulnerable to rising seas, drought, and extreme weather are demanding payment of climate debt by the wealthy nations. Youth leaders are organizing demonstrations and nonviolent direct actions and demanding strong and effective action by world leaders to stop climate change. Indigenous communities are resisting fossil-fuel extraction and linking Indigenous rights with the rights of Mother Earth. Women activists in developing nations are leading struggles for the right to clean water, land for small farms, and a stable climate.

Many people-powered movements are springing up, calling us to acknowledge and repent from our participation in systems that cause suffering and to join with others to act for justice. Climate justice is one such movement, but others are also gaining ground: Idle No More, Black Lives Matter, the Fight for $15 (a minimum wage campaign), Health Care for All, struggles for immigrant rights, prison reform, marriage equality, pro-democracy campaigns, the peace movement, and many more. Working for climate justice means coming together with many constituencies for whom the current system is not working and exploring together where compassionate and just action lies.

Many of the people working for justice in these and similar movements have historically been dismissed and discounted. It may be that these are the very neighbors who will save us.

9

Tradition: Social Holiness on a Warming Planet

Better no trade than trade procured by villainy. . . . Better is honest poverty, than all the riches bought by the tears, and sweat, and blood, of our fellow creatures.[1]

—John Wesley

When Jesus introduced his public ministry in the synagogue of his home town of Nazareth, he stood up, opened a scroll, and read from the prophet Isaiah:

"The Spirit of the Lord is upon me,
because he has anointed me
to bring good news to the poor.
He has sent me to proclaim release to the captives
and recovery of sight to the blind,
to let the oppressed go free,
to proclaim the year of the Lord's favor."
(Luke 4:18–19)

1. John Wesley, *Thoughts upon Slavery* (London, 1773), 45-46. Electronic Edition, Documenting the American South, University of North Carolina at Chapel Hill, http://docsouth.unc.edu/church/wesley/wesley.html.

He then rolled up the scroll and gave it to the attendant. He sat back down and said, "Today this scripture has been fulfilled in your hearing" (Luke 4:21).

For those who yearn for justice, these words of Jesus inspire and uplift. The Holy Spirit confirms their power and inspires us to want to follow Jesus on the path of justice and love. But for his original hearers, these were fighting words, especially when he made it clear that his neighbors were not entitled to special privileges (Luke 4:22-30). Even today, love requires us to bring good news to poor and oppressed people, as Jesus did. Even now reactionary forces are trying to stop those who seek to establish justice, as they tried to stop Jesus in his day.

Working for justice always involves controversy because it requires us to look upstream at the causes and conditions of injustice and act to set things right. This is likely to put us at odds with people who benefit from the status quo. Climate change complicates this dynamic because all who live in the industrialized world are deeply enmeshed in fossil-fuel-based systems of development, agriculture, transportation, and trade. Likewise, those who live comfortably with decent salaries, health insurance, and pensions benefit from the current economic system, which is characterized by great and growing income and wealth inequalities.

These conflicts of interest, however, need not hold us back. By putting our faith first and courageously seeking truth, we can face the situation, explore options, and make informed choices based on our deepest values. A mature faith requires us to use our heads and our hearts, studying scripture and reflecting on our faith traditions as we struggle with the issues of our day, form opinions, and choose what actions to take.

This chapter explores the theme of justice in Christian tradition, especially focusing on John Wesley's concept of *social holiness*, which emphasizes the connection between personal spirituality, community, and social concern. In this chapter we explore what social holiness means on a warming planet and what it requires of us. Wesley's responses to the social issues of his day often brought him into the center of controversy. This chapter describes some of those struggles and relates them to struggles for justice today. It also presents contemporary interpretations of Wesleyan tradition related to justice that are relevant to the movement for climate justice today.

Working for climate justice takes us into the midst of controversy because it includes a critique of the dominant system and seeks to establish alternative ways of organizing the human family based on mercy, justice, creation care, and participatory democracy. There is a prophetic edge to this movement that puts climate justice activists at odds with the status quo. This is not always comfortable in the local church or community, but we can take heart from the Hebrew prophets, Jesus, John Wesley, and contemporary prophets as well.

Justice and Injustice in Christian Tradition

Although Jesus geared his primary message of love and inclusion toward those who were sick, poor, devalued, outcaste, and dispossessed, the theme of *justice* in Christian tradition is tragically mixed. We cannot speak of justice within the Christian tradition without acknowledging the injustices that have been perpetrated by institutionalized Christianity throughout its two-thousand-year history.

When weighing the authority of tradition, John Wesley believed that the early Christians most clearly exemplified "true religion," because they demonstrated the love that was evident in the life and message of Jesus. Early Christians followed Christ, shared their possessions, and reached out in mercy to those who were in need. Many were martyred for refusing to pledge allegiance to the Emperor or serve in the Roman Army.

When Constantine imposed Christianity as the religion of the Roman Empire in the fourth century, everything shifted. Christianity became a religion of Empire. As it spread, church leaders largely adapted to, supported, and benefited from whomever was in power. One example of church support for empire is the fifteenth-century religious doctrine now known as the *Doctrine of Discovery*, through which the Roman Catholic Church gave Christian explorers the right to claim for their monarchs any lands that they "discovered." Indigenous peoples inhabiting the lands might be spared if they converted to Christianity; otherwise they could be driven off the land, enslaved, or killed.[2] Missionaries were complicit in this colonization project. In 1823, the Doctrine of Discovery was adopted into US law. It was referenced in a Supreme Court ruling as recently as 2005.[3]

Many other forms of injustice are attributed to Christian influence,

---

2. "Doctrine of Discovery: What's That?" Doctrine of Discovery Study Group, Jamesville, NY, http://www.doctrineofdiscovery.org/.

3. Steven Newcomb, "Christian Discovery and Indian Sovereignty," in *Cultural Survival Quarterly* 29, no. 2 (Summer 2005), Cultural Survival, https://www.culturalsurvival.org/publications/cultural-survival-quarterly/united-states/christian-discovery-and-indian-sovereignty.

including crusades and holy wars, genocide, slavery, racism and anti-Semitism, sexism, homophobia, and environmental destruction. It is no wonder that many people today reject Christianity and consider it to be a regressive force. In *A Short History of Christian Thought*, Linwood Urban wrote: "Cultural imperialism, anti-Semitism, capitalism and resulting economic injustice, and male chauvinism are perceived by some contemporary critics to result from Christian teaching and to be woven into the very fabric of the intellectual and emotional conscious-ness of Christians; and because of this they seem to be all the more dan-gerous—hence the intensity of the debate."[4]

"At the same time," said Linwood, "many of those in the traditional church believe that their faith impels them toward egalitarianism and concern for the poor. . . . At times traditionalists and reformers have seen themselves in a life and death struggle."[5] These words point to an alternate strand of Christian tradition, grounded in the love of Christ and supporting a view of justice for all. Throughout the centuries, many Christians have opposed imperialism, domination, and violence, and have taken strong stands for justice, even at great risk to them-selves and sometimes at the cost of their own lives.

These conflicting dynamics continue today. Some forms of Chris-tianity condone or actively promote reactionary and oppressive atti-tudes, practices, and social policies. The overwhelming white Evan-gelical support for Donald Trump's presidential campaign will only reinforce the perception of Christianity as bigoted, unjust, anti-sci-ence, and destructive of the earth.

At the same time, many who seek to follow Jesus dedicate them-selves to working for peace, justice, and the healing of creation. Those who value justice will be heartened by the teachings and example of John Wesley.

Justice in the Life and Teachings of John Wesley

John Wesley (1703–1791), an Anglican priest, was a central figure in the eighteenth-century Methodist movement in Great Britain, during one of the greatest religious revivals in history. He sought out and preached to the unchurched in factory towns, mining communities, depressed rural areas, and city slums. Many who were poor and dispos-sessed and had been excluded by the Anglican Church establishment

---

4. Linwood Urban, *A Short History of Christian Thought* (New York: Oxford University Press, 1986), 256.
5. Ibid.

listened with joy to his message that they were people of dignity and worth, children of God.

In *Good News to the Poor: John Wesley's Evangelical Economics*, Theodore W. Jennings Jr. describes John Wesley's stance on justice as the "demystification of wealth and power."[6] Wesley criticized the institutionalized church's traditional alliance with the wealthy and powerful and lived out what Jennings calls an "evangelical economics"[7] based on frugal living and generosity toward the poor.

Wesley lived simply, gave away most of his money, and went door to door begging for food and clothes for the poor. After learning the basics of medicine, he offered free health care and created simple medical manuals for those who could not afford to pay. He started an orphanage, founded a "poor house" for widows and others who were destitute, organized literacy classes, and formed a credit union.[8] He identified with the poor, lived in solidarity with them, and worked tirelessly for justice on their behalf.

As a social reformer, Wesley was a strong advocate for human rights and a passionate abolitionist. He spoke out for the rights of women and included them as preachers and in other leadership roles in the Methodist Societies. He spoke out against the causes of poverty and oppression, denounced materialism and luxury, worked to reform prisons, and organized factory workers to end child labor and other abuses of newly industrializing England. He worked with the Royal Society for the Prevention of Cruelty to Animals, founded by his friend and fellow abolitionist William Wilberforce, to alleviate animal suffering.

Although Wesley was loyal to the Church of England throughout his life, he was often banned from preaching in churches. Wesley alienated many by his unorthodox style of field preaching, his critique of wealth and power, and his radically inclusive message of God's love. While some rich and powerful people also gathered to hear him, many were appalled. The Duchess of Buckingham wrote of the Methodists: "Their doctrines are most repulsive, and strongly tinctured with impertinence and disrespect toward their superiors, in perpetually endeavoring to level all ranks, and to do away with all distinctions. It is monstrous to

---

6. Theodore W. Jennings Jr., "Wesley and the Poor: An Agenda for Wesleyans," in *The Portion of the Poor: Good News to the Poor in the Wesleyan Tradition*, ed. Douglas Meeks (Nashville: Abingdon, 1995), 32.

7. Ibid., 22.

8. Donald A. D. Thorsen, *The Wesleyan Quadrilateral: Scripture, Tradition, Reason, & Experience as a Model of Evangelical Theology* (Grand Rapids: Zondervan, 1990), 94.

be told that you have a heart as sinful as the common wretches that crawl on the earth. This is highly offensive and insulting. . . ."[9]

A friend once challenged Wesley after he had preached to an affluent and genteel congregation on the text from Matthew 23:33: "Ye serpents, ye generation of vipers, how can you escape the damnation of hell?" His offended friend rebuked him, saying, "Sir, such a sermon would have been suitable in Billingsgate, but it was highly improper here." (Billingsgate was a slum area populated by criminals, alcoholics, and prostitutes.) Wesley replied, "If I had been in Billingsgate, my text would have been, 'Behold the Lamb of God which taketh away the sin of the world'" (John 1:29).[10]

Wesley had a critical view of colonialism, the system of institutionalized domination that was built on the appropriation of land of Indigenous peoples and the enslavement of people from African nations. His clearest statements on human rights were made in the context of his opposition to the slave trade, "that execrable sum of all villainies,"[11] especially chattel slavery in the American colonies, which he called "the vilest that ever saw the sun."[12] He pointed to the lust for profits to determine who was responsible for the detestable institution of slavery. In *Thoughts upon Slavery* he wrote to merchants, charging: "It is you that induce the African villain to sell his countrymen; and in order thereto, to steal, rob, murder men, women, and children without number, by enabling the English villain to pay him for so doing. . . ."[13] Likewise, to plantation owners he wrote: "Now, it is your money that pays the merchant, and through him the captain and the African butcher. You therefore are guilty, yea, principally guilty. . . . You are the spring that puts all the rest in motion; they would not stir a step without you; therefore the blood of all these wretches who die before their time, whether in their country or elsewhere, lies upon your head."[14]

Wesley also used economic analysis to search out the root causes of other social issues. He decried the emerging system of industrializing capitalism, which enriched the wealthy at the expense of the poor.

---

9. Aaron C. H. Seymour, *The Life and Times of Selina, Countess of Huntingdon* (1884), 1:27, as cited by Oscar Sherwin, *John Wesley: Friend of the People* (New York: Twayne Publishers, 1961), 40–41.
10. John Telford, "Preacher, Writer, and Philanthropist," in *The Life of John Wesley* (Epworth, 1929), chapter 20, Wesley Center Online, Northwest Nazarene University, http://wesley.nnu.edu/john-wesley/the-life-of-john-wesley-by-john-telford/.
11. "Wesley to Wilberforce: John Wesley's Last Letter from His Deathbed," written February 24, 1791, as quoted in *Christianity Today*, http://www.christianitytoday.com/history/issues/issue-2/wesley-to-wilberforce.html.
12. Ibid.
13. Wesley, *Thoughts upon Slavery*, 54.
14. Ibid., 55.

English lawmakers had passed enclosure laws that allowed landowners to enclose publicly shared lands, or *commons*, in order to grow cash crops and raise carriage horses for profit. This practice deprived peasants of the common lands upon which they had subsisted for generations by growing vegetables and grazing animals. When they could no longer sustain their families, peasants migrated to the cities where they were forced to seek factory work. Unemployment was high, so labor had little bargaining power and conditions were miserable.[15]

In his critique of these conditions, Wesley looked at those who benefited financially in order to determine who was responsible and what could be done to set things right. When the cost of grains went sky-high, Wesley attributed it to the competition created by farmers growing wheat for alcohol and oats to feed horses raised to pull coaches for the emerging middle classes in England and France. He blamed rising costs of meat, poultry, and eggs on "the monopolization of farms: perhaps as mischievous a monopoly as was ever introduced into these kingdoms."[16] He called on the government to act by intervening in the economy. His suggestions included raising taxes on carriages and on horses exported to France, and putting a ceiling on the amount of rent charged for land use so that small farms could become viable again.[17] His proposals suggest similar measures that could be enacted today, if economic justice was the goal of public policy.

John Wesley taught that God's intention is the fulfillment of creation, not its destruction. His vision of "the fullness of time" was a vision of personal transformation, justice, and peace. He said:

> Suppose now the fullness of time to be come, and the prophecies to be accomplished. What a prospect is this! All is peace. . . . Wars are ceased from the earth . . . ; no brother rising up against brother; no country or city divided against itself, and tearing out its own bowels. Here is no oppression to make even "the wise man mad"; no extortion to "grind the face of the poor"; no robbery or wrong; no rapine or injustice; for all are "content with such things as they possess." Thus "righteousness and peace have kissed each other" (Ps. 85:10); they have "taken root and filled the land"; "righteousness flourishing out of the earth"; and "peace looking down from heaven."[18]

15. Theodore Runyan, *The New Creation: John Wesley's Theology Today* (Nashville: Abingdon, 1998), 186.
16. John Wesley, "Thoughts on the Present Scarcity of Provisions," in *The Works of the Reverend John Wesley* (London: Methodist Book Room, 1773), 11:56. Online at http://ufdc.ufl.edu/UF00076196/00011/61.
17. Ibid., 58.
18. John Wesley, Sermon 4, "Scriptural Christianity," ed. Albert C. Outler, *The Works of John Wesley* (Nashville: Abingdon, 1986), 1:170–71.

Commenting on this passage, Theodore Runyan says, "Hence, in contrast with the present order of things, Wesley envisions a society of economic justice. . . . Religion is not to be viewed, therefore, as alienated humanity's means of escape to a more tolerable, heavenly realm, but as participation in God's own redemptive enterprise, transforming alienated servants into liberated sons and daughters, whose works are at one and the same time the expression of their own life in the Spirit and the sign of the new age of justice and love that is to come."[19]

Wesley's vision supports a hopeful view of personal and social transformation that is relevant to our time. We turn now to a consideration of justice in light of Wesley's theology and contemporary theologies of liberation. Surely, social holiness today includes "liberated sons and daughters" engaged in ongoing spiritual growth, living in integrity, honoring creation, and taking action for peace and justice in the world. Love in a time of climate change demands nothing less.

Social Holiness Today

Social holiness today means considering the effects of our lifestyles and actions in the context of global warming, the worsening plight of the poor and vulnerable, harm to other beings and God's creation, and threats to future generations. It includes studying and acknowledging the underlying systemic causes of these interrelated problems and taking action toward their resolution. In addition to hands-on acts of mercy, social holiness calls us to engage in acts of justice.

Wesley's condemnation of the slave trade in its pursuit of profit at the expense of justice is relevant today. We participate in a global trading system that provides those of us who are privileged with countless consumer goods. These goods are acquired through supply chains that are mostly invisible. They depend on largely unregulated resource extraction and the exploitation of cheap labor, sometimes slave labor. They are shipped around the world via transportation networks that burn vast quantities of fossil fuels, exacerbating climate change and all the suffering that comes with it. Wesley's words should strike to the heart: "Better no trade than trade procured by villainy. . . . Better is honest poverty, than all the riches bought by the tears, and sweat, and blood, of our fellow creatures."[20]

In this era of advanced, unregulated free-market capitalism, the

19. Runyan, "Preface," *Sanctification and Liberation*, 46.
20. Wesley, *Thoughts upon Slavery*, 45–46.

idols of wealth and power are alive and well. Economic injustice abounds. According to Wesleyan scholar M. Douglas Meeks:

> In the new situation of market capitalism spreading throughout the world the poor are increasingly subjected to the laws and necessities of the market and free trade. In the economic "logic" of capitalism, capital and the laws of the market come first. Human beings and the satisfaction of their basic needs and the right to life for all come second. This is true also in First World countries as capital flight causes a restructuring that means many are dropping out of the middle class while the plight of the poor becomes more desperate.

Here again is a reminder of the need to work for social and economic policies that allow families to survive and thrive and that offer a social safety net for those abandoned by extreme capitalism. Meanwhile, as the rich get richer and the poor get poorer, the planet continues to heat up.

Theodore Jennings links this global "economy of death" with the destruction of creation:

> The vicious cycle of impoverishment and violence feeds upon itself. This same economy of death meanwhile is rapidly destroying the earth itself. . . . Certainly no minor adjustments to this mechanism of death will transform it into something that nourishes life. Without a radical transformation of our ways of dealing with one another and the earth, God's teeming creation may become a lifeless rock hurtling through the void of space. But from whence can such a radical transformation come?[21]

Jennings points to John Wesley's theology as a direction of hope for the earth: "A Wesleyan theology of transformation which takes seriously the importance of future redemption . . . will issue not only in protest against the violation of the earth but also in the practice of transformation of the earth as evidence of the truth of the gospel."[22]

Wesley's concept of *social holiness* requires us to respond to the increasingly severe impacts of a warming world with acts of mercy and acts of justice. His concept of the *world parish* reinforces the conviction that our call is to love as Christ loves, with care and concern extending out beyond the walls of our churches, boundaries of our communities, and borders of our nations. Wesley was considering human beings when he expanded the concept of parish to include the whole world,

21. Jennings, "Wesley and the Poor," 26.
22. Ibid., 34.

which in itself is applicable to our work as we consider the people harmed most by climate change. But, as discussed earlier, we must also extend our circle of concern to future generations and to all living things. As Theodore Runyan said in *The New Creation: Wesley for Today*: "For 'social holiness' today includes not only our link to all present inhabitants of the planet but to future generations for whom, as stewards, we hold the earth in trust. There can be no holiness today that is not social holiness shaped by this task. . . ."[23]

Meanwhile, the legacy of colonialism continues today, as does resistance to the injustices of institutionalized domination and greed. A faithful response to climate change requires us to commit ourselves to struggles for justice. We must each decide where to take our stand. We are invited to join in the struggles of Indigenous people fighting to defend the rights of Mother Earth; in ongoing demonstrations against racism; in working to abolish modern-day slavery that manifests as human trafficking; in struggles for immigrant rights; in movements for marriage equality; in pro-democracy networks working against corporate rule and toxic trade agreements; in living wage campaigns, in organizations working for peace; and in the climate justice movement that is gaining ground on every continent. People of every faith tradition and philosophical perspective are joining together to build broad-based coalitions that include these and other causes and are working to create a world that reflects comprehensive justice, peace, and a healthy environment for all.

As we continue to explore social holiness in our time, we turn to contemporary liberation theologies, which have emerged in the twentieth and twenty-first centuries as theological and practical responses to injustice in various contexts. As contemporary manifestations of Christian tradition that focus on justice, liberation theologies enrich our understanding of what social holiness on a warming planet requires. These varied perspectives make clear that climate justice will have to incorporate social, economic, racial, gender, and environmental justice in order to build a movement that is broad enough to shake the foundations of the dominant culture, demonstrate participatory democracy, and help lay the groundwork for the new world to come.

23. Runyan, *New Creation*, 207.

Liberation Theologies

Scholars have explored the intersections between John Wesley's theology and contemporary theologies of liberation. As an Englishman, Wesley was no revolutionary. He opposed the Revolutionary War because he believed that war in the American colonies would create great suffering and chaos and would further extend the power of "merchant princes" and the institution of slavery, which he deplored.[24] He lived in a pre-democracy world and had no confidence that democratic governance was possible. Nevertheless, liberation theologians have found a kindred spirit in Wesley because of his strong critique of wealth and privilege, his affirmation of human rights, and his solidarity with the poor and oppressed.

As we have seen, Wesley taught that God's grace extends to all people and all parts of creation. At the same time, he demonstrated a focused and concrete concern for poor and marginalized people in all aspects of his ministry, and insisted that the early Methodist societies do so as well. This focus is consistent with a key concept in liberation theology: God's "preferential option for the poor."[25] While God's grace encompasses all, God reaches out with particular concern to those who suffer from poverty and other forms of injustice. Latin American liberation theologian Gustavo Gutiérrez explains:

> God's preferential option for the poor, the weak, the least members of society, runs throughout the Bible. . . . The gratuitous love of God requires that we establish an authentic justice for all, while giving privileged place to a concern for the unimportant members of society—that is, for those whose rights are not recognized either in theory (by a set of laws) or in practice (in the way society conducts itself).[26]

Liberation theology is undertaken in the context of injustice; it recognizes that the experiences of oppressed people have authority and can provide a starting point for theology. Latin American liberation theology originates in the context of colonialist exploitation, black theology in the context of white supremacy and racial discrimination, Native American theology in the context of colonization and genocide, feminist theology in the context of male domination and the oppression of women, and womanist theology in the context of the oppres-

---

24. Ibid., 28.
25. Gustavo Gutiérrez, *The God of Life*, trans. Matthew J. O'Connell (Maryknoll, NY: Orbis, 1991), 116.
26. Ibid., 116–17.

sion of women of color based on gender, class, and race. Each of these forms of liberation theology originates in the experience of injustice and includes a critical approach to the established social, economic, and political order. Scripture is read from the perspective of the oppressed—with reasoned analysis and critique of historical and contextual realities—while considering the effects of particular passages on marginalized people. Christian tradition is considered critically, while acknowledging ways that the church and its theology have historically contributed to oppression and have served to legitimate unjust social structures, extending to today.

Some contemporary liberation theologians link concern for human justice with concern for the earth. Latin American theologian Leonardo Boff said:

> Just as conventional theology developed unrelated to its social context, current theologies, including liberation theology, have developed without reference to the environmental context. It is important now to complement these perspectives with a coherent and holistic vision. The logic that leads the dominant classes to oppress peoples and discriminate against persons is the same as that which leads to the exploitation of nature.[27]

Latin American liberation theologies include a critique of capitalism, which has generated massive wealth while creating poverty and ravaging the earth. In a recent article, "The Earth Will Defeat Capitalism," Boff decries its consolidation of power over the earth:

> There is an indisputable and sad fact: capitalism as a mode of production and its political ideology, neoliberalism, are so thoroughly established globally that it seems to make any real alternative impossible. It has in fact occupied every space and aligned almost every country to its global interests. Since society has been commercialized and turned everything, even the most sacred things, such as human organs, water and the capacity of flowers to be pollinated, into an opportunity to gain wealth, most countries feel obliged to participate in the globally integrated macro-economy and much less inclined to serve the common good of their people. . . .[28]
>
> Meanwhile, our task is, within the system, to widen the openings, exploring all its contradictions to guarantee the essentials for subsistence: nourishment, work, housing, education, basic services and some free time,

27. Leonardo Boff, "Social Ecology: Poverty and Misery," in *Ecotheology: Voices from North and South*, ed. David G. Hallman (Eugene, OR: Wipf & Stock, 1994), 245.
28. Leonardo Boff, "The Earth Will Defeat Capitalism," *Tikkun Magazine* (January 5, 2016), Tikkun.org, http://www.tikkun.org/nextgen/the-earth-will-defeat-capitalism.

especially to the humble peoples of the Earth. . . . And also, we must pray and be prepared for the worst.

James H. Cone speaks and writes extensively on the topic of black liberation theology. In *A Black Theology of Liberation*, Cone claims that theology must never be neutral, but must take a stand on issues related to justice for the oppressed. Unfortunately, he says, American white theology has failed in this task:

> American white theology has not been involved in the struggle for black liberation. It has been basically a theology of the white oppressor, giving religious sanction to the genocide of Amerindians and the enslavement of Africans. From the very beginning to the present day, American white theological thought has been "patriotic," either by defining the theological task independently of black suffering (the liberal northern approach) or by defining Christianity as compatible with white racism (the southern approach). In both cases theology becomes a servant of the state, and that can only mean death to blacks.[29]

A 2007 article titled "Whose Earth Is It, Anyway?," critiques the logic that leads to both racial oppression and the destruction of the natural world. Not only are the ideological causes of these issues interwoven, but struggles for their solutions must be undertaken together as well.

> The logic that led to slavery and segregation in the Americas, colonization and apartheid in Africa, and the rule of white supremacy throughout the world is the same one that leads to the exploitation of animals and the ravaging of nature. It is a mechanistic and instrumental logic that defines everything and everybody in terms of their contribution to the development and defense of white world supremacy. People who fight against white racism but fail to connect it to the degradation of the earth are anti-ecological, whether they know it or not. People who struggle against ecological injustice but do not incorporate in it a disciplined and sustained fight against white supremacy are racists, whether they acknowledge it or not. The fight for justice cannot be segregated but must be integrated with the fight for life in all its forms.[30]

Cone also points to white privilege as a blind spot of theologians who write about caring for the earth:

---

29. James H. Cone, *A Black Theology of Liberation* (Maryknoll, NY: Orbis, 2010), 4.
30. James H. Cone, "Whose Earth Is It, Anyway?" in *Sojourners Magazine* (July 2007).

> Now that humanity has reached the possibility of extinction, one would think that a critical assessment of how we got to where we are would be the next step for sensitive and caring theologians of the earth. . . . What is absent from much of the talk about the environment in First World countries is a truly radical critique of the culture most responsible for the ecological crisis. . . . Only when white theologians realize that a fight against racism is a fight for *their* humanity will we be able to create a coalition of blacks, whites and other people of color in the struggle to save the earth.[31]

Fortunately, there has been growing momentum recently that is bringing together just such a coalition, willing to fight for justice and for "life in all its forms," perhaps despite of white theologians. Black Lives Matter demonstrations are taking place around the country, fueled by ongoing police shooting deaths of black men and women and supported by people of various races. Various movements that coordinate actions across racial and ethnic boundaries and across issues now work to raise awareness among participants by offering diversity trainings and establishing anti-oppression protocols for leadership, meetings, and actions. It is becoming clear to many that justice for people and the earth will require a diverse movement with a commitment to mutual well-being that is strong enough to change the dominant system, which causes so many harms.

Native American theology has much to contribute to our understanding of creation in this time of climate change, with its critique of anthropocentrism, its view of the Creator as immanent within creation, and its spatial rather than temporal focus. Indigenous wisdom is grounded in the sacredness of the earth, the inherent value of each part of creation, and our interrelatedness with the whole. At the same time, Indigenous liberation theologies begin with the contemporary context and include a call for justice. In his book *Spirit and Resistance: Political Theology and American Indian Liberation*, Native American theologian George Tinker writes:

> The contemporary Native American experience of disintegration and alienation derives from the ongoing history of conquest, oppression, and poverty, with all of their ongoing consequences. . . . Thus, an Indian theology must begin with the present-day social disintegration experienced by every Indian community, and begin to name the causes for the disintegration. . . . This situation reasonably requires that a Native American theology begin with this context as political reality and move quickly to press

31. Ibid.

to a new vision of health and well-being (what some might call salvation) for the people. Thus, an American Indian theology must be a theology of liberation. It must be overtly political.[32]

As mentioned earlier, the church was complicit in the historical colonization of Indigenous lands. It was a primary tool for conquest and provided moral justification for systematic removal of Indigenous communities from their homelands, forced conversions, slavery, cultural genocide, and death. Indigenous people today often reject Christianity, the religion imposed by colonizers, but there are still many Native American churches on or near reservations that continue to foster Christ-centered community. By including traditional practices in their services of worship they demonstrate a form of resistance to cultural domination. Native American liberation theology also critiques capitalism. According to Tinker, "It is not, then, that American Indian peoples have been unable to understand the basics of the capitalist, developmentalist system that has dominated the world since 1492; rather, American Indian societies have had no cultural room for that fundamental ingredient, greed, which fires up the whole capitalist system."

In fact, the whole concept of development, including *sustainable development* discussed in climate negotiations, "already represents a cultural imposition on American Indian and other indigenous peoples" because it is limited by the "cultural commitment to temporality and the dictates of perceived economic forces that always function temporally in the modern world system." Rather, George Tinker suggests alternative ways of organizing human society. He suggests, "Ultimately, I would like to see a vision emerge in the world of small, local, autonomous communities as the basic political unit recognized and respected by everyone, with tolerance for a wide variety of politically organized configurations."[33]

Feminist and womanist theologians point to patriarchy as a primary system of oppression. Eco-feminist theologians claim that the problem is not just *anthropocentrism* (human-centeredness), but *androcentrism* (male-centeredness) because the domination of women and domination of the earth go together. Rosemary Radford Ruether explains:

The theology of eco-feminism brings feminist theology into dialogue with

---

32. George E. Tinker, *Spirit and Resistance: Political Theology and American Indian Liberation* (Minneapolis: Augsburg Fortress, 2004), 3–4.
33. Ibid., 13.

a culturally based critique of the ecological crisis. Patriarchal ideology perceives the earth or nature as a female or as a feminine reality. As such, nature is considered to be inferior to men. As a material being having no spirit, no life in and of itself, nature is only a tool to be exploited by men. The cultural roots of the ecological crisis can be found in this common perception of both women and nature as realities without spirit and tools to be exploited by the dominant males.[34]

God is often considered in masculine terms, as active, controlling, and initiating, while nature is identified with opposite qualities that are considered feminine. "Mother Earth" is seen as passive, receptive, and nurturing; environmental destruction is referred to as "rape" of the earth. From an eco-feminist perspective, male domination of both women and nature are dual expressions of patriarchal values and systems that rule the world today.

The competitive, controlling, dominating qualities that have traditionally been considered masculine characterize the institutions that make up the dominant global system, which is leading us toward disaster. Eco-feminists argue that the only way to bring about the needed transformation is to incorporate so-called "feminine" qualities, such as compassion, cooperation, and nurture into our social structures in order to bring about a humane and ecologically sustainable world order. This will provide a more balanced and sane foundation for societies where humans and other parts of creation can thrive.

Part of this work requires us to expand our images and understanding of God. Using inclusive God-language or a variety of metaphors, such as those from Isaiah 66 portraying God as midwife and mother, enables us to become aware of feminine aspects of the divine. According to Ruether:

> In order to create an ecological culture and society, we must transform relationships of domination and exploitation into relationships of mutual support. This transformation will not occur without a parallel change in our image of God, our image of the relationship between God and creation in all its dimensions. . . . Only when we have come to understand that God is the source and the foundation calling us to live in relationships of mutual support can we effectively rebuild our vision of the world.[35]

---

34. Rosemary Radford Ruether, "Eco-feminism and Theology," in *Ecotheology*, 199.
35. Ibid., 204.

Many African American women and other women of color identify more as *womanist* than as *feminist* because the term *womanist* acknowledges their experience of oppression due to race as well as gender. Alice Walker explained: "Womanism is simply another shade of feminism. It helps give visibility to the experience of black women and other women of color who have always been at the forefront of the feminist movement yet marginalized and rendered invisible in historical texts and the media." Or, using a more poetic phrase, Walker said, "Womanist is to feminist as purple is to lavender."[36]

Many womanist theologians connect racism with the degradation of the earth. In "Sin, Nature, and Black Women's Bodies," Delores Williams explains how the historic oppression of enslaved women parallels the exploitation of nature. She writes:

> This defilement of nature's body and of black women's bodies is sin, since its occurrence denies that black women and nature are made in the image of God. Its occurrence is an assault upon the spirit of creation in women and nature. Whereas theologians such as Paul Tillich spoke of sin as man's [sic] estrangement from God and from other humans, womanist theologians can claim that humanity in the Western world has fallen to deeper states of degradation and depravity. Western Christians, some of whom are the manipulators of technology and concepts of development, no longer have to struggle only with the despair of being alienated from God (or the ground of being). They must now struggle with the attack Western man has waged against creation itself. They must struggle against the sin of defilement (evidenced today in nature and in the history of black women)—the sin that now threatens to destroy all life on the planet.[37]

It takes courage to face the extent of harm being done to people and the earth, and to rise in faith to take action for justice. Liberation theologians point in the direction of faithfulness to the liberating and transforming God of justice and love. Several Wesleyan scholars link liberation theologies with Wesley's teachings on sanctification, his emphasis on social holiness, and his hope for the redemption of creation. In his preface to a book of essays titled *Sanctification and Liberation: Liberation Theologies in Light of the Wesleyan Tradition*, Theodore Runyan explains:

36. "What is A Womanist?" in The Progress a Progressive Pupil Blog, https://progressivepupil.wordpress.com/2014/03/04/what-is-a-womanist/.
37. Delores Williams, "Sin, Nature, and Black Women's Bodies," in Ecofeminism and the Sacred, ed. Carol J. Adams (New York: Continuum, 1993), 29.

> The thesis advanced by some . . . is that there is a peculiar affinity between Wesleyan theology—especially Wesley's doctrine of sanctification—and movements for social change. When Christian perfection becomes the goal of the individual, a fundamental hope is engendered that the future can surpass the present. Concomitantly, a holy dissatisfaction is aroused with regard to any present state of affairs—a dissatisfaction that supplies the critical edge necessary to keep the process of individual transformation moving. Moreover, this holy dissatisfaction is readily transferable from the realm of the individual to that of society—as was evident in Wesley's own time—where it provides a persistent motivation for reform in the light of 'a more perfect way' that transcends any status quo.[38]

Liberation theologies emerge in situations of oppression, where "holy dissatisfaction" and faith in God inspire hope for liberation. Such hope involves personal transformation and motivation for action to bring social change. As we have seen, Wesley taught and lived out a similar vision. Liberation theologies inform us more specifically of the kinds of liberation that people yearn for, and may motivate us to take actions "in light of a more perfect way" that transcend the status quo.

Guided by Tradition: Actions That Transcend the Status Quo

John Wesley's teachings about economics are pertinent today, since climate justice requires reducing consumption among the wealthy, sharing the earth's resources justly, advocating for the needy, caring for creation, and working to transform the way we order our political, economic, and social affairs. In an essay titled "Reading Wesley with the Poor," Douglas Meeks said:

> If persons are to make a genuine difference in the conditions of an economy that oppresses the poor, they must be freed from their own idolatrous captivities and practice the disciplines of "evangelical economics" in their own lives. Without the development of a personal and communal ethic of frugality, simplicity, generosity, and solidarity with the poor, no persons or communities will have the courage to challenge the "economy of death."[39]

Meeks is not just talking about what we can do as individuals, but also as communities. We need to apply the ethic of which he speaks not

---

38. Theodore Runyan, "Preface," in *Sanctification and Liberation: Liberation Theologies in Light of the Wesleyan Tradition*, ed. Theodore Runyan (Nashville: Abingdon, 1981), 10.
39. Meeks, "On Reading Wesley with the Poor," 15.

just to ourselves, but to our churches. As followers of Jesus, we need to move our churches to adopt practices that reflect God's love and that challenge the "economy of death," for the sake of the larger human community. We can only do this effectively if we adopt these practices ourselves.

Frugality frees us from "idolatrous captivities," such as overconsumption, shopping as entertainment, the demand for instant gratification, and greed. Like John Wesley did in his day, we can follow the money to search out root causes of climate change and other social ills. Living frugally means making conscious choices based on values and spending money accordingly.

Simplicity is a traditional spiritual discipline that is highly valuable in the contemporary Western context of busy-ness and overconsumption. Practicing simplicity reveals our struggles with idolatrous desires while reducing our harmful impacts on the earth. Simplicity includes frugality, but there is also an inner aspect to simplicity that enables us to acknowledge our dependence on God and to commit ourselves to seeking and following God's will in all things. This may mean asking for support in releasing compulsive behaviors that continue to plague us in spite of our best intentions. There is also an outer aspect to simplicity, which includes living simply, reducing our carbon footprint, and reducing harm caused by irresponsible purchases and mindless consumption. We "live simply so others may simply live."[40]

Living frugally and practicing simplicity are even more powerful when linked with *generosity* and *solidarity* with poor and oppressed people, which take us further in developing the strength of character and courage to challenge "the economy of death." Generosity means sharing with people in need; acting in solidarity with them means entering into mutual relationship and speaking and acting for justice together. By working for justice, we make it possible for those who are marginalized or excluded to survive and improve their lives. By working for systemic change, we make justice possible in the world.

"Holy dissatisfaction" with the present state of affairs motivates us to take a critical stance toward policies, institutions, and systems that violate the poor, threaten the future, and damage creation. This means working to demystify and dethrone the idols of wealth and power that enthrall people and dominate the ruling institutions of our world. In

---

40. Widely attributed to Mohandas Gandhi, as quoted in Natural Living School, https://naturallivingschool.com/2012/04/22/live-simply-so-others-may-simply-live-gandhi/.

the next chapter, we will identify some of these idols and explore the ruling institutions that perpetuate climate change.

Climate justice means establishing justice for those who live in regions most vulnerable to a changing climate, those who live in sacrifice zones polluted by fossil-fuel extraction, younger generations living on the cusp of runaway climate change, and species facing extinction. We must enter into communion with these frontline communities and make their cause our own. This is solidarity. This is faithfulness. This is love.

10

Reason: Climate Justice and Common Sense

What the climate needs to avoid collapse is a contraction in humanity's use of resources; what our economic model demands to avoid collapse is unfettered expansion. Only one of these sets of rules can be changed, and it's not the laws of nature.[1]

—Naomi Klein

For people who honor creation and seek justice, the election of Donald Trump to the US presidency has brought a darkness that continues to descend as he appoints people to carry out his agenda, which includes institutionalizing discrimination, endangering the most vulnerable people, and undoing environmental protections. Climate change deniers and oil company executives are now in position to establish climate policy. During these first chaotic months, the Administration has proposed or enacted policy changes that include: dismantling policies that limit greenhouse gas emissions, approving the Keystone XL and Dakota Access crude oil pipelines, slashing funding for science and the environment, appointing a climate change skeptic as head of the Environmental Protection Agency and the CEO of Exxon Mobil as Secretary of State. Changes to US environmental policies are happening so fast

1. Naomi Klein, *This Changes Everything: Capitalism vs. the Climate* (New York: Simon and Schuster, 2014), 21.

that *National Geographic* is keeping a running list to help the public keep up with them.[2]

Now that the divisive 2016 election is over, it is easy to forget that Republicans opposed to President Obama were not the only voters who wanted a dramatic shift in public policy. During the primary, many Democrats and Independents enthusiastically supported the candidacy of Bernie Sanders, whose call for political "revolution" mobilized a broad and diverse constituency eager for systemic change. One of his campaign promises was to create strong policies that would reduce the dangers of planetary warming.

Because of his strong showing in the Democratic primaries and caucuses, Sanders was able to nominate several high-profile progressives to the Democratic Party Platform Committee. To represent concerns about climate change, he nominated Bill McKibben, founder of the climate action organization 350.org. McKibben wrote an article in which he describes what happened as he attempted to add specific climate policy proposals to the platform:

> At which point we got (about 11 p.m., in a half-deserted hotel ballroom) to the climate section of the platform, and that's where things got particularly obvious. We all agreed that America should be operating on 100 percent clean energy by 2050, but then I proposed, in one amendment after another, a series of ways we might actually get there. A carbon tax? Voted down 7–6. . . . A ban on fracking? Voted down 7–6. An effort to keep fossil fuels in the ground, at least on federal land? Voted down 7–6. A measure to mandate that federal agencies weigh the climate impact of their decisions? Voted down 7–6. Even a plan to keep fossil fuel companies from taking private land by eminent domain: voted down 7–6. (We did, however, reach unanimous consent on more bike paths!)[3]

Of course, Hillary Clinton ultimately became the Democratic presidential nominee and Donald Trump won the election. But it is important to see that this all took place in the context of a deeply flawed election process. Regardless of which party spent more in 2016 (and regardless of who won), the process through which people are elected to high office in the United States is deeply corrupted by the rule of money

---

2. Michael Greshko, "A Running List of How Trump Is Changing the Environment," *National Geographic*, March 31, 2017. http://news.nationalgeographic.com/2017/03/how-trump-is-changing-science-environment/.

3. Bill McKibben, "The Clinton Campaign Is Obstructing Change to the Democratic Platform," *Politico* (June 27, 2016), http://www.politico.com/magazine/story/2016/06/hillary-clinton-2016-democratic-platform-213993#ixzz4DQ4qQbwz.

and its distorting effects on democracy. The growing power of corporations and of wealthy individuals pooling vast sums of dark money allow them to manipulate elections, the media (and with it, public opinion), and public policies at the local, state, federal, and international level.

This chapter uses reason to explore these dynamics in the context of how they affect climate policy. Long before the 2016 election, underlying systemic dynamics have prevented policies from being enacted that could significantly reduce greenhouse gas emissions and mitigate global warming. Under both Democratic and Republican leadership truly effective climate policies have been impossible. This is one reason why some find the call for political revolution so appealing.

Two Kinds of Climate Change Denial

As we saw in earlier chapters, many people deny the reality of climate change or downplay its implications. Various psychological and social mechanisms prevent people from facing the extent of current damage or future dangers of a warming world. Major oil and gas corporations deliberately sow doubt so they can continue profiting from the fossil-fuel-based economy. Right-wing religious organizations reject both climate science and basic evolutionary biology, insisting that their members do the same. These dynamics combine to confuse the public about whether or not they should be concerned.

Another form of denial accepts the evidence and conclusions of climate science but imagines that the problem can be solved with small incremental changes, preserving the world as we know it without changing the overall direction of the current global system. This form of denial sustains an illusion of stability, diverts people into focusing solely on personal lifestyle change, and prevents well-meaning people from seeing what effective climate action might entail.

Of course, if we are concerned about global warming, cutting back on our personal use of fossil fuel makes sense, but that will not bring about the profound changes that are required. In her groundbreaking book *This Changes Everything: Capitalism vs. the Climate*, Naomi Klein challenges this form of denial, which keeps our focus on asking individuals to "voluntarily 'green' the minutiae of their lives,"[4] while corporations and the super-rich pollute on a large scale and benefit from the current system. If we take the authority of reason seriously, we need to break free of denial of every kind and squarely face not only the reality of cli-

4. Klein, *This Changes Everything*, 46.

mate change but its underlying causes. The dominant system and its ideological underpinnings will have to be unmasked, challenged, and transformed. Establishing economic, social, and environmental justice is an essential part of effective action to address climate change.

This chapter explores global warming and related injustice through the lens of reason, reveals links that bind these problems together, and shows why effective climate action includes justice for poor and vulnerable human beings, future generations, and all creation. This process of exploration includes analyzing some of the underlying systemic conditions that cause and perpetuate climate change and other forms of injustice. It means looking at how the dominant ideologies of our time make possible both the exploitation of human beings and the destruction of the earth. Seeking truth in these areas clearly reveals that working for climate justice is a matter of common sense, and that action to combat climate change, relieve suffering, and build a cooperative global community go together.

Justice for People, Justice for the Earth

Justice for people and justice for the earth go together. The principles of fairness and equity have been understood as basic to international efforts to combat climate change since international climate negotiations began in the early 1990s. Even then it was clear to world leaders that issues of the environment, poverty, and development were linked, and that global cooperation on climate change would only be possible if proposed solutions were just and equitable.

This principle was incorporated into the Framework Convention on Climate Change, the foundational climate treaty, which was agreed upon at the United Nations Conference on Environment and Development in Rio de Janeiro in 1992. Nations of the world acknowledged that the only way to lower global greenhouse gas emissions to 1990 levels (the goal at the time) was to work to alleviate poverty and to foster sustainable development simultaneously. Wealthy nations, which had historically emitted most greenhouse gases into the atmosphere through fossil-fuel-intensive industrialization, agreed in principle that they had a responsibility to help developing nations adapt to climate change and mitigate further planetary warming. Such help would include transferring renewable technologies to poor nations, enabling them to leapfrog over fossil-fuel-intensive technologies and develop along climate-friendly lines, to the benefit of all nations. Sadly, these many years later, effective mechanisms for such technology transfers are still not in place.

More recently, in December 2015, representatives from 175 nations traveled to Paris to offer voluntary greenhouse gas reduction targets. The Paris accord restated the goal of keeping overall warming below 2 degrees Celsius, while also acknowledging the importance of pursuing a stricter limit of 1.5 degrees. The talks were hailed as a success. Spokespersons gave optimistic public statements, and celebrations accompanied the signing ceremony on Earth Day, 2016.[5]

But the Paris agreement will not prevent climate chaos. Since the targets are strictly voluntary, there is no way to hold countries to their stated goals. The transition from the Obama Administration to the Trump Administration highlights this dilemma. Furthermore, the targets fall far short of what is needed. Even if all countries were to stay within their stated goals, average planetary warming would continue climbing to 3.5 degrees or higher. To those who take seriously the calls for climate justice, this soft agreement is not a proportionate response to the unfolding disasters that we already see with just a 1 degree average global temperature rise.

Another unresolved issue that was still on the table in Paris is the ongoing demand for a mechanism that ensures justice for countries that are experiencing dramatic climactic changes. People are suffering disproportionately in countries that have contributed little to the atmospheric burden of greenhouse gas pollution. Clearly, rich nations have greater responsibility for current levels of planetary warming, since we have emitted most of the greenhouse gases currently in the atmosphere. At the same time, poor nations now bearing the brunt of climate disasters are unable to afford clean technologies that would enable them to bypass fossil fuels, and are calling for assistance from wealthy nations. Climate justice advocates call on wealthy nations to consider such assistance not as charity but as payment for a climate debt and as a reasonable response that will benefit us all.

What are the reasons for this ongoing failure to act? Why has international progress in addressing climate change stalled when the stakes are so high? What has prevented effective action that the nations of the world agreed to in principle so long ago? Why is there such failure on the part of wealthy nations to do what justice, national self-interest, and the well-being of life on earth require?

---

5. Doyle Rice, "175 nations sign historic Paris climate deal on Earth Day," *USA Today* (April 22, 2016).

We need to exercise our God-given faculty of reason as we search for answers to these confounding questions. It might seem easier to simply accept conventional answers, but a deeper search requires us to explore underlying systemic conditions that cause or aggravate both injustice and accelerating climate change. One way to do this is to follow the money, to see whose interests are served by the current order. This rigorous search for the truth of our situation may lead to surprising conclusions.

Corporate Influence on Climate Policy

Transnational corporations greatly influence government policies, both domestically and in the international arena. The United States has granted corporations the status of *persons* under the law.[6] But *corporate persons* have great advantages over flesh-and-blood human beings, for they can span the globe, hold several nationalities at once, exist in numerous places simultaneously, live in perpetuity, control vast wealth, and dominate the policies of many different governments at the same time.

Corporate influence on local, state, and national governments is immense. Corporations use their wealth and power to sway public opinion through the media, elect candidates of their choice, and lobby to establish policies that benefit corporations at the expense of people and the earth. This dynamic ensures that many elected officials see their interests as tied to corporate interests and so are unwilling to stand up against their demands.

As mentioned earlier, fossil-fuel companies have been effective in fostering doubt about the reality of climate change, blocking legislation to reduce greenhouse gas emissions, and slowing global climate negotiations. Several state attorneys general are currently pressing charges against Exxon Mobil, claiming that the company fraudulently misled its investors and the public about the reality of climate change.[7] Internal documents recently made public reveal that in the 1970s, Exxon's own internal studies showed that greenhouse gas emissions from their products would cause the warming of the earth's atmosphere. Instead of switching to renewable technologies or encouraging

---

6. Rob Kall, "Is the USA the Only Nation in the World with Corporate Personhood?" *Huffington Post* (April 9, 2012), http://www.huffingtonpost.com/rob-kall/is-the-usa-the-only-natio_b_1262525.html.

7. John Schwartz, "Exxon Mobil Climate Inquiry in New York Gains Allies," *New York Times* (March 29, 2016).

people to conserve, the Exxon corporation invested millions to build a worldwide public relations machine to promote the denial of climate science.[8] Corporate obfuscation of climate science and undermining of climate policy has greatly contributed to the logjam on climate action. Nevertheless, representatives of Exxon Mobil, Chevron, Shell, and other oil companies sit at the negotiation table as official participants in international climate summits. And now, in a move that seems surreal, President Trump has appointed Rex Tillerson, former CEO of Exxon Mobil, as Secretary of State.

In the United States, wealthy private individuals like the Koch brothers also have undue influence. They can pool their fortunes in non-transparent, tax-deductible "philanthropic" organizations that fund causes and campaigns to benefit the one percent. This vast dark money network, together with corporate capital, distorts democracy. In addition, conservative lawmakers work with corporate leaders to pass legislation on a variety of issues, including climate and energy policy. As mentioned earlier, the American Legislative Council (ALEC) brings together heads of industry with elected officials to draft model legislation to present to state legislatures around the country. Together, these tactics result in the domination of politics by the wealthy few, the corporate capture of democracy, and failure to facilitate effective climate action. They reveal the bankruptcy of the current global system of unrestrained free-market capitalism.

The Bankruptcy of Free-Market Capitalism

In my previous book, *Shaking the Gates of Hell: Faith-Led Resistance to Corporate Globalization*, I presented an overview and theological critique of the global economy. I described the system in detail and claimed "The system is designed for the results it is getting. The architects, rule makers, and enforcers of the global economy are reaping the benefits of what they have designed."[9]

The functioning of the global economic system is based on a system of finance, trade, and public policy rules that governments agree to follow. These rules of the global economy press governments to establish laws protecting corporate investments and removing laws that interfere with the free movement of corporations, the free flow of goods,

8. Justin Gillis and John Schwartz, "Exxon Mobil Accused of Misleading Public on Climate Change Risks," *New York Times* (October 30, 2015).

9. Sharon Delgado, *Shaking the Gates of Hell: Faith-Led Resistance to Corporate Globalization* (Minneapolis: Fortress Press, 2007), 108.

and especially the free flow of capital. These rules include: privatization, deregulation, cutbacks in social services, tax breaks for corporations, export-led development, incentives and protections for corporate investment, elimination of currency controls, and limitations on consumer safety, health, labor, and environmental laws that could be construed as barriers to trade. Many of these rules make effective climate action impossible.

The International Monetary Fund (IMF) and the World Bank, dominated by the United States and European Union, have imposed rules like these on developing nations for generations. The World Bank meets its lending targets by loaning money to poor governments, often for large, expensive industrial development projects such as dams and power plants. When these countries find themselves unable to pay the interest, the World Bank and IMF step in to give them new loans or guarantee loans from private banks so they can refinance their debt and infuse additional money into their economies. But these loans are conditional, given only to countries that enact *austerity measures* based on the *structural adjustment policies* that these global institutions dictate. These already-poor nations are told that they must tighten their belts, cut social spending, privatize public services (such as education, health care, and access to water), and follow the other rules. These policies have resulted in a global debt crisis that keeps poor nations in an ever-spiraling cycle of debt and misery. These countries, already strapped by years of such policies, are the ones most severely impacted by climate change. Unable to afford the cost of cleanup and recovery, they will be forced into additional "aid" and loan packages with ever-more stringent rules, thus reinforcing the dominance of the United States and Europe in this inequitable global system.

The World Trade Organization (WTO), the North American Free Trade Agreement (NAFTA), the proposed Trans-Pacific Partnership (TPP) and Trans-Atlantic Trade and Investment Partnership (TTIP), and other free trade agreements impose similar rules on member nations. Negotiations to institute the WTO and NAFTA began in the late 1980s, at the same time as global climate negotiations began. As we have seen, the decades-long climate negotiations have resulted in non-binding agreements, without effective enforcement mechanisms. In contrast, free trade agreements are binding. They are enforced by a dispute-settlement system that penalizes countries that do not comply.

Free trade agreements have been remarkably effective in instituting and enforcing the rules of the global economy, which limit the power of governments to achieve the stated goals of international climate summits. They limit government regulation by penalizing governments that pass laws that interfere with corporate profits. NAFTA has an investor-state dispute settlement (ISDS) clause that allows corporations to directly sue national governments for lost profits—past, present, and future—if they do not comply.[10] For example, a Canadian subsidiary of Lone Pine Resources Inc., a US company incorporated in Delaware, acquired fracking permits in Quebec, including a permit to frack under the St. Lawrence River. In 2011, after studies showed potentially serious environmental impacts, Quebec instituted a moratorium on fracking under the river. In response, Lone Pine is suing the Canadian government under NAFTA for $118.9 million.[11] Such suits are tried by non-transparent dispute panels, and the resulting judgment is binding. This binding dispute process has a chilling effect on legislation of all kinds, including climate legislation. The US government's policy is that it will change its laws to comply.

Why would governments agree to such limitations on national sovereignty? The track record has shown that these economic rules have led to growing inequity both within and among nations and a *race to the bottom* in wages, environmental standards, and consumer protections around the world. If our goal is to create a peaceful and just world with a stable climate, the rule-making institutions of the global economy are leading us in precisely the wrong direction. The very policies that they promote and enforce are incompatible with effective action to limit greenhouse gas emissions. It is irrational to believe that we can reduce greenhouse gas emissions and achieve a stable climate if unrestrained free-market capitalism continues along its current course.

Here are two examples of the irrationality and dysfunction of the current global system and the need for system change: As mentioned earlier, the World Bank warns that we are on track for a disastrous 4 to 6 degree Celsius rise in global temperatures. Meanwhile, the IMF recently announced that the governments of the world subsidize the fossil-fuel industry at the rate of ten million dollars per minute.[12] Yet

---

10. David Dayen, "The Scariest Trade Deal Nobody's Talking About Just Suffered a Big Leak," *New Republic* (June 4, 2015), https://newrepublic.com/article/121967/whats-really-going-trade-services-agreement.

11. "Lone Pine Resources Inc. v. Government of Canada," Global Affairs Canada, http://www.international.gc.ca/trade-agreements-accords-commerciaux/topics-domaines/disp-diff/lone.aspx?lang=eng.

12. Damian Carrington, "Fossil fuels subsidized by $10m a minute, says IMF," *The Guardian* (May

these rule-making institutions of the global economy continue on in the same dysfunctional direction with policies that exacerbate planetary warming.

Clearly, there are people within these institutions who understand the extent of the problem, factors that perpetuate it, and the threat of runaway climate change. Yet in the current global system, driven by institutional inertia and constrained by free-market ideology, there seems to be nothing they can do. Changing direction would require acknowledging that the whole experiment of organizing society around the market for the past thirty years has been a failure. And indeed, climate change does represent a profound failure of free-market capitalism.

Climate change also threatens to disrupt global capitalism. The US military is the primary enforcer of the global economy, securing access to oil, water, and other resources and keeping the global trading system running smoothly. But climate change is already bringing chaos and exacerbating conflicts all over the world.[13] Meanwhile, the US Defense Department and CIA are planning how to respond to advancing climate change. Their plans are not based on establishing justice or protecting creation, but rather on preserving access to diminishing resources, providing security from the many expected climate refugees, and intervening militarily in regional conflicts made worse by planetary warming and extreme weather events.[14] In other words, current policies will be strengthened and reinforced to preserve global dominance.

Another problem with unrestrained free-market capitalism is that it demands unlimited economic growth on a finite planet. In an article titled "Clean energy won't save us—only a new economic system can," Jason Hickel wrote:

> The root problem is the fact that our economic system demands ever-increasing levels of extraction, production and consumption. Our politicians tell us that we need to keep the global economy growing at more than 3% each year—the minimum necessary for large firms to make aggregate profits. That means every 20 years we need to double the size of the global economy—double the cars, double the fishing, double the mining,

18, 2015), https://www.theguardian.com/environment/2015/may/18/fossil-fuel-companies-getting-10m-a-minute-in-subsidies-says-imf.

13. Christian Parenti, *Tropic of Chaos: Climate Change and the New Geography of Violence* (New York: Perseus, 2011), 14–17.

14. Ibid.

double the McFlurries and double the iPads. And then double them again over the next 20 years from their already doubled state.[15]

If we are to be reasonable, we must be open to evidence, even if such evidence challenges our core beliefs or worldview. The question is, will we be able to halt the progression of climate change and create climate justice while also following the path of unregulated capitalism? Common sense says no. We cannot halt and reverse climate change without transforming or replacing the system that is perpetuating climate change.

Although climate change is an unintended consequence of industrial development propelled by advancing capitalism, the global economic system is still functioning quite well in fulfilling the wealth-generating purpose for which it is designed. It may appear that the system is being blindly propelled by anonymous forces and that there is nothing anyone can do to stop it. But as I wrote in *Shaking the Gates of Hell*: "The machine of the global economy is not simply out of control. It is not malfunctioning. It is functioning according to its own rules, and continually expanding those rules and making new ones. As William Greider points out, there is a 'manic logic' to global capitalism. The system is not just out of control. It is insane."[16]

Or, as a popular saying goes, "The system isn't broken. It's 'fixed.'"

However, the global economic system is rational and consistent with the principles upon which it is based. The problem is that the ideological foundation of this system is idolatrous, short-sighted, violent, and unjust. In our search for the deeper truths about the underlying conditions that perpetuate climate change, we need to critique the logic of free-market capitalism.

Market Fundamentalism

The underlying ideology that propels climate change is Market Fundamentalism, which professes faith in the market above all else. This dominant economic theory has been gaining ground since the Reagan Revolution of the 1980s. It is presented as logical and mathematical, as if it were a science, but it is not. Although proven wrong countless times, most notably in the United States by the 2008 economic collapse

---

15. Jason Hickel, "Clean energy won't save us—only a new economic system can," *The Guardian* U.S. ed. (July 15, 2016), https://www.theguardian.com/global-development-professionals-network/2016/jul/15/clean-energy-wont-save-us-economic-system-can?CMP=share_btn_tw.
16. Delgado, *Shaking the Gates of Hell*, 109.

and subsequent bank bailout, this economic belief system persists and continues to serve as the dominant secular religion of our time.

Market Fundamentalism does not recognize the intrinsic value of God's creation. Its view is purely utilitarian, based on turning plants, animals, land, and even water into commodities to be bought and sold. It reduces the value of everything to the economic bottom line. This ideology desacralizes life and creates a framework that allows creation, including human beings, to be exploited for financial gain.

Corporate profits, stock values, and economic growth continue to be the primary governmental measures of national well-being, despite growing poverty, inequity, deficits, trade imbalances, indebtedness, job loss, homelessness, and destruction of the environment, including planetary warming. Discontent, anxiety, and fear are also prevalent. All expenditures, whether they have positive or negative impacts on people or the earth, contribute to the Gross National Product (GNP). According to this logic, an old-growth forest is an *underperforming asset* that adds nothing to the GNP until it has been harvested and sold, while the cost of cleaning up an oil spill counts as positive because it adds to the GNP. This creates a distorted view and ignores alternative economic measurements that take account of economic, environmental, and social well-being.

Climate change, toxic pollution, habitat destruction, species loss, and other environmental damages are not reflected in the costs of doing business or in the prices we pay. Standard economic measurements ignore *externalities*, that is, the environmental and social costs that come about through the process of extracting resources and producing, packaging, transporting, and disposing of consumer goods. It would make sense to include these costs in the total calculations and prices of goods, but this is not done.

In addition to devaluing creation, Market Fundamentalism rationalizes policies and practices that lead to injustice. Standard economic calculations do not measure the value of sectors of society upon which the formal economy rests: unpaid household work, volunteer labor, government-supported infrastructure, the nonprofit sector, cultural resources, or the "services" provided by the natural world. Furthermore, the current market-based approach does not measure human need, but only supply and demand based on what people can afford to buy. Those with economic and political power manipulate the market, creating advantages for the wealthy and for large corporations at the expense of small businesses, working people, and the poor. When the values of unrestrained free-market capitalism dominate public policy, economic relationships take priority and the social fabric is torn apart. When the market is the primary measurement of value, those without money are left behind.

This is idolatry that places money at the pinnacle of values and relationships, and discounts human, social, and environmental needs. We need a public discussion of values that go beyond profit and self-interest, and an exploration and change of policies leading to a transformed economy and world.

Do the Math: The Movement to Divest from Fossil Fuels

To reasonably discuss what might constitute effective climate action, there is a simple mathematical formula that calculates what might make it possible to move away from the threshold of climate chaos. This math comes from economists and scientists, but was given widespread attention when Bill McKibben wrote an article called "Global Warming's Terrifying New Math."[17] These calculations became the foundation for a movement calling on churches, universities, and other institutions to take a moral stand against climate change by divesting from fossil fuels. The catchphrase of this movement is "It is wrong to profit from wrecking the planet."

To review: Average global temperatures have risen by 1 degree Celsius (1.8 degrees Fahrenheit) since the Industrial Revolution began. Scientists have warned and the nations of the world have agreed that global warming should be limited to 2 degrees Celsius (3.6 degrees Fahrenheit) to prevent runaway climate change.[18] Because the life-support systems of the planet are already being damaged faster than had been projected, many scientists say that even 2 degrees of warming will be disastrous.

The math itself is simple. If we use 2 degrees Celsius as an upper limit, we can set a *carbon budget* to calculate how much more carbon can be released into the atmosphere before we reach that point. Scientists have determined that number to be 565 gigatons (565 billion tons). Globally, we can burn fossil fuels releasing 565 gigatons of carbon, and

---

17. Bill McKibben, "Global Warming's Terrifying New Math," *Rolling Stone Magazine* (July 19, 2012), http://www.rollingstone.com/politics/news/global-warmings-terrifying-new-math-20120719.
18. Copenhagen Accord, article 9, Conference of the Parties, 15th session (December 18, 2009) United Nations Framework Convention on Climate Change, http://unfccc.int/resource/docs/2009/cop15/eng/l07.pdf.

no more, for there to be any likelihood of staying within the 2 degree limit we have set.

The problem is that known reserves of coal, oil, and gas amount to five times that much, or 2,795 gigatons. Most of those reserves are held by fossil-fuel corporations, which are planning to extract, sell, and burn them all. In fact, their stock values depend upon it. If laws to protect the climate are enacted, many of those reserves will become *stranded assets*. No wonder fossil-fuel companies fund projects to sow doubt about climate change!

It follows from these calculations that to stay within our carbon budget we must keep most coal, oil, and gas in the ground. Yet fossil-fuel companies continue searching for new reserves and building infrastructure for extreme forms of extraction to access oil from offshore oil drilling, bitumen from tar sands, coal from mountaintop removal, and natural gas from fracking. The math makes it clear. We cannot give fossil-fuel corporations free rein to mine and burn all their reserves and, by doing so, polluting communities, warming the planet, and causing massive harm. This is the foundation of the moral argument for churches to join other organizations in divesting from fossil fuels; it is morally wrong to invest in corporations whose products and business models cause massive suffering and destroy the ability of the earth to sustain life as we know it.

Divestment from fossil fuels may sound radical to those who believe that we should work to reduce greenhouse gas emissions gradually. Anjali Appaduri, an eloquent young climate justice activist, challenged that view when she spoke to gathered world leaders at the 2011 Climate Summit in Durban, South Africa. She said, "Real ambition [on climate change] is dismissed as radical, deemed not politically possible. . . . Long-term thinking is not radical. What's radical is to completely alter the planet's climate, to betray the future of my generation, and to condemn millions to death by climate change."[19]

Out of Denial, into Action

Cap and trade is a market-based approach to limiting carbon emissions that is known in international climate negotiations as *The Clean Development Mechanism*. This is the leading approach of climate negotiators.

19. Brendan DeMelle, "Youth Delegate Anjali Appadurai Speaks Truth to Power at Conclusion of COP17 in Durban," DESMOG: Clearing the PR Pollution That Clouds Climate Science (December 9, 2011), http://www.desmogblog.com/youth-delegate-anjali-appadurai-speaks-truth-power-conclusion-cop17-durban.

It involves the buying and selling of *carbon credits* to help companies (and countries) lower their aggregate greenhouse gas emissions.[20]

This mechanism was created by financial institutions, like Lehman Brothers, and is based on creating a carbon market so that investors can trade carbon credits, that is, permits that allow them to pollute. Permits are given (not sold) to big polluters, allowing these corporate polluters to release a certain amount of greenhouse gases into the atmosphere. The idea is to eventually reduce the number of permits; theoretically, they would become scarcer and more expensive, giving polluting companies the incentive to reduce their emissions. If a corporation wants to emit additional greenhouse gases, it can show that emissions are being reduced elsewhere in the company or the corporation can buy additional carbon credits (permits to pollute) on the open market. Carbon credits can come from projects that reduce greenhouse gas emissions—for instance, a forest preserve, recycling plant, or a solar development project.

But climate change will not be solved through the market mechanism of cap and trade. Carbon trading regimes are dominated by big corporations and are easily gamed. In Indonesia, companies that clear-cut mature forests are given carbon credits for planting palm oil plantations. Companies can easily claim carbon credits under false pretenses. If a polluting company claims that it plans to expand by 200 percent and only expands by 100 percent, it can claim carbon credits for that claim.

California, the state that I call home, has instituted a cap and trade system as one piece of its overall program to reduce emissions.[21] I live in the Sierra Nevada Mountain Range in a temperate forest severely threatened by climate change. It is also threatened by logging. The Sierra Pacific Corporation, the largest landowner in California, is in process of turning diverse forest ecosystems into tree plantations. Sierra Pacific's Timber Harvest Plans call them *even-aged forests* and describe how they create them. First, they clear-cut and bulldoze the intact forests, then treat the ground with herbicides to suppress native vegetation. Finally, they plant crops of single species, same-aged trees. Sierra Pacific receives carbon credits for these even-aged forests because the company claims that they will sequester more carbon over

---

20. "Training Seminars for Climate Mitigation Actions in the Caribbean," United Nations Framework Convention on Climate Change (UNFCCC), https://cdm.unfccc.int/press/newsroom/latestnews/releases/2016/0208_index.html.
21. "California Cap and Trade," Center for Climate and Energy Solutions, http://www.c2es.org/us-states-regions/key-legislation/california-cap-trade.

a period of eighty years than intact forests. Although this point is disputed, California's cap and trade mechanism gives Sierra Pacific carbon credits for this process. Clearcutting temperate forest ecosystems, killing the native plants with herbicides, and converting them into tree farms are supported by the dominant cultural worldview and by law.[22]

There are many other reasons that cap and trade is not a reasonable approach to solving the problem of climate change. First, there is no internationally agreed-upon cap, which is the basis for the whole idea. Second, carbon trading is subject to the fluctuations of the market, which can lead to times of boom or bust. Finally, cap and trade is a distraction from real solutions, such as strong laws, solid caps, and fees on carbon. It leads people to think that something effective is being done to address climate change. In a short, animated video called "The Story of Cap and Trade," narrator Annie Leonard says: "We can't solve the climate crisis with the mindset (their mindset) that got us into this mess. We need something new. It won't be easy, but it's time we dreamed bigger. It's time we designed a climate solution that will really work."[23]

Furthermore, it is irrational and many say futile to try to control greenhouse gas emissions *at the tailpipe*, as they are released into the atmosphere after fossil fuels have been burned. A much simpler and more effective approach to limiting emissions is to control them *at the tap*, by keeping most fossil-fuel reserves in the ground.[24]

Many reasonable, workable, and just policy responses to climate change have been proposed. Some are being enacted at the local and state level in various jurisdictions. But so far, the US government has not approached climate change as a crisis or instituted policies that will move the world toward climate justice.

Let's briefly consider what the federal government could do to keep fossil fuels in the ground and lessen the dangers of runaway climate change, if it were politically possible. The proposals that Bill McKibben made to the Democratic Platform Committee would have been a good start. A carbon tax or a fee on carbon would provide an incentive at every level of the economy to reduce the use of fossil fuels and invest in alternative sources of power. The *carbon fee and dividend* proposal supported by climate scientist James Hansen and the Citizens' Climate

22. "Forest clearcutters hop on cap and trade," Forests Forever, http://www.forestsforever.org/archives_resources/climate_crisis/Climate_Crises-Clearcutters_Hop_on_Cap_&_Trade.html.
23. Annie Leonard, "The Story of Cap and Trade," The Story of Stuff Project, http://storyofstuff.org/movies/story-of-cap-and-trade/.
24. Noelle Sedor, "Why fee and dividend is better than cap and trade at fighting climate change," *L.A. Times* (March 5, 2015).

Lobby would collect fees at the wellhead, mineshaft, or point of entry, then return the proceeds gathered in fees to the people to offset rising fuel costs.[25] Others suggest using some of the fees to offset fuel costs for poor and working people, and some to subsidize renewable sources of power.

A national ban on hydraulic fracturing (fracking) would prevent the widespread methane leaks that come through the extraction, storage, and transporting of natural gas. Such a ban would also protect water from being polluted with the chemicals injected into fracking wells and would prevent earthquakes from being triggered by the process.

Keeping fossil fuels in the ground on federal land could cut CO_2 emissions by one hundred million tons by 2030.[26] This would require the Interior Department to stop issuing or renewing leases that allow corporations to extract fossil fuels from federal waters and lands. Mandating that federal agencies weigh the climate impact of their decisions is reasonable and workable. Preventing fossil-fuel companies from taking private land by eminent domain is another policy that makes sense. But as of the writing of this book, none of the above decisions have been acceptable to either the Democrat or Republican Party.

There are other policies that the federal government could enact that would keep fossil fuels in the ground, reduce emissions, and set an example for other nations to follow. We could stop subsidizing fossil fuels and use the money saved to subsidize renewable technologies and public transportation systems. We could require coal, oil, and gas companies to comply with the Clean Air Act, Clean Water Act, and Safe Drinking Water Act. (They are currently exempt from these and several other environmental laws.[27]) We could end government subsidies to agribusiness corporations, which monopolize seeds, use fossil-fuel-intensive fertilizers and pesticides, and ship products around the world. Instead, we could subsidize small family farms that grow organic foods or practice permaculture, sequestering carbon in the soil while providing food to local communities. We could engage in good-

25. "The Basics of Carbon Fee and Dividend," Citizens Climate Lobby, http://citizensclimatelobby.org/basics-carbon-fee-dividend/.
26. Peter Erickson and Michael Lazarus, "How would phasing out U.S. federal leases for fossil fuel extraction affect CO2 emissions and 2°C goals?" Stockholm Environment Institute, (Seattle, May 2016), https://www.sei-international.org/mediamanager/documents/Publications/Climate/SEI-WP-2016-US-fossilfuel-leases-climate.pdf.
27. Renee Lewis Kosnik, Research Director, Oil and Gas Accountability Project, "The Oil and Gas Industry's Exclusions and Exemptions to Major Environmental Statutes," A joint project of Earthworks (Washington, DC) and Oil & Gas Accountability Project (Durango, CO), http://www.shalegas.energy.gov/resources/060211_earthworks_petroleumexemptions.pdf.

faith negotiations toward an international treaty with binding limits on greenhouse gas emissions and mechanisms for renewable technology transfers to developing nations. Finally, we could stop using the US military to gain and preserve access to foreign oil.

What stands in the way of instituting any of these measures on a large scale is systemic inertia and lack of political will. If powerful interests that benefit from the present system can control the narrative, define the options, and limit the possibilities, significant change is impossible. If well-intentioned people believe the dominant narrative and feel personally powerless (and thus off the hook), things continue in the same direction. But as we face the truth about climate change and its profound implications, faith provides the resources we need to find guidance, courage, and strength for whatever actions we are called to take.

Making Connections through Reason: Thinking outside the Box

When making connections through reason, education is a good place to start. As mentioned earlier, speakers, documentaries, or book studies provide an opportunity for congregations and communities to wrestle with issues related to climate change.

Email subscriptions, social media networks, and independent media such as *Democracy Now!*[28] offer information and perspectives not covered by the mainstream media, while keeping people informed and up to date about action opportunities. By connecting with the movement for climate justice, we show solidarity and make the movement stronger.

One strong action is to organize within our denominations to divest from fossil fuels. The *Go Fossil Free* campaign offers background material, resources, and up-to-date information on campaigns in churches, colleges and universities, foundations, and nonprofit organizations.[29] This growing movement is an effective way for faith communities that are concerned about the environment to practice what they preach about climate change.

Engaging in political advocacy by writing, calling, or visiting public officials registers public opinion on specific legislation. Demonstrations or sit-ins at their offices highlight the urgency of issues and

28. Democracy Now, Independent Global News, http://www.democracynow.org/.
29. "About Fossil Free," Fossil Free: Divest from Fossil Fuels, http://gofossilfree.org/about-fossil-free/.

add additional pressure on public figures to support compassionate, just, and climate-friendly policies. Getting people to think outside the box often requires creative, symbolic, and energetic nonviolent action. These methods of political action can expand possibilities and build momentum for systemic transformation. As moneyed interests dominate government and drown out the voices of the people, nonviolent direct action has become an even more important expression of democracy.

Whatever we do, it is important to keep in mind that we are not acting in isolation, but contributing to the larger movement for climate justice. We are doing our small part to awaken people to what is at stake and to point in the direction of hope.

Reason makes clear that building a strong movement to stabilize the climate means working in coalition with justice-oriented groups that have other priorities. By joining with pro-democracy organizations, we help to end corporate domination of government and build a people's democracy. Another natural ally is the peace movement. War is deadly for humans and all life, and the US military is one of the world's largest consumers of fossil fuels. It also makes sense to work with groups that oppose toxic trade deals like the TPP. Websites of specific groups are listed in the Suggested Reading List at the back of this book. Working together in a broad coalition of groups builds strength in solidarity and makes it possible to influence public policy in areas of trade, economics, racial justice, immigration reform, prison reform, war and peace, and climate justice. It also makes systemic change more likely.

The movement for climate justice, together with allies in the broader movement for global justice, embodies faith that "another world is possible." Together we seek to establish justice and build a global community in which all human lives, local communities, and the natural world are valued for themselves and not for how much wealth they deliver upwards. As we consider God's call to climate justice, we turn now to the experiences of people living and working on the front lines of climate change.

11

Experience: On the Front Lines of Climate Change

It was love that brought me to this jail cell.[1]

—Sandra Steingraber

When my granddaughter Nikayla was ten years old, climate change became real to her. She learned that glaciers and ice sheets are melting, endangering the habitats of polar bears and emperor penguins. She loves animals, as most children do, so she created a poster with pictures of hearts, the earth, and animals. The poster said:

> Save our earth! We all know our earth is at stake! We need to do something about it. Try not killing animals or grow a garden. We need our earth to live on. We need you to help save our earth. There are many endangered species of animals. Please save our animals. There is a Polar bear for instance and all of a sudden the ice melts under his feet and he sinks in. There is no land for thousands of miles so there is nothing to do. He just dies. We need to save our animals, too. Save our earth. Save our animals.

My granddaughter empathized with the penguins and polar bears, felt

---

1. Sandra Steingraber, "Letters from Chemung County Jail #2," *Marcellus Effect* (April 23, 2013), http://marcelluseffect.blogspot.com/2013/04/letters-from-chemung-county-jail.html.

grief when she thought about their suffering, and responded by making a poster. Her feelings motivated her to action. Her response brings to mind John Wesley's counsel to reflect on the suffering of animals to "soften and enlarge our hearts." The resulting empathy involves an experiential change: a change of attitude and an increase of love.

I referred earlier to studies showing that for people to be motivated to act on climate change, their knowledge and concern must move from the head to the heart. Those of us whose lives are still intact may not realize the grave implications of a warming world. Even if we understand climate change intellectually and accept the conclusions of climate scientists, we may not internalize the dangers if we experience relative stability in our day-to-day lives. This disconnection between our head and our heart may prevent us from responding in a way that is proportional to the dangers we face.

In this chapter, we focus on justice through the lens of experience. We have seen that scripture, tradition, and reason uphold the call for justice, but how can we internalize this knowledge so that it is confirmed at the level of our own experience? What will lift us out of denial, self-centeredness, despair, and paralysis, and motivate us to respond to the suffering of others by joining in the work for climate justice?

The answer is love. According to Michael Lodahl, "For Wesley the love of God is to be experienced, in some sense felt, deep within our beings. Wesley was not content with a purely intellectual faith, nor even with a simply volitional faith, but with a faith of conscious and experienced relation to God and neighbor."[2]

Wesley spoke of salvation as "deliverance from a blind, unfeeling heart, quite insensible of God and the things of God."[3] Religious faith is not simply a rational assent to a belief or doctrine, but as Wesley said, it is "no other than love, the love of God and of all mankind; the loving God with all our heart, and soul, and strength, as having first loved us . . ., as the fountain of all the good we have received, and of all we ever hope to enjoy; and the loving every soul which God hath made, every man on earth as our own soul. This love is the great medicine of life; the never failing remedy for all the evils of a disordered world; for all the miseries and vices of men."[4]

2. Michael Lodahl, *God of Nature and of Grace: Reading the World in a Wesleyan Way* (Nashville: Abingdon, 2003), 206.
3. John Wesley, Sermon 85, "On Working Out Our Own Salvation," ed. Albert C. Outler, *The Works of John Wesley* (Nashville: Abingdon, 1986), 3:204.
4. Wesley, Sermon 112, "On Laying the Foundation of the New Chapel," *Works,* 3:577.

This love is real in human experience. We have explored the experience of God as revealed through creation and the experience of assurance of God's forgiveness and love. In this chapter, we focus on the experience of God's love within us, moving us to compassion for others. Compassion motivates us to acts of mercy and justice that witness to God's love, embody hope, and positively influence the world. Love is the only foundation strong enough to carry us through the difficulties posed by climate change with courage, compassion, persistence, and hope.

This chapter summarizes a few stories of people who live and work on the front lines of the climate crisis. Listening to their stories may touch our hearts and bring home to us the human impacts of this global challenge. Some people may fear being swallowed up by pain, guilt, or the inability to cope if they open their hearts to the magnitude of suffering caused by climate change. Denial and suppression of such feelings may seem to be the only way to carry on with current responsibilities as a functional human being. But as we grow spiritually and mature in faith, our capacity for both joy and sorrow expand. As we become more fully alive and connected with others, we come to recognize the presence of love in the full range of human emotion. We move out of denial through faith and are carried by love. The climate crisis presents us with opportunities to demonstrate that love in a variety of ways, in solidarity with people on the front lines of the struggle for climate justice. As Joan Baez said, "Action is the antidote to despair."[5]

Working for Climate Justice

Our changing climate brings life-threatening challenges to people in the very regions of the world where churches and other charitable organizations seek to alleviate suffering. Many of these same people are at the forefront of struggles for climate justice and are seeking to defend both people and the earth. Their experiences carry a weight of authority as we seek to understand the effects and implications of climate change. As we hear of their experiences and consider their perspectives, we may find our hearts softened, our minds opened, and our lives transformed.

As mentioned in chapter 1, a massive typhoon devastated the Philippines in November 2013, just days before the COP 19 climate con-

---

5. Jone Johnson Lewis, "Joan Baez Quotes," About History: Women's History, http://womenshistory.about.com/od/joanbaez/a/joan_baez_quotes.htm.

ference in Warsaw. Typhoon Haiyan, known in the Philippines as "Yolanda," was one of the largest storms ever recorded, killing over six thousand and displacing over four million people.[6] Yeb Sano, the lead delegate from the Philippines who fasted throughout the climate talks in Warsaw, wept openly as he spoke passionately to the gathered delegates just days after the typhoon hit:

> If anyone continues to deny the reality that is climate change, I dare you to get off your ivory tower and away from the comfort of your armchair. I dare you to go to the islands of the Pacific, the islands of the Caribbean and the islands of the Indian ocean and see the impacts of rising sea levels; to the mountainous regions of the Himalayas and the Andes to see communities confronting glacial floods, to the Arctic where communities grapple with the fast dwindling polar ice caps, to the large deltas of the Mekong, the Ganges, the Amazon, and the Nile where lives and livelihoods are drowned, to the hills of Central America that confront similar monstrous hurricanes, to the vast savannas of Africa where climate change has likewise become a matter of life and death as food and water becomes scarce. . . . Not to forget the massive hurricanes in the Gulf of Mexico and the eastern seaboard of North America. And if that is not enough, you may want to pay a visit to the Philippines right now. . . . What my country is going through as a result of this extreme climate event is madness. The climate crisis is madness. We can stop this madness. Right here in Warsaw.[7]

Joy Hayag, a United Methodist Deaconess from the Philippines, spoke about her home country when I interviewed her at a climate justice training in May 2016. She said,

> There are so many problems in my country: pollution, a "Smokey Mountain" of garbage, extreme poverty. I also see climate change happening in my lifetime. . . . Every time I saw scenes of Yolanda on TV, my heart was broken. So many people died. It was crushing to see the people, especially the kids.[8]
>
> Recently a monsoon rain caused a big flood. Tall buildings were flooded and cars were floating. Kids who wanted to go home from school were stranded from morning until nighttime. This wasn't a big storm, just a

6. U.S. AID Fact Sheet on Typhoon Haiyan/Yolanda in The Philippines, U.S. Agency for International Development, http://iipdigital.usembassy.gov/st/english/texttrans/2013/11/20131112286248.html.

7. Tierney Smith, "Must watch: Philippines speech moves COP19 plenary to tears," *Tcktcktck* (November 11, 2013), the Global Call for Climate Action, http://tcktcktck.org/2013/11/cop19-philippines-speech-moves-plenary-tears/#sthash.quuri27n.dpuf.

8. Joy Hayag, in an interview by Sharon Delgado, May 6, 2016, St. Louis, MO.

constant rain. Even places that don't regularly flood were flooding. And the weird thing is that other provinces have droughts. The land is cracking—it's barren and dry. You can't plant anything. Everyone's thinking "there's something going on."[9]

Droughts, floods, and other weather-related disasters can lead to hunger, conflict, migration, and repression. In April 2016, the Spottswood United Methodist Mission Center in Mindanao became a sanctuary to 4,000 farmers and Indigenous people after security forces fired on a crowd demonstrating for food relief for those facing starvation from drought.[10] According to Ms. Hayag:

These people were just looking for rice, to feed them. The government is holding tons of rice. The military killed some of them, and they were so peaceful. They were asking for rice: "that's our rice, give us our rice, just rice, you can't give it?" Did they hurt anyone, did they kill anyone? They were just hungry. They were looking for food—rice, r-i-c-e. It's like in Syria, they left because they were looking for food. It's the revolution of the poor people, the revolution of the hungry people. This is what will happen if we don't have climate justice.[11]

Although a strong and binding international treaty has still not been signed, Yeb Sano continues to be a powerful force for climate justice. His "fast for the climate" has continued on in a different form with people fasting worldwide on the first day of each month as a way to raise awareness, reflect on, and internalize the reality of climate change.[12] In late 2015, Yeb and his brother, Philippine artist AG Sano, walked with other climate activists from Rome to Paris, where the COP 21 climate summit was being held. Their purpose was to highlight the urgency of the climate crisis, the suffering being experienced by poor and vulnerable nations, and the necessity for strong and binding action. As they prepared to set out on the 900-mile pilgrimage, Yeb Sano was received by Pope Francis in Rome. He wrote of his experience with the Pope:

The sun made his face glow and his smile was just so magical, imbued with deep sincerity and love. In the midst of the jostling around him, I presented to him a replica of his Encyclical, *Laudato Si'*, written in my own

9. Ibid.
10. Gladys Mangiduyos and Kathy L. Gilbert, "United Methodist church sheltering farmers in Philippines," *United Methodist News* (April 4, 2016), http://www.umc.org/news-and-media/united-methodist-church-sheltering-farmers-in-philippines.
11. Ibid.
12. "News and Updates," Fast for the Climate, http://fastfortheclimate.org/en/.

handwriting. He smiled and looked at it intently. Then he held my hand. His left hand held my right hand. His grip was firm and as he held my hand for a full minute—I was speechless.

I was going to tell him so many things about thanking him for his courage and leadership on the climate issue and that our group of pilgrims would be carrying the encyclical to Paris. But no words came out of my mouth. Instead, I reciprocated his grip on my hand and tears welled in my eyes. I had received his blessings, and this inspiration will carry us from Rome to Paris and for our whole lives.[13]

Also in 2015, led by the Philippines, twenty nations most vulnerable to climate change came together to form the V20 group, representing nations with the following features: low and middle income, least developed, arid, isthmus, landlocked, mountainous and small island developing countries from Africa, Asia, the Caribbean, Latin America, and the Pacific. Member nations include Afghanistan, Bangladesh, Barbados, Bhutan, Costa Rica, Ethiopia, Ghana, Kenya, Kiribati, Madagascar, Maldives, Nepal, Philippines, Rwanda, Saint Lucia, Tanzania, Timor-Leste, Tuvalu, Vanuatu, and Vietnam. World Bank Group President Jim Yong Kim affirmed this effort: "The world needs stronger voices from developing countries to draw more attention to their great needs for investment in fighting the impacts from climate change. This new group of 20 countries, led by the Philippines, will play an important role in pushing for greater investment in climate resiliency and low carbon growth at home and internationally."[14] Let us pray that this will be so.

Poor people and people of color within wealthy industrialized nations also suffer the impacts of climate change disproportionately. In 2005, Hurricane Katrina hit the U.S. Gulf Coast, resulting in over 2,000 deaths, the displacement of hundreds of thousands of people, and more than $100 billion in damage. The worst destruction occurred in New Orleans, a predominately African American city, where many people lived in poverty. There was widespread criticism of the Federal Emergency Management Agency (FEMA) for its flawed handling of rescue operations, as scenes of desperate survivors suffering for days without

---

13. Yeb Saño, "Face to Face with Pope Francis," The People's Pilgrimage (October 1, 2015), http://peoplespilgrimage.org/evoke/blog/face-to-face-with-Pope-francis/view?category=PeoplesPilgrimage#sthash.YAC85nkg.klHWH567.dpuf.

14. "'Vulnerable Twenty' Ministers Call for More Action and Investment in Climate Resiliency and Low-Emissions Development," World Bank (October 8, 2015), http://www.worldbank.org/en/news/feature/2015/10/08/vulnerable-twenty-ministers-more-action-investment-climate-resilience-low-emissions-development.

aid shocked people around the world.[15] Eleven years later, in 2016, historic floods devastated Baton Rouge, a majority African American city just eighty miles from New Orleans.

In 2012, Hurricane Sandy made its calamitous landfall on the East Coast. The superstorm impacted more than a dozen states, killed 159 people, damaged or destroyed 650,000 homes, and caused $65 billion in damage.[16] Those who fared worst were people living in low-lying coastal areas, predominately in poor neighborhoods of color. They experienced the greatest damage and waited the longest for services to be restored. In the Rockaway neighborhood of Queens, activists from the recently evicted Occupy Wall Street encampment organized to provide relief, even going door to door to identify people who might need care.[17]

Yotam Maram, who lived through Hurricane Sandy in his hometown of Hoboken, New Jersey, joined with other Occupy Sandy volunteers to help organize and provide relief to the hardest-hit areas of New York. In an article entitled "Occupy Sandy: From Relief to Resistance," he wrote of the importance of local actions:

> Welcome to the climate crisis. There's nothing abstract about it. It isn't some apocalypse decades away or an event that comes down like one big hurricane to wipe us all out. It's Hurricane Sandy. It's all the economic, political and social conditions that were already in place. And it's the opportunity for forces of profit and repression to push their agenda forward in the aftermath.
>
> But guess what: The climate justice movement isn't so abstract either. This is it. It's dedicated organizers recognizing how their work can be aligned across issues. It's relief providers and hard-working volunteers transforming into activists and community leaders. It's the hardest hit neighborhoods taking control of their own liberation. It's local community institutions with deep roots and long histories connecting to one another and mobilizing their efforts as part of a movement. It's all of that alongside so many other fights for climate justice—from the blockade of the Keystone XL pipeline to the fight for water rights in Bolivia, from Indian women standing up to corporate seed monopolies to youth from 350.org launching campaigns to divest from fossil fuel companies.
>
> There is much work to do. But people are doing it—day by day, block by block. Windows of opportunity have opened here in New York, just as

---

15. Mike M. Ahlers, "Report: Criticism of FEMA's Katrina response deserved," *CNN* (April 14, 2006).
16. Doyle Rice and Alia E. Dastagir, "One year after Sandy, 9 devastating facts," *USA TODAY* (October 29, 2013).
17. Alan Feuer, "Occupy Sandy: A Movement Moves to Relief," *New York Times* (November 12, 2012), http://wagingnonviolence.org/feature/occupy-sandy-from-relief-to-resistance/#more-19879.

they have in other places around the world. Many people are working to keep those windows open and continue the transformation that is already underway—from volunteer work to organizing, from emergency response to a genuine recovery, from relief to resistance.[18]

Clearly, compassion requires us to provide relief to those who suffer first and worst from climate disasters, but also to act in solidarity with them by working for climate justice and for systemic transformation. We need to move from volunteer work to organizing, from emergency response to a genuine recovery, from relief to resistance.

Women and Their Dependent Children

Wherever climatic changes or extreme weather make life harder, women and their dependent children are disproportionately impacted. Women are on the front lines of coping with the impacts of climate change because of their economic status and because of the particular roles they play in society. In poor nations on every continent, women are the primary caretakers of food, water, and fuel for their families and communities. They lose the ability to fulfill these roles as lakes and rivers evaporate, soils dry up, and food becomes scarce.[19] Women and children also face increased risk in other forms of disaster, including extreme weather events that are more likely with global warming.

In some areas women are excluded from official decision-making. Nevertheless, they are often at the forefront of struggles for climate justice. The roles of women as subsistence farmers, caregivers, providers, and community workers place them in positions to manage risk, foresee problems, create alternative adaptation strategies, and organize to promote solutions and demand government action.[20]

A Bolivian farmer named Rosario helps lead a community-based company that produces native cacao, reforests native tree species, and sustainably harvests woods and fruits. Extreme floods have recently devastated the area. She said, "I feel sad because although we didn't really contribute to climate change, we are the ones suffering. . . ." Her call is for people to work together for climate justice: "I speak as a farmer, but we all need to get together to pressure the people in power.

18. Ibid.
19. "Women at the Forefront," *Climate Change Connections*, a project of the United Nations Population Fund (UNPF) and Women's Environment and Development Organization (WEDO), http://www.unfpa.org/sites/default/files/pub-pdf/climateconnections_1_overview.pdf.
20. "Women and Climate Change," Church World Service publication, http://hunger.cwsglobal.org/site/DocServer/CWS_Enough2.pdf?docID=1521.

. . . If you want something, you can get it—it's just about the power inside you to go and do things. So my message to people would be 'let's get organized, let's get together, let's talk and move forward towards the same point.'"[21]

Amina Mohammed, from Nigeria, is a special adviser to United Nations Secretary-General Ban Ki-Moon on post-2015 development planning. She said, "In Africa, you don't just think about the children that you bear. Every child is yours." She said that climate change has exacerbated poverty and set the stage for violence in Nigeria: "It has come together as the perfect storm to create situations that have fueled Boko Haram, the terrorists that live in my part of the country." But Ms. Mohammed refuses to give up hope, saying, "I think we're getting nearer the light at the end of the tunnel."[22]

Kathy Jetnil-Kijiner is a poet and climate activist from the Marshall Islands, which has been hit with severe coastal erosion, sea-level rise, storm surges, and drought. Aid agencies respond by bringing emergency food and water, but future prospects for the Pacific island nation are grim. "It's hard to confront the fear that your island could be gone permanently and that your people would be wandering," said Jetnil-Kijiner. "There are people who will say, 'It's done. It's a done deal. There's no way you can turn it back. The islands are basically gone.' And then there are those who say, 'It's not done. There's still hope. You can still fight for it.' I'm just going to go with hope. At some point you've got to choose which story you want to believe in."[23] In 2014, during the opening ceremony of the international climate conference in Lima (COP 20), Jetnil-Kijiner brought participants to tears when she read "Dear Matafele Peinem," a poem dedicated to her baby daughter. A dramatic video version of the poem is available online.[24]

Women are coming together, locally, regionally, and across continents to form networks of education and action. The Women's Environment and Development Organization (WEDO)[25] and the Women's Earth and Climate Action Network (WECAN International) work with women around the world, especially in developing nations, to take

21. Alison Woodhead, "Celebrating female climate change fighters," OXFAM International, https://blogs.oxfam.org/en/blogs/15-03-08-celebrating-female-climate-change-fighters.
22. Cameron Russell, "Climate Warriors," no. 12, Amina Mohammed, *Vogue* (November 30, 2015), http://www.vogue.com/projects/13373340/climate-change-summit-women-cop21-warriors-global-warming.
23. Ibid., no. 6, Kathy Jetnil-Kiliner.
24. Kathy Jetnil-Kiliner, "Dear Matafele Peinem," Creative Resistance, http://www.creativeresistance.org/dear-matafele-peinem/.
25. Women's Environment and Development Organization (WEDO), http://wedo.org/.

actions to mitigate, adapt to, and resolve challenges of climate change. WECAN's declaration states: "We are committed to a transition from a future of peril to a future of promise, to rally the women around the world to join together in action at all levels until the climate crisis is solved."[26]

Extreme Extraction and Sacrifice Zones

Climate activists continue to pressure governments to take strong climate action since there is no substitute for an international agreement. As demands for climate justice at the international level intensify, many people are also acting outside official channels, often by supporting regional struggles.

Some of the most ardent climate justice advocates live in or near areas that are being exploited by fossil-fuel companies in their search for corporate profits. Throughout the fossil-fuel era, extraction, transport, and refining operations have polluted poor communities and countries, harmed vulnerable ecosystems, and endangered the health of people who live and work there. These sacrifices zones have been largely hidden from the view of those who are privileged enough to afford the benefits of a lifestyle based on abundant access to fossil fuels, but now that is changing. As conventional extraction methods yield less fuel, advanced technologies make possible extreme extraction techniques such as mountaintop-removal coal mining, offshore oil drilling, tar sands mining, and hydraulic fracturing ("fracking") of underground shale to extract oil and natural gas. Scenes of devastation caused by these unconventional fuels sear the conscience and create grief, concern, and outrage among people who love the earth. With globalized news and the Internet, sacrifice zones are harder to hide as these operations expand and as activists use social media to expand and coordinate resistance actions.

Around the world, climate activists are making common cause with those who have always been on the front lines of the fossil-fuel economy—people living in sacrifice zones, where the land, air, and water are polluted by the extraction, transportation, processing, and storage of coal, oil, and gas, and where natural systems that sequester carbon are being destroyed. From oil operations in Nigeria to forest clearcutting projects in the Amazon, from mountaintop removal sites in

---

26. Women's Earth and Climate Action Network, International (WECAN), http://wecaninternational.org/.

Appalachia to fracking sites in California, from coal-fired power plants in Europe to crude oil pipelines in the United States, from Palm Oil plantations in Thailand to tar sands extraction mines on Indigenous lands in Canada, and in communities around the world, people are engaging in local struggles to stop economic exploitation, environmental pollution, and global warming caused by corporate profiteers. These local struggles have come to be known as *Blockadia,* a term used to represent a dispersed, diverse, and shifting community of people who engage in blockades and other nonviolent resistance actions.

In *This Changes Everything,* Naomi Klein describes several Blockadia actions. She quotes Alexis Bonogofsky, who is working with others in southeastern Montana to protect the region from mining companies like Arch Coal: "That connection to this place and the love that people have for it, that's what Arch Coal doesn't get. It's not the hatred of the coal companies, or anger, but love will save that place."[27] Klein writes of the power of this love based on connection to a particular place:

> The power of this ferocious love is what the resource companies and their advocates in government inevitably underestimate. . . . And though this kind of connection to place is surely strongest in Indigenous communities where the ties to the land go back thousands of years, it is in fact Blockadia's defining feature.[28]

Recent Blockadia actions include blockades of tracks along the routes of trains carrying highly explosive crude oil, hundreds of *kayactivists* paddling out in kayaks to block a gigantic Shell Oil icebreaker headed for the Arctic, demonstrations at refineries to prevent their expansion, direct interference at tar sands extraction sites, disruption of oil pipeline construction, and countless other creative nonviolent actions. These organized actions are a direct response to lack of regulation, lack of transparency, and lack of democratic input into government decisions that affect both people and the earth. Such nonviolent actions help draw attention to the local and global dangers of ever-increasing exploitation of fossil fuels.

What ties these local struggles together with the global movement for climate justice is the realization that fossil fuels are damaging, especially for poor and vulnerable people during the process of extraction, as they are transported, when they are burned, in their disposal, and at

---

27. Naomi Klein, *This Changes Everything: Capitalism vs. the Climate* (New York: Simon & Schuster, 2014), 343.
28. Ibid., 342.

every stage in between. There is widespread agreement among climate justice activists that in order to stay within the earth's carbon budget and avoid climate chaos we need to keep the majority of fossil fuels in the ground.

Sacrifice zones are no longer hidden. As extreme forms of extraction expand and dangerous forms of transport and storage become more common, the risks are becoming obvious for all to see. In 2015, a massive methane leak from a natural gas storage site near Porter Ranch, an affluent suburb of Los Angeles, made thousands sick, caused over 2,000 families to be relocated, and contributed more to global warming than the BP Deep Horizon Oil Spill of 2010.[29] Such disasters make clear that we all live on the front lines of climate change.

The Rights of Indigenous Peoples and the Rights of the Earth

Indigenous communities are at the forefront of struggles to prevent extreme forms of extraction of fossil fuels that produce climate change. The historic assault on Indigenous lands continues today in countries around the world, often through the violation of treaty rights and the exploitation of native lands by extractive industries. Large corporations have repeatedly violated treaty rights by extracting resources and polluting traditional lands that have sustained Indigenous peoples for millennia.[30]

In 2012, the Canadian government passed legislation that violated treaty rights and removed environmental protections on lands upon which Indigenous communities depend.[31] This legislation gave more power to mining, logging, fishing, and oil companies, which were already extracting resources and polluting Canadian lands and waters. Of major concern was the tar sands industry, which destroys forests and creates vast wastelands to extract a tar-like fuel called *bitumen*, to send via pipelines to refineries in the United States for export to the global market.

In response to this legislation, Attawapiskat Chief Theresa Spence began a hunger strike calling on the Canadian government to honor First Nations' treaty rights and to protect the lands and water from cor-

---

29. Nathaniel Rich, "The Invisible Catastrophe," *New York Times* (March 31, 2016).
30. Clayton Thomas-Muller, "Energy Exploitation on Sacred Native Lands," *Race, Poverty, and the Environment (RP&E), A Journal of Social and Environmental Justice* (Winter 2005), Reimagine, http://reimaginerpe.org/node/307.
31. Terry Pedwell, "Idle No More vs. Bill C-45: First Nations Leaders Launch National Protest in Ottawa as Movement Grows," *The Canadian Press* (December 21, 2012).

porate exploitation. "I am willing to die for my people because the pain is too much and it's time for the government to realize what it's doing to us," she said. "I am not afraid to die. If that's the journey for me to go, then I will go."[32]

Chief Spence's fast gave impetus to the Idle No More Movement, which links the rights of Indigenous people with the rights of Mother Earth. The movement has now become global in scope, with Indigenous people rising up around the world to resist the exploitation of their lands by extreme forms of fossil-fuel extraction, the construction of oil and gas pipelines, deforestation, pollution, and the development of harmful infrastructure systems that pollute the land, air, and water. Climate activists have joined them in solidarity on the front lines of local resistance actions, recognizing that Indigenous leadership and teachings about protecting the earth are essential for transitioning to a life-enhancing way of being in the world. Even when stopping climate change is not the primary purpose of such actions, they express resistance to the unbridled use of fossil fuels.

As mentioned in chapter 1, in 2016 thousands of people, including members of over 300 Indigenous tribes, traveled to join the Standing Rock Sioux "water protectors" in their camp in North Dakota. The tribe welcomed allies and engaged in peaceful and prayerful actions of resistance to the construction of the Dakota Access Pipeline, which if completed would transport crude oil under the Missouri River near the Standing Rock reservation, endangering their water supply as well as the waters downstream. Leaders from many different religious groups issued statements in support of the Standing Rock Sioux. The United Nations issued a statement calling on the United States to ensure their right to participate in decision-making about the pipeline, since its construction would negatively impact their rights, lives, and land.[33] Hundreds were arrested in nonviolent actions. People around the country and world sent money, transported supplies, and engaged in solidarity demonstrations. The Standing Rock rallying cry was "Mni Wiconi," meaning "Water is Life."

In early November 2016, five hundred clergy gathered at Standing Rock to engage in acts of repentance and reconciliation. They publicly

32. Terry Pedwell, "'Idle No More': Hunger-striking Attawapiskat chief vows to 'die' for her people as aboriginal protests spread," *The Canadian Press* (December 11, 2012).
33. "Statement from the Chair and PFII Members Dalee Dorough and Chief Edward John on the Protests on the Dakota Access Pipeline" (August 31, 2016), Division for Social Policy and Development, Indigenous Peoples, United Nations, https://www.un.org/development/desa/indigenous-peoples/news/2016/08/statement-on-protests/.

repudiated the Doctrine of Discovery, and then gave a copy of the doctrine to tribal elders, who burned it. They also memorialized and lamented the execution of thirty-eight Dakota Sioux men who were hanged by the U.S. government in 1862 after an uprising. As the condemned men stood upon the gallows awaiting death, many of them sang a hymn: "Wakantanka" or "Many and Great" (currently Hymn 148 in the United Methodist Hymnal). As an act of repentance, the clergy at Standing Rock sang that same hymn, both in English and in the Dakota language. They told law enforcement officials, "You're standing on Dakota land." Several were arrested and spent time in jail. This gathering of clergy at Standing Rock demonstrated repentance for past harms, the desire for reconciliation, and a commitment to Indigenous rights and care for the earth.

Just days later, on Election Day, I arrived at Standing Rock with eight friends. The tribe had asked for people to come who were trained in nonviolent action, so we responded to their call.

We watched the election results come in that night at a nearby casino, and woke up in the morning to the specter of a Trump presidency. It was a good day to be with friends, engaged in positive action for change.

We spent the next few days getting oriented at the camp. We attended the newcomer orientation and daily community briefings, media trainings, legal trainings, and nonviolence trainings. We were reminded again and again that we were guests, that we needed to follow the guidance of the elders, and that we were part of a peaceful gathering based in prayer. We contributed as we could—working in the kitchens, painting signs and banners, washing dishes, filling potholes, stacking wood. We sat at the sacred fire.

One day a contingent of Indigenous Canadian women processed into camp. The women, representing every tribe in Canada, carried a large banner that had symbols of species from their different regions. They sang songs and gave gifts of support to the Standing Rock Sioux. Each woman spoke of the struggles of the people in her region to protect the land, air, water, and the species upon which they depend for life. We then had the privilege of walking through the welcome line, shaking hands, giving hugs, and exchanging words of greeting and appreciation.

Finally, on the day before we were scheduled to go home, we were invited to participate in a nonviolent resistance action. I was arrested for blocking a road near the pipeline construction site with over thirty others, including several other members of the clergy. I spent four days in Bismarck County Jail.[34] Our trials have been delayed. Mine is now scheduled for December 2018.

Regardless of the outcome of the struggle, Standing Rock has become a symbol of Indigenous resistance to the degradation of creation for the sake of profit. It is also a model that will be replicated as people seek to protect the rights of Native peoples and the gifts of creation in this critical time. Standing Rock represents the much larger struggle of bringing peace, justice, and healing to the earth. It demonstrates that when people come together in peace and in prayer, there is hope that creation may be protected and justice may prevail against the principalities and powers of this and any age.

Intergenerational Justice and Justice for All Creation

One emphasis of climate justice is *intergenerational justice*, that is, justice for children, young people, and future generations. In my own experience as a grandmother, retired pastor, and Sunday school teacher, concerns for the children are paramount—the children of today and the children of tomorrow. If climate change continues to accelerate they will face the ongoing degradation of creation and diminishing prospects for the future.

Diana Davis, a climate justice leader for United Methodist Women and a preschool teacher in Chicago, is greatly concerned about the children there: "They have so many health issues: asthma, allergies, rodents, families that can't afford medication. I'm concerned about poor nutrition and how it affects comprehension and development. We've had unseasonably warm weather; that affects the quality and costs of food. We're already dealing with food deserts. With climate change that will only get worse." Ms. Davis adds a note of hope and speaks of her motivation for action: "I'm concerned about when these children grow up, but through education, advocacy, and community there is hope. I feel that it is my responsibility to reflect the image of God that encompasses all that I've been given, especially to the children."

Scientist Sandra Steinbgraber, author of *Living Downstream*, was a passionate force behind the successful campaign to establish a moratorium on fracking in the state of New York. While spending a night in

---

34. To read about my experiences at Standing Rock, go to my blog at https://sharondelgado.org/category/standing-rock/.

jail for engaging in nonviolent direct action to protest a fracking operation near her home, she wrote an open letter explaining why she had been willing to risk arrest for this cause. After explaining the details of the situation, she wrote of her grief, determination, and motivation for taking action:

> Seven years ago, when my son was four years old, he asked to be a polar bear for Halloween, and so I went to work sewing him a costume from a chenille bedspread. It was with the knowledge that the costume would almost certainly outlast the species. Out on the street that night—holding a plastic pumpkin with KitKat bars—I saw many species heading towards extinction; children dressed as frogs, bees, monarch butterflies, and the icon of Halloween itself—the little brown bat.
>
> The kinship that children feel for animals and their ongoing disappearance from us literally brought me to my knees that night, on a sidewalk in my own village. It was love that got me back up. It was love that brought me to this jail cell.
>
> My children need a world with pollinators and plankton stocks and a stable climate. They need lake shores that do not have explosive hydrocarbon gases buried underneath. The fossil fuel party must come to an end. I am shouting at an iron door. Can you hear me now?[35]

Many young people today are aware that they face a very hard future because of the impacts of climate change. If greenhouse gas emissions continue unabated, they will face almost unimaginable challenges. Even school children face the grief of knowing that the world is being diminished day by day. It should be no surprise, then, that young people are among the most ardent warriors for climate justice. They are demanding that state, national, and world leaders take action for the preservation of other species and the living systems of the earth as their rightful inheritance and birthright.

In a passionate speech that transfixed delegates of the COP 17 climate summit in Durban, South Africa in 2011, a young woman named Anjali Appadurai, mentioned earlier, said:

> I speak for more than half the world's population. We are the silent majority. You've given us a seat in this hall, but our interests are not on the table. What does it take to get a stake in this game? Lobbyists? Corporate influence? Money? You have been negotiating all of my life. In that time, you've failed to meet pledges, you've missed targets, and you've broken

---

35. Sandra Steingraber, "Letters from Chemung County Jail #2," *Marcellus Effect* (April 23, 2013), http://marcelluseffect.blogspot.com/2013/04/letters-from-chemung-county-jail.html.

promises. . . . So, distinguished delegates and governments of the developed world: deep cuts now. Get it done.[36]

After rousing applause, most of the delegates took their seats, while fifty young people remained standing. Ms. Appadurai stepped away from the podium, dropped the pages of her speech, and used the "people's mic," a way to communicate with large crowds popularized by Occupy Wall Street. She shouted: "Mic check." The young people in the audience called back: "Mic check." As she called out each phrase, they echoed her words: "Equity now. You've run out of excuses. And we're running out of time. Get it done. *Get it done.* Get it done. *Get it done.*"[37]

College students are at the forefront of the movement to get colleges, universities, and other institutions to divest from corporations that produce coal, oil, and gas. To date, several trillion dollars have been divested from the investment portfolios of colleges, seminaries, faith communities, foundations, businesses, pension funds, cities, and counties. Young people are taking the lead in many areas of community organizing, planning mass demonstrations, engaging in dramatic actions for climate justice, and employing a variety of creative nonviolent tactics to make clear that they demand strong action to safeguard their future from the worst effects of climate change.

In 2008, Tim DeChristopher, then in his twenties, engaged in an act of civil resistance by bidding on several publicly owned parcels of pristine Utah lands that were being auctioned off to be leased to oil and gas companies. As the result of his courageous action, the auction was later ruled illegal and the land was spared. Those responsible for the illegal auction were not prosecuted, but DeChristopher served twenty months in federal prison. After he was released, he entered seminary and founded Peaceful Uprising, an organization dedicated to creative nonviolent direct action for climate justice. At his sentencing hearing, DeChristopher spoke about hope, patriotism, love, and personal choice. He said:

This is not going away. At this point of unimaginable threats on the horizon, this is what hope looks like. In these times of a morally bankrupt government that has sold out its principles, this is what patriotism looks like.

---

36. Brendan DeMelle, "Youth Delegate Anjali Appadurai Speaks Truth to Power at Conclusion of COP17 in Durban," *DESMOG* (December 9, 2011), http://www.desmogblog.com/youth-delegate-anjali-appadurai-speaks-truth-power-conclusion-cop17-durban.
37. Ibid.

With countless lives on the line, this is what love looks like, and it will only grow. The choice you are making today is what side are you on.[38]

A Movement That Is Strong and Growing

These stories make clear that there is a global movement for climate justice that is strong and growing. Around the world, small, local, human-scaled groups are joining together for education and action on these issues. In turn, these groups are forming coalitions across demographics and across borders and are taking coordinated actions that both demand and demonstrate hope for systemic transformation.

Thousands of autonomous groups on every continent organize coordinated climate actions with the help of 350.org and other groups to demonstrate global solidarity and to raise awareness about the urgency of the climate crisis. On September 21, 2014, over 400,000 people demonstrated in New York City in the historic People's Climate March, including youth leaders, members of faith communities, Indigenous groups, women's organizations, labor unions, environmental activists, and human rights groups.[39] It was the largest of over 2,500 demonstrations taking place that day in 162 countries, showing the coordination, power, and determination of the climate justice movement.[40] In May 2016, tens of thousands of people participated in coordinated nonviolent actions for climate justice on six continents. The actions focused on keeping coal, oil, and gas in the ground and on creating a just transition to a 100 percent renewable economy. They organized around the theme "Break Free from Fossil Fuels."[41]

Another example of coordinated action was the extended campaign against the proposed Keystone XL Pipeline, which would have carried bitumen, a heavy form of petroleum, from tar sands in Canada through the United States to the Gulf of Mexico for export around the world.[42] Idle No More, Peaceful Uprising, Tar Sands Blockade, 350.org, and many other climate activists, environmental organizations, and Indige-

---

38. Jake Hanson, "Tim's official statement at his sentencing hearing," Peaceful Uprising (July 26, 2011), http://www.peacefuluprising.org/tims-official-statement-at-his-sentencing-hearing-2011 0726.

39. Daquel Harris, "Marching in the Light of God," United Methodist Women (September 23, 2014), http://www.unitedmethodistwomen.org/news/marching-in-the-light-of-god.

40. "People's Climate March Wrap Up," on the 350.org website: http://2014.peoplesclimate.org/wrap-up/.

41. "May 3–15, On Six Continents, Thousands of People Took Bold Action to Break Free from Fossil Fuels," Break Free 2016, https://breakfree2016.org/.

42. Keystone XL Pipeline, Friends of the Earth, http://www.foe.org/projects/climate-and-energy/tar-sands/keystone-xl-pipeline.

nous rights groups coordinated actions to prevent this pipeline from being built. Thousands of people trained in nonviolent direct action and signed a "pledge of resistance," promising to engage in nonviolent resistance actions if the pipeline was approved. The Sierra Club, for the first time in its history, called on its members to take nonviolent direct action to prevent its construction.[43] Finally, after coordinated and widespread public opposition and action, the State Department under the Obama Administration halted construction on the pipeline. Around the country, people concerned about climate change celebrated this victory.

However, immediately after taking office as president, Donald Trump moved to reverse this decision, along with the Obama Administration's decision in late 2016 to halt construction on the Dakota Access Pipeline. One of Trump's first actions as president was to sign executive orders attempting to revive and expedite the construction of both pipelines.[44] These and similar struggles are ongoing. This reversal of policy highlights the problem of "winner-take-all politics"[45] that comes from the corruption of democracy by money, including money organized in the form of corporations.

Climate justice activists understand that an effective response to climate change includes working to change the overarching system that perpetuates climate change and many other interrelated problems. The climate justice movement is one part of a larger movement for social change that encompasses struggles for participatory democracy, fair trade, human rights, racial and economic justice, prison reform, immigration reform, just international relations, and peace. This broad coalition of organized networks that support each other as allies and coordinate actions is a direct challenge to the dominant system, which is based on unrestrained free-market capitalism, ruled by trade agreements that promote corporate interests, and enforced by police and military power. Changing the system that perpetuates multiple forms of injustice requires the building of a global justice movement strong enough to pressure those at the apex of political and economic power. This growing movement is gaining momentum and bringing hope

43. "Sierra Club, Allies, Engage in Historic Act Civil Disobedience to Stop Keystone XL," Sierra Club (February 13, 2013), http://content.sierraclub.org/press-releases/2013/02/sierra-club-allies-engage-historic-act-civil-disobedience-stop-keystone-xl.

44. Steven Musfson and Juliet Eilperin, "Trump Seeks to Revive Dakota Access, Keystone XL Pipelines," Washington Post, January 24, 2017.

45. Jacob S. Hacker and Paul Pierson, Winner-Take-All Politics: How Washington Made the Rich Richer—And Turned Its Back on the Middle Class (New York: Simon & Schuster, 2010.

for transformation. In this time of dangerous planetary warming, God's grace is at work, raising people up to bring healing to creation and climate justice to our world.

In *What We're Fighting for Now Is Each Other: Dispatches from the Front Lines of Climate Justice*, Wen Stephenson presents an overview of the US climate justice movement that includes stories of climate activists, along with interviews that shed light on their motivations for action. The book is a call to action, solidarity, and love. He writes:

> . . . if there is to be any hope of such solidarity, then "climate justice" will need to be defined broadly enough, inclusively enough, to encompass everyone. . . . Because what we are fighting for now is each other. We have to fight for the person sitting next to us and the person living next door to us, for the person across town and across the tracks from us, and for the person across the continent and across the ocean from us. Because we're fighting for our humanity. That's what solidarity is. That's what love looks like.

For those of us who are searching for a faith response to climate change, the motivation for action is love—love of God and our neighbors near and far, human and nonhuman, present and future. . . . Love takes us out of ourselves and motivates us to take courageous actions to establish justice in the world.

Experiences That Transform: Love in Action

What actions will we take? Churches contribute to struggles for climate justice by offering institutional resources, spiritual support, practical assistance and advocacy, actions of solidarity, and a theological perspective that upholds the values of honoring creation and establishing justice.

Joining the *Fast for the Climate* is a way to enter into solidarity with others who care. Fasting on the first day of the month with people around the world sensitizes us and establishes our mutual connection and commitment to working for a just resolution to climate change.[46] This can be a full or partial fast.

Volunteering for short-term mission work with people whose homes and lives have been devastated by floods, hurricanes, and other extreme weather events is an expression of compassion and solidarity. Hands-on assistance expresses mercy in the name of Christ, comforts

---

46. "News and Updates," Fast for the Climate, http://fastfortheclimate.org/en/.

victims, and brings the impacts of climate change to life for those who engage in such ministries. Likewise, visiting sacrifice zones and participating in actions with those whose communities are being threatened or polluted demonstrates solidarity and hope.

Listening to activists who are engaging in strong, courageous, nonviolent climate action brings to mind the obvious question: What would it take for the rest of us to move beyond safe ministries of creation care and acts of mercy and take a strong and courageous stand for justice on the front lines of climate change? Bill McKibben said,

> You're not a member of the Resistance just because you drive a Prius. You don't need to go to jail but you do need to do more than change your light bulbs. You need to try to change the system that is raising the temperature, the sea level, the extinction rate—even raising the question of how well civilization will survive this century.[47]

Short of risking arrest, there are many forms of creative nonviolent actions, including speeches, petitions, strikes, rallies, marches, picketing, street theater, boycotts, teach-ins, singing, religious processions, mock funerals, and many others. The late Gene Sharp, founder of the Albert Einstein Institute, wrote extensively on various forms of nonviolent struggle. His list of "198 Methods of Nonviolent Action" can be found online.[48]

It is true that "you don't need to go to jail," and circumstances prevent some people from risking arrest. But readers who are able may choose to consider under what circumstances that risk might be acceptable. Although controversial when undertaken, organized nonviolent resistance actions, including civil disobedience, have a long and successful history of adding impetus to social movements and helping to bring about social change.

On May 25, 2016, sixteen clergy from different faith traditions came together in West Roxbury, Massachusetts to pray, speak out, sing sacred songs, and take action by putting their bodies in the way of the construction of a controversial natural gas pipeline. Their joint statement said: "As global temperatures rise, and the world's poorest citizens are being affected, we stand together to demand that our federal, state and local government stop investing in the fossil fuel industry. . . . While civil disobedience is not a common method for any of us, we are

---

47. Bill McKibben, "The Fossil Fuel Resistance," *Rolling Stone Magazine* (April 11, 2013).
48. Gene Sharp, "198 Methods of Nonviolent Action," Albert Einstein Institution, http://www.aeinstein.org/nonviolentaction/198-methods-of-nonviolent-action/.

called by our faith and positions of leadership to take bold, visionary action. . . . The tide is rising and so are we."[49]

Ian Mevorach, minister and co-founder of Common Street Spiritual Center in Natick, Massachusetts, wrote an article describing his experience as a participant in the protest and challenging others to join in resistance actions for climate justice. He said:

> This was my first time getting arrested and I don't believe it will be my last. We're fighting for the survival of life on our planet, and we're up against a corporate power structure that does not care about us and has co-opted our government. This is the same corporate power structure that sucks the blood out of the Earth, that imprisons the poor and people of color for profits, and that makes war and builds weapons of mass destruction for the sake of greed. This military-industrial-prison complex does all these misguided and destructive things and many more in the name of maximizing return on investment for millionaires and billionaires who don't need or deserve another penny, but who instead need to learn how to share with everyone else on this planet, including human and non-human forms of life. So let me ask you directly: Are you willing to join us in this movement of protest and resistance? Are you willing to join us in envisioning and manifesting new, life-sustaining ways of life?
>
> One more personal note: when our feet were dangling in that trench, and construction was halted, I knew in my bones that I was right where God was calling me to be. We were in the Spirit, worshiping not only with words and songs, but with our very bodies and souls. The sun was shining and it was a glorious day to be arrested for a just cause.[50]

As people of faith, the climate crisis demands that each of us decide where we stand and what love requires. In each moment, we have a choice: to follow where love leads or to relinquish our responsibility to choose. Each prayer and each action has significance. With each decision we move the world closer to climate chaos or to climate justice. In each moment we stand on the front lines of climate change.

Love brought Sandra Steingraber to a jail cell. Love brought Jesus to the cross. Where will love bring you?

---

49. Ian Mevorach, "16 Clergy Arrested for Blocking Pipeline Construction: Here's Why," *Huffington Post* (June 2, 2016), http://www.huffingtonpost.com/ian-mevorach/16-clergy-arrested-for-bl_b _10182052.html.
50. Ibid.

12

Conclusion: Love of God and Neighbor— A Faithful Response to Climate Change

Faith working by love is the length and breadth and depth and height of Christian perfection.[1]

—John Wesley

As I conclude this book, spring has arrived. After the wet winter, the grass is lush and green, trees are in blossom, wildflowers are in bloom, and our early vegetable garden is thriving. Bees are at work, birds and squirrels are at the feeders, and my grandchildren are playing outside.

I am grateful for these days, so full of life. I am grateful to be able to "let go of the world and love all the things that climate can't change,"[2] or at least what the climate hasn't changed so far. I am glad that Easter is coming, reminding me that it's not up to me to bring life out of death, but to be willing to surrender to God, to die into life, to live and love

---

1. John Wesley, *Hymns and Sacred Poems* (London: William Strathan, 1739), viii, at Eighteenth Century Collections Online, http://quod.lib.umich.edu/e/ecco/004800840.0001.000/1:2?rgn=div1;view=fulltext.
2. Josh Fox, "How to Let Go of the World and Love All the Things That Climate Can't Change," http://www.howtoletgomovie.com/.

in the present and do what I can for this precious world, regardless of what the future holds.

Still, we do face climate-related challenges. Last fall and winter brought rain and snow to Northern California, bringing relief to people, plants, and animals, refreshing the thirsty ground, filling lakes and rivers to overflowing, and replenishing the snowpack to record levels.[3] But the record-breaking storms also brought massive flooding and major damage to roads, dams, and other infrastructure throughout the state. This damage included the failure of the emergency spillway of the Oroville Dam, just one hour away from my home, leading to the evacuation of over 200,000 people. People here and people in other areas responded to flood evacuees with great generosity, the rain slowed and the spillway held, and the people returned home. Still, the widespread damage to California's infrastructure has grave financial implications. The American Society of Civil Engineers says that fixing and maintaining California's aging and neglected infrastructure would cost the state an astounding $65 billion per year.[4]

Furthermore, climate change continues to progress. Last summer was California's warmest since record-keeping began,[5] while the snowpack is one of the deepest ever recorded in California's history. Officials warn that summer heat could melt the snow dramatically and cause further flooding.[6] Dried-out and dead trees, still standing, mean that fire is still a constant danger. There are one hundred million dead trees in California alone.[7]

Now our community is facing another challenge. Ironically, the local water district is planning to build a dam and create another reservoir. This project is being billed as a solution to water shortages that are expected to result from ongoing climate change. We can expect many more such proposed solutions as the planet continues to warm.

Last fall, my husband and I spent time with our daughter and several

3. "California's Snowpack, One of Deepest Recorded in State History, Now Poses Flooding Risk," KTLA TV, March 30, 2017. http://ktla.com/2017/03/30/californias-snowpack-one-of-deepest-recorded-in-state-history-poses-flooding-risk/.
4. Katy Murphy, "Oroville Dam drags California's billion infrastructure annual price tag into the open," *San Jose Mercury News*, February 14, 2017.
5. Craig Miller, "California's Warmest Summer: This Is It," KQED Science (Sept 8, 2016), https://ww2.kqed.org/science/2016/09/08/californias-warmest-summer-this-is-it/.
6. "California's Snowpack, One of Deepest Recorded in State History, Now Poses Flooding Risk," KTLA TV, March 30, 2017. http://ktla.com/2017/03/30/californias-snowpack-one-of-deepest-recorded-in-state-history-poses-flooding-risk/.
7. Mike McPhate, "California Today: More Than 100 Million Trees Are Dead. Now What?" *New York Times* (November 21, 2016), http://www.nytimes.com/2016/11/21/us/california-today-dead-trees-forests.html?_r=0.

grandchildren at a nearby campground on the banks of the Bear River, in an area that will be submerged if the project goes forward. Concerned people opposing the dam displayed maps and charts showing the areas that would be taken by eminent domain, destroyed, and submerged: 125 existing homes, trees and native plants, downstream waterways, ecosystems, and various species that thrive here. Members of the local Indigenous community told the children stories and demonstrated traditional uses of stones found on the river bank, then invited everyone into a circle for a ritual of protection for all the beings who inhabit this place, and for our descendants who will come after.

Whether to build this dam is a climate justice issue. The idea of another dam and reservoir makes sense from one perspective, since precipitation is less dependable and the snowpack no longer ensures a continuous supply of water. But there would be great social and environmental costs, including the loss of people's homes, destruction of native cultural sites, loss of habitat for many plant and animal species, damage downstream to fish and other wildlife, and the forfeiture of people's ability to enjoy the natural world in this place. Furthermore, logging the trees, bulldozing the plants, scraping the soil, building the dam, and flooding the region would release stored carbon into the atmosphere and eliminate the carbon sequestration function that the living trees, plants, and soil provide. There are alternatives that would avoid these social and environmental costs, including making existing reservoirs higher and recharging groundwater that has been depleted by over-pumping in recent years. The dam is an example of a so-called solution that exacerbates the problem of climate change.

This proposal to build a dam as a response to the threat of climate change, along with the opposition it is generating, is an example of the difficult policy decisions that will have to be made for the foreseeable future. It is also an example of a regional struggle to prevent ecosystem destruction, block further carbon pollution, and link the rights of Indigenous people with the rights of the earth. Like people in other parts of the world, we are doing what we can to preserve the integrity of the place that we call home.

Meanwhile, news on the climate front is getting worse. Rising average global temperatures have broken records each year for the past three years.[8] The year 2016 surpassed 2015 as the hottest year ever recorded.[9] February 2016 was "the most anomalously hot month ever

8. Justin Gillis, "Earth Sets a Temperature Record for the Third Straight Year," *New York Times*, January 18, 2017.

recorded on the planet, crushing all records," wrote Bill McKibben. "The world had pledged in Paris in December [2015] to try to hold global temperature increases to 1.5 degrees Celsius—well, February was just about at that level already."[10] McKibben calls for a worldwide wartime mobilization against further warming. "It's not that global warming is *like* a world war," he said. "It *is* a world war. And we are losing. . . . We're under attack from climate change—and our only hope is to mobilize like we did in World War II."[11] So far, among the political establishment, the will for such a mobilization is not there, as evidenced by the absence of the topic from the presidential debates and the election of Donald Trump as president.[12]

We return here to the question presented in the Introduction: "How can we face these realities about climate change, discern their practical and spiritual implications, emerge with our faith intact, and respond with words and actions that demonstrate God's loving intentions for the world?" Those who have read this book have made a beginning on the first three questions. Readers have faced the realities of climate change, reflected on its implications, and continue to be open to the language of faith. The final question is one that we will be asking and answering for the rest of our lives: How can we live, speak, and act in ways that demonstrate God's loving intentions for the world?

The answer to this question is not static. In this book I have demonstrated a theological method that enables us to discern the truth, develop a sound perspective, and determine a faith response to the climate crisis. By utilizing scripture, tradition, reason, and experience as sources of authority, we have embarked on an ongoing process of discernment. Our conclusions may differ, but even our disagreements can help us expand our knowledge, examine our biases, and formulate a deeper and more mature perspective. Each person has the dignity of choice in assuming responsibility, discerning the Spirit's call, and taking responsive action. That is the essence of mature faith.

I have made the case throughout this book that insights gained through this process confirm the necessity of honoring creation and establishing justice for the human family, future generations, and all

9. Fiona Harvey, "2016 locked in to being hottest year on record, NASA says," *The Guardian*, October 18, 2016, https://www.theguardian.com/environment/2016/oct/18/2016-locked-into-being-hottest-year-on-record-nasa-says.

10. Bill McKibben, "Signs of Things to Come," *Sojourners Magazine* (June 2016), 39.

11. Bill McKibben, "A World at War," *The New Republic* (August 15, 2016), https://newrepublic.com/article/135684/declare-war-climate-change-mobilize-wwii.

12. Justin Gillis, "Earth Sets a Temperature Record for the Third Year Straight," *New York Times*, January 18, 2017.

living things. Each chapter has built upon the learnings of previous chapters, enabling readers to integrate the subject matter, find clarity, and form conclusions while moving through this book. The approach I have demonstrated requires each of us to do the hard work of becoming informed, reflecting theologically, and choosing our response. This concluding chapter synthesizes the major themes that have been presented, encourages ongoing development of these ideas, and suggests a general framework for considering actions that express love in this time of climate change.

Creation and Justice: A Synthesis Based on Love

A strong sense of the value of creation provides a foundation for actions to preserve, defend, and renew the natural world. To have our eyes opened to the God of love who is mediated to us through creation is to experience awe. To witness God's creation being diminished brings outrage and grief. From this perspective, creation has value for us not simply because scripture and tradition tell us that God cares for creation and we should care for the earth, or even because reason tells us that we will perish if we do not preserve the natural world. Rather, creation has value for us because we love it and because through it we experience the divine. We protect and defend creation not because we should, but because we care. This sense of caring includes the human family and extends to all parts of creation.

Likewise, our hearts are opened if we expand our understanding of *neighbor* to include current victims of climate change, vulnerable people around the world, our neighbors of the future, and our non-human neighbors with whom we share this earthly home. Concern for neighbors near and far gives us a foundation for loving action. Our motivation to work for justice on their behalf is not based simply on morality but on compassionate concern for their well-being. In short, a way of life that upholds the inherent value of creation and the ethical requirement of justice is based on love of God and neighbor. Such love is essential to clarify, guide, and motivate faithful action in the context of climate change.

I have presented ideas for action at the end of each chapter, but this book offers no prescribed path. However, I do suggest that readers keep in mind two essential points. First, for those who seek to follow Jesus, the decision to commit ourselves to the struggle for climate justice is a spiritual one. A Christian response to climate change must be firmly based on faith, with a progressive awakening to the realities presented in this book and ongoing growth in love. As we cultivate spiritual awareness, we perceive the Spirit's call and are empowered to do what love requires.

Second, the commitment to climate justice is no small thing, for it will require a cultural shift and a reordering of values, priorities, and public policies. This will only be possible with the ongoing growth of a people's movement strong enough to bring about the transformation of the ideologies, institutions, and systems that perpetuate climate change and a host of other ills. I am convinced that God is active in this transformative movement, that churches are vital in this struggle for the earth and for humanity, and that each of us has a part to play. Keeping this big picture in mind enables us to trust that our limited and partial contributions further the needed transformation. By adding our prayers, words, and actions to this movement of embodied love, we contribute to the awakening that must take place.

Discerning a Faithful Response

The foundation of spiritual awakening is openness to God, who is present throughout creation (prevenient grace), and acceptance of God's forgiveness and love (justifying grace). But that is just the beginning of a process of maturing faith and ongoing growth in love of God and neighbor (sanctifying grace). Faith is expressed through loving actions in the world. Taking actions that honor creation and working to establish justice are ways to demonstrate love in a time of climate change.

Still, each of us must determine what, specifically, love requires of us at this pivotal time. Just as spiritual and theological understanding involves personal responsibility and choice, so do decisions related to spiritual practice, lifestyle, and action in the world. We each have our own path and our own context, and God calls each of us in the direction that will lead to the greatest well-being for us and for all.

When considering what actions to take in response to climate change, I offer a note of caution: Please resist the temptation to focus solely on what you can do as an individual. Although each of us is called to discern what our unique contribution to climate justice can be, it is important to be grounded in a community of care and concern and connected with the larger movement for climate justice.

Likewise, our actions in the outer world need the support that regular prayer, meditation, and other spiritual practices can bring. The

Spirit is our guide as each of us determines what spiritual practices to commit ourselves to and what actions of mercy and justice to take in the world. At the same time, the voice of the Spirit may be easier to discern in community, and actions that we take with the support or participation of others may be stronger than actions we undertake alone.

In approaching climate justice from a faith perspective, one way to start is to find or create a small group of people who can share experience, learn together, and offer mutual support in the process of discernment and action. Leading a discussion group focused on this book is one way to identify like-minded people and begin the process of engaging with these issues at a spiritual level. It is a great blessing to find even a single friend or two with whom to share this journey, for wherever two or three are gathered in his name, Jesus is there in our midst (Matt 18:20).

A Merciful, Just, and Proportional Response

Love of God and neighbor requires a merciful, just, and proportional response to climate change. We need to continue to care for creation in simple ways and to reach out in mercy to those who are suffering. By simplifying our lifestyles and reducing our carbon footprints we reject overconsumption, live with integrity, and assume personal responsibility for changing cultural patterns that harm God's beloved creation. By greening our churches and working with others to build resilient communities we act in support of the common good, demonstrate the church's relevance, and witness to God's love for all creation.

By engaging in relief efforts wherever disaster hits, including weather-related disasters that come more frequently with climate change, we demonstrate mercy while relieving suffering in the name of Christ. As conditions become intolerable in various regions, we must challenge our churches and the larger society to refrain from persecuting, excluding, or turning a blind eye to people fleeing regions made uninhabitable by a warming world. Ongoing climate change will bring far greater demands on ministries of mercy to those who are suffering, but as followers of Jesus we must see his face in each person and act accordingly, for he said, "Truly I tell you, just as you did it to one of the least of these my brothers and sisters, you did it to me" (Matt 25:40).

Our response must also be just. We must face the degree to which our culture has been built upon historic and current patterns of injustice. One example is industrial development based on fossil fuels, which has benefited some at the expense of others and has caused greenhouse gases to accumulate in the atmosphere. Those of us who benefit from the current system at the expense of poor and vulnerable people must stand in solidarity with those who live and work on the front lines of climate change. This includes listening to their stories, speaking out and acting as allies, working to change unjust policies, and challenging the ideologies, institutions, and systems that support and perpetuate the fossil-fuel-based global economy with all of its deadly effects.

Finally, we cannot settle for so-called solutions that will have little effect on actual conditions. Our response must be sufficient for the magnitude of the problems we face. Naomi Klein correctly makes the case that the challenge of climate change is so great and its implications so grave that it calls into question all of the assumptions upon which our global society has been built. It changes everything, and if our response is to be proportional to the threat, our assumptions, our habits, and the way we live our lives must be called into question as well. The dangers posed by climate change also provide motivation for strong and effective communal action. In the words of climate activist Russell Greene, "There is no time left for gradualism. That window has passed. This is a climate emergency—the moment to make a stand for the future. For each other. For our children."[13]

In speaking about climate change, this is no time to mince words or try to craft a message that is palatable. This is no time to use words or images that will be less controversial or to downplay the seriousness or urgency or radical changes that are necessary to meet this challenge. We must not falsely imply that we can simply make small lifestyle changes or that the systems we take for granted can stay the same. It is time for prophetic words and courageous actions that demonstrate the extremity of our situation and the need for deep and lasting cultural, political, economic, and spiritual transformation.

In a 2014 interview on Moyers and Company, Bill McKibben made the case for building a people's movement strong enough to transform the global system, prevent catastrophic climate change, and change the world. "Most people understand that we're in a serious fix," he said. "There's nothing you can do as individuals that will really slow down this juggernaut. . . . You can say the same thing about the challenges

---

13. John Quealy, "McKibben: Time to Declare a War (Literally) on Climate Change," *Common Dreams*, August 15, 2016, http://commondreams.org/news/2016/08/15/mckibben-time-declare-war-literally-climate-change.

faced by people in the civil rights or the abolition movement, or the gay rights movement or the women's movement. In each case, a movement arose; if we can build a movement, then we have a chance."[14]

Fortunately, the rapidly advancing movement for climate justice is part of a great awakening taking place among the peoples of the earth to the dangers and opportunities of this pivotal time. The church of Jesus Christ must not sit on the sidelines! It is time for those of us who know what is at stake to insist that our churches provide spiritual, moral, and physical support for this awakening. We must work with other people around the world to protect creation, resist the forces that threaten life on earth, support those who are most vulnerable to climate change, and join with those who are on the front lines of the struggle for climate justice. As it grows in power, this movement may, with God's help, enable us to reverse course, reveal the bankruptcy of the current system, and lay the foundations for its transformation.

God's Love at Work through Us

As we join together with each other in small groups, in our congregations, in denominational gatherings, and with interfaith allies, we bring blessings of faith, life-giving values, and spiritual power that help to create the broad cultural shift that is needed. As we join our voices with the voices of women and youth, Indigenous peoples defending Mother Earth, people living in sacrifice zones, and people from regions harmed and threatened by climate change, we amplify their voices and make their cries our own. As we call for systemic changes that must be made for the sake of those who are most vulnerable today, for future generations, and for the whole interconnected web of life, we make such changes more likely. As we join in this work we become part of the movement for global justice, gathering momentum as people working together on various issues for peace, justice, and the healing of creation.

God's love is at work through us as we respond to the challenges of climate change. Giving up hope is not an option. The beleaguered and suffering peoples of the world are calling us, future generations are calling us, and other species facing extinction are calling us. Through all these voices God is calling us to allow Christ's love to work through

---

14. Candace White, producer, "Bill McKibben to Obama: Say No to Big Oil," interview on Moyers and Company (February 7, 2014), http://billmoyers.com/episode/bill-mckibben-to-obama-say-no-to-big-oil/.

us for the sake of the whole creation. In this way, we help create a more hopeful future for everyone and everything that we hold dear. In the hopeful words of author and activist Arundhati Roy, "Another world is not only possible, she is on her way. On a quiet day I can hear her breathing."[15]

15. Arundhati Roy, "Confronting Empire," Speech at the World Social Forum, Puerto Allegro, Brazil, January 27, 2003 *Ratville, Times,* https://ratical.org/ratville/CAH/AR012703.html.

Suggested Reading List

Books

Adams, Carol J., ed. *Ecofeminism and the Sacred*. New York: Continuum, 1993.

Brother Lawrence of the Resurrection. *The Practice of the Presence of God,* trans. Donald Attwater. Springfield, IL: Templegate, 1974.

Building Bridges Collective. *Space for Movement? Reflections from Bolivia on Climate Justice, Social Movements, and the State*. Leeds: Footprint Workers Co-op. https://spaceformovement.files.wordpress.com/2010/08/space_for_move ment1.pdf.

Capra, Fritjof, and David Steindl-Rast. *Belonging to the Universe: Explorations on the Frontiers of Science and Spirituality*. San Francisco: HarperSanFrancisco, 1992.

Cobb Jr., John B. *Grace and Responsibility: A Wesleyan Theology for Today*. Nashville: Abingdon, 1995.

Crossan, John Dominic. *The Power of Parable: How Fiction by Jesus Became Fiction about Jesus*. New York: HarperCollins, 2012.

Delgado, Sharon. *Shaking the Gates of Hell: Faith-Led Resistance to Corporate Globalization*. Minneapolis: Fortress Press, 2007.

Denis, Edward. *Jesus and the Cosmos*. Mahwah, NJ: Paulist, 1991.

Engler, Mark, and Paul Engler. *This Is an Uprising: How Nonviolent Revolt Is Shaping the Twenty-First Century*. New York: Nation Books, 2016.

Frank, Thomas. *Listen, Liberal: What Ever Happened to the Party of the People?* New York: Macmillan, 2016.

Gore, Albert Jr. *An Inconvenient Truth: The Crisis of Global Warming*. New York: Rodale, 2007.

Gutiérrez, Gustavo. *The God of Life*. Translated by Matthew J. O'Connell. Maryknoll, NY: Orbis, 1991.

Hallman, David G., ed. *Ecotheology: Voices from North and South*. Eugene, OR: Wipf & Stock, 2009.

Harper, Fletcher. *Greenfaith: Mobilizing God's People to Save the Planet*. Nashville: Abindgon, 2010.

Jennings Jr., Theodore W. *Good News to the Poor: John Wesley's Evangelical Economics*. Nashville: Abingdon, 1990.

Joranson, Philip N., and Ken Butigan, ed. *Cry of the Environment: Rebuilding the Christian Creation Tradition*. Rochester, NY: Bear and Company, 1984.

Klein, Naomi. *This Changes Everything: Capitalism vs. the Climate*. New York: Simon and Schuster, 2014.

Kolbert, Elizabeth. *The Sixth Extinction*. New York: Henry Holt and Company, 2014.

Lodahl, Michael, *God of Nature and of Grace: Reading the World in a Wesleyan Way* (Nashville: Abingdon, 2003), 213–14.

Lofgren, Mike. *The Deep State: The Fall of the Constitution and the Rise of a Shadow Government*. New York: Penguin Random House, 2016.

Lonergan, Anne, and Caroline Richards, eds. *Thomas Berry and the New Cosmology*. Mystic, CT: Twenty-Third Publications, 1988.

Mann, Michael, and Tom Toles. *The Madhouse Effect: How Climate Change Denial Is Threatening Our Planet, Destroying Our Politics, and Driving Us Crazy*. New York: Columbia University Press, 2016.

Marshall, George. *Don't Even Think About It: Why Our Brains Are Wired to Ignore Climate Change*. New York: Bloomsbury, 2014.

Mayer, Jane. *Dark Money: The Hidden History of the Billionaires behind the Rise of the Radical Right*. New York: Doubleday, 2016.

McKibben, Bill, ed. *The Global Warming Reader: A Century of Writing about Climate Change*. London: Penguin, 2011.

_____. *Oil and Honey: The Education of an Unlikely Activist*. New York: Henry Holt, 2013.

Meeks, Douglas, ed. *The Portion of the Poor: Good News to the Poor in the Wesleyan Tradition*. Nashville: Abingdon, 1995.

Mirowski, Philip. *Never Let a Serious Crisis Go to Waste: How Neoliberalism Survived the Financial Meltdown*. London, New York: Verso, 2013.

Monbiot, George, *How Did We Get into This Mess?* London, New York: Verso, 2016.

Moore, Kathleen Dean. *Great Tide Rising: Towards Clarity and Moral Courage in a Time of Planetary Change*. Berkeley: Counterpoint, 2016.

Moe-Lobeda, Cynthia D. *Resisting Structural Evil: Love as Ecological-Economic Vocation*. Minneapolis: Fortress Press, 2013.

Northcott, Michael S. *A Moral Climate: The Ethics of Global Warming: The Ethics of Global Warming*. Maryknoll, NY: Orbis, 2007.

O'Connell, Maureen H. *Compassion: Loving Our Neighbor in an Age of Globalization.* Maryknoll, NY: Orbis, 2009.

Outler, Albert C., and Richard P. Heitzenrater, ed. *John Wesley's Sermons: An Anthology.* Nashville: Abingdon, 1991.

Parenti, Christian. *Tropic of Chaos: Climate Change and the New Geography of Violence.* New York: Perseus, 2011.

Pope Francis. *Laudito Si, Encyclical on Climate Change and Inequality: On Care for Our Common Home.* Brooklyn and London: Melville House, 2015.

Postele, Denis. *Fabric of the Universe.* New York: Crown, 1976.

Runyan, Theodore, ed. *Sanctification and Liberation: Liberation Theologies in Light of the Wesleyan Tradition.* Nashville: Abingdon, 1981.

_____. *The New Creation: John Wesley's Theology Today.* Nashville: Abingdon, 1998.

Shiva, Vandana. *Soil not Oil: Environmental Justice in an Age of Climate Crisis.* Berkeley: North Atlantic Books, 2015.

Simon Peter, Rebekah. *Green Church: Reduce, Reuse, Recycle, Rejoice.* Nashville: Abingdon, 2010.

Stephenson, Wen. *What We Are Fighting for Now Is Each Other: Dispatches from the Front Lines of Climate Justice.* Boston: Beacon, 2015.

Stone, Bryan P. Stone, and Thomas J. Oord, eds. *Thy Nature and Thy Name Is Love: Wesleyan and Process Theologies in Dialogue.* Nashville: Abingdon, 2001.

Thorsen, Donald A. D. *The Wesleyan Quadrilateral: Scripture, Tradition, Reason, & Experience as a Model of Evangelical Theology.* Grand Rapids: Zondervan, 1990.

Tinker, George E. *Spirit and Resistance: Political Theology and American Indian Liberation.* Minneapolis: Augsburg Fortress Press, 2004.

Tokar, Brian. *Toward Climate Justice.* Porsgrunn, Norway: Communalism Press, June 16, 2010.

Wesley, John. *A Plain Account of Christian Perfection*, print version. ReadaClassic.com.

_____. *A Survey of the Wisdom of God in the Creation: A Compendium of Natural Philosophy.* Lancaster, PA: William Hamilton, 1810. Available online at http://wesley.nnu.edu/john-wesley/a-compendium-of-natural-philosophy/.

Children's Books

Burton, Virginia Lee. *Life Story.* New York: Houghton Mifflin and Co., 1962.

Hickman , Martha Whitmore. *And God Created Squash: How the World Began.* Morton Grove, IL: Albert Whitman and Co., 1993.

Ray, Jane. *Adam and Eve and the Garden of Eden.* Grand Rapids: Eerdmans, 2005.

Root, Phyllis Root. *Big Momma Makes the World.* Cambridge, MA: Candlewick, 2002.

Articles

Carrington, Damian. "Fossil fuels subsidized by $10m a minute, says IMF." *The Guardian*, May 18, 2015. https://www.theguardian.com/environment/2015/may/18/fossil-fuel-companies-getting-10m-a-minute-in-subsidies-says-imf.

Cone, James H. "Whose Earth Is It, Anyway?" in *Sojourners Magazine*, July 2007. https://sojo.net/magazine/july-2007/whose-earth-it-anyway.

Delonge, Marsha. "Soil Carbon Can't Fix Climate Change by Itself, But It Needs to Be Part of the Solution." Union of Concerned Scientists, September 26, 2016. http://blog.ucsusa.org/marcia-delonge/soil-carbon-cant-fix-climate-change-by-itself-but-it-needs-to-be-part-of-the-solution?_ga=1.219593561.179871221.1472596472.

Gillis, Justin John Schwartz. "Exxon Mobil Accused of Misleading Public on Climate Change Risks." *New York Times*, October 30, 2015. http://www.nytimes.com/2015/10/31/science/exxon-mobil-accused-of-misleading-public-on-climate-change-risks.html.

Hickel, Jason. "Clean energy won't save us—only a new economic system can." *The Guardian* U.S. ed., July 15, 2016. https://www.theguardian.com/global-development-professionals-network/2016/jul/15/clean-energy-wont-save-us-economic-system-can?.

Klein, Naomi, and Frank Barat. "We are going backwards, COP21 is the opposite of progress." *The New Internationalist*, December 10, 2015. https://newint.org/features/web-exclusive/2015/12/10/naomi-klein-cop21-is-the-opposite-of-progress/.

McKibben, Bill. "Global Warming's Terrifying New Math." *Rolling Stone Magazine*, July 19, 2012. http://www.rollingstone.com/politics/news/global-warmings-terrifying-new-math-20120719.

_____. "The Fossil Fuel Resistance." *Rolling Stone Magazine*, April 11, 2013. http://www.rollingstone.com/politics/news/the-fossil-fuel-resistance-20130411.

_____. "A World at War." *The New Republic*, August 15, 2016. https://newrepublic.com/article/135684/declare-war-climate-change-mobilize-wwii.

Mevorach, Ian. "16 Clergy Arrested for Blocking Pipeline Construction: Here's Why." *Huffington Post*, June 2, 2016. http://www.huffingtonpost.com/ian-mevorach/16-clergy-arrested-for-bl_b_10182052.html.

Nuwer, Rachel. "The Rising Murder Count of Environmental Activists." *New York Times*, June 20, 2016. http://www.nytimes.com/2016/06/21/science/berta-caceres-environmental-activists-murders.html?_r=0.

Olive Hamilton, "Geoengineering Is Not a Solution to Climate Change." *Scientific*

American, March 10, 2015. http://www.scientificamerican.com/article/geo-engineering-is-not-a-solution-to-climate-change/.

Phillips, Jenny. "The Last Beneficiary." Fossil Free UMC blog, http://www.fossilfreeumc.org/blog/2014/11/13/thelastbeneficiary.

Sammon, Alexander. "A History of Native Americans Protesting the Dakota Access Pipeline." *Mother Jones*, September 9, 2016. http://www.motherjones.com/environment/2016/09/dakota-access-pipeline-protest-timeline-sioux-standing-rock-jill-stein.

Sandra Steingraber. "Letters from Chemung County Jail #2." *Marcellus Effect* (April 23, 2013), http://marcelluseffect.blogspot.com/2013/04/letters-from-chemung-county-jail.html.

Sedor, Noelle. "Why fee and dividend is better than cap and trade at fighting climate change." *L.A. Times*, March 5, 2015. http://www.latimes.com/opinion/op-ed/la-oe-sedor-climate-change-fee-and-dividend-vs–cap-and-trade-20150306-story.html .

Stewart, Katherine. "America's Theologians of Climate Science Denial." *The Guardian*, November 4, 2012. https://www.theguardian.com/commentisfree/2012/nov/04/america-theologians-climate-science-denial.

Thomas-Muller, Clayton. "Energy Exploitation on Sacred Native Lands." *Race, Poverty, and the Environment (RP&E), A Journal of Social and Environmental Justice* (Winter 2005), Reimagine, http://reimaginerpe.org/node/307 .

Online Resources

350.org. http://350.org/.

Citizens Climate Lobby: http://citizensclimatelobby.org/.

"Climate Change and Church: How Global Climate Change Will Impact Core Church Ministries," National Council of Churches, http://interfaithpowerandlight.org/wp-content/uploads/2009/11/ClimateWhitePaper_finalREV.pdf.

"Climate extremes, regional impacts, and the case for resilience," World Bank. "Consensus Statement from Global Scientists," Millennium Alliance for Humanity and Biosphere (MAHB), http://mahb.stanford.edu/consensus-statement-from-global-scientists.

Climate Reality Project: http://climaterealityproject.org/.

Common Dreams: Breaking News and Views for the Progressive Community. http://commondreams.org/.

Creation Justice Ministries (National Council of Churches), http://www.creationjustice.org/.

Democracy Now, Independent Global News, http://www.democracynow.org/.

Fast for the Climate. http://fastfortheclimate.org/en/.

Fossil Free: Divest from Fossil Fuels. http://gofossilfree.org/.

Global Trade Watch, Public Citizen. http://www.citizen.org/trade/.

Greenfaith, Interfaith Resources for the Environment, website: http://green-faith.org/.

Idle No More: http://www.idlenomore.ca/.

Interfaith Power and Light, an interfaith ministry. http://www.interfaith-powerandlight.org/.

Intergovernmental Panel on Climate Change: www.ipcc.ch/.

Jetnil-Kiliner, Kathy. Video presentation of poem "Dear Matafele Peinem." http://www.creativeresistance.org/dear-matafele-peinem/.

Leonard, Annie, narrator. "The Story of Cap and Trade" and other short animated videos at The Story of Stuff Project. http://storyofstuff.org/movies/story-of-cap-and-trade/.

"Minute for Climate Justice." World Council of Churches, November 8, 2013. https://www.oikoumene.org/en/resources/documents/assembly/2013-busan/adopted-documents-statements/minute-on-climate-justice.

Rajendra K. Pachauri (Chair), Myles R. Allen (United Kingdom), Vicente R. Barros (Argentina), John Broome (United Kingdom), Wolfgang Cramer (Germany/France), Renate Christ (Austria/WMO), John A. Church (Australia) et al., eds, "Climate Change 2014 Synthesis Report," The Intergovernmental Panel on Climate Change, https://www.ipcc.ch/pdf/assessment-report/ar5/syr/SYR_AR5_FINAL_full.pdf.

Peaceful Uprising. www.peacefuluprising.org/.

Popular Resistance. https://www.popularresistance.org/.

Soil Not Oil Coalition. Includes videos of past conferences. http://soilnotoil-coalition.org/.

Skeptical Science. www.skepticalscience.com/.

Standing Rock Sioux (opposition to Dakota Access Pipeline). http://standingrock.org/.

"Statement from the Chair and PFII Members Dalee Dorough and Chief Edward John on the Protests on the Dakota Access Pipeline" (August 31, 2016), Division for Social Policy and Development, Indigenous Peoples, United Nations, https://www.un.org/development/desa/indigenouspeoples/news/2016/08/statement-on-protests/.

The Consensus Project: http://theconsensusproject.com/.

"Turn Down the Heat: Climate Extremes, Regional Impacts, and the Case for Resilience," World Bank, http://documents.worldbank.org/curated/en/2013/06/17862361/turn-down-heat-climate-extremes-regional-impacts-case-resilience-full-report.

"Turn Down the Heat: Why a 4°C Warmer World Must Be Avoided," The World Bank, http://documents.worldbank.org/curated/en/2012/11/17097815/turn-down-heat-4%C2%B0c-warmer-world-must-avoided.

"What you can do about Global Warming." Union of Concerned Scientists. http://www.ucsusa.org/what-can-i-do-about-climate-change#.V-3KyPArKUk.

"Women and Climate Change," Church World Service, http://hunger.cws-global.org/site/DocServer/CWS_Enough2.pdf?docID=1521.

Women at the Forefront," *Climate Change Connections*, a project of the United Nations Population Fund (UNPF) and Women's Environment and Development Organization (WEDO), http://www.unfpa.org/sites/default/files/pub-pdf/climateconnections_1_overview.pdf.

Women's Earth and Climate Action Network, International (WECAN), http://wecaninternational.org/.

Women's Environment and Development Organization (WEDO), http://wedo.org/.

Index